THE ORGANIZATION OF
THE BRITISH ARMY IN THE
AMERICAN REVOLUTION

THE ORGANIZATION OF
THE BRITISH ARMY IN THE
AMERICAN REVOLUTION

By
EDWARD E. CURTIS, Ph.D.

Republished EP Publishing Ltd., 1972
First published New Haven and London, 1926

Republished 1972 by EP Publishing Limited
East Ardsley, Wakefield
Yorkshire, England,

by kind permission of the original
publishers Yale University Press,
New Haven,
Connecticut

ISBN 0 85409 906 9

Please address all enquiries to EP Publishing Ltd.
(address as above)

Reprinted in Great Britain by
Scolar Press Limited, Menston, Yorkshire

YALE
HISTORICAL PUBLICATIONS

MISCELLANY

XIX

PUBLISHED UNDER THE DIRECTION OF
THE DEPARTMENT OF HISTORY
FROM THE INCOME OF
THE FREDERICK JOHN KINGSBURY
MEMORIAL FUND

THE ORGANIZATION OF THE BRITISH ARMY IN THE AMERICAN REVOLUTION

They came three thousand miles and died,
To keep the past upon its throne;
Unheard, beyond the ocean tide,
Their English mother made her moan.

INSCRIPTION ON THE GRAVE OF THE RED–COATS
WHO FELL AT CONCORD BRIDGE

BY
EDWARD E. CURTIS, Ph.D.
Associate Professor of History, Wellesley College

NEW HAVEN: YALE UNIVERSITY PRESS
LONDON: HUMPHREY MILFORD
OXFORD UNIVERSITY PRESS
MDCCCCXXVI

IN MEMORIAM
E. A. C.

PREFACE

THE author wishes to express gratitude to the authorities of the Yale University Library and the British Museum for giving him access to a mass of printed material relative to the subject of this volume, which in its original form was presented as a doctoral dissertation at Yale University. More especially thanks are due to the best friend of American historical scholars in England, Mr. Hubert Hall, who facilitated the author's examination of the rich collection of manuscript papers relative to the British army in the Public Record Office, London. These constituted, indeed, his chief source of information. No words seem adequate to express the author's sense of obligation to Professor Wilbur C. Abbott, of Harvard University, whose keen interest in the subject has been an inspiration, and to Professor Charles M. Andrews, of Yale University, whose criticisms and suggestions, based upon an unrivaled knowledge of American colonial history, have been of assistance at every stage of the work.

Lochmere, N. H.
September 6, 1925.

TABLE OF CONTENTS

CHAPTER I[1]

THE BRITISH ARMY AT THE OUTBREAK OF THE REVOLUTION: A GENERAL SURVEY

EVER since the American Revolution became a subject of investigation, no little attention has been paid to the Continental army. The British army on the other hand has received but passing notice. Writers have frequently assumed that it was a smooth-running fighting machine which failed because badly directed. The impression has been created that it wanted in nothing save success. We are asked to picture Washington's men as ragged and half-starved while Howe's are to be imagined as warmly clothed and well-fed. In fact the well-equipped forces of the crown, in scarlet coats and gold braid, have traditionally been used as a foil to set off the wants and sufferings of the tattered Continentals. To test the accuracy of this view and also to shed light upon the methods employed by the British government in recruiting, transporting, and subsisting its army in America is the purpose of the present study.

At the outbreak of the Revolution, the total land forces of Great Britain exclusive of militia numbered on paper 48,647 men, of which 39,294 were infantry; 6,869 cavalry; and 2,484 artillery. These troops were unequally divided

---

[1] In this work the citations Adm. (Admiralty), A.O. (Audit Office), H.O. (Home Office), C.O. (Colonial Office), T. (Treasury), and W.O. (War Office), refer to MSS. in the P.R.O. (Public Record Office, London). The reference, Addit. MSS., refers to collections in the British Museum. When a printed work is frequently referred to, only the name of the author is given. The complete title of the work may be found by consulting the Bibliography. Other references are self-explanatory.

between two separate military establishments—the English establishment and the Irish establishment. The Scottish establishment had been abolished in 1707. The English establishment comprised 25,871 infantry organized into 46 regiments and 20 independent companies; 4,151 cavalry organized into 16 regiments; and 2,256 artillerymen organized into one regiment of 4 battalions. Of the aforesaid infantry one regiment of 482 men (the 41st) and the 20 independent companies of 1,040 were largely non-effective, being composed of "invalids"[2] doing garrison duty in Great Britain and the Scilly Islands.[3]

The Irish establishment consisted of 13,423 infantry divided into 28 regiments; 2,718 cavalry divided into 12 regiments; and 228 artillerymen embodied into one regiment of four companies.

Such were the numbers of the British army in 1775 and such they had approximately been ever since the close of the Seven Years' War.

An examination of the location of the British army in 1775 reveals the fact that while small detachments of it were to be found in many distant quarters of the globe, the bulk of it was distributed unequally among three different countries. There were roughly speaking 15,000 men in England, 12,000 in Ireland, and 8,000 in America. The remaining 10,000 were distributed among the West Indies, Africa, Minorca, Gibraltar, and Scotland. The following table indicates the situation in detail:

---

2 "The invalids in the British forces . . . consist of soldiers partly disabled by wounds and veterans, who from old age and length of service are rendered incapable of the duties of an active campaign, but are still judged fit for garrison duty." Grose, *Military Antiquities*, I, 164. In 1775 a detachment of invalids was dispatched to garrison Newfoundland. Duncan, *History of the Royal Artillery*, I, 268.

3 The statistics in this and the next few paragraphs have been compiled from the *Court and City Register*, 1775, and 35 *Commons Journal*, pp. 35-37.

SUMMARY OF THE LOCATION OF THE BRITISH ARMY IN 1775

England,	19 Regs.	Infy.	11,396	16 Regs. Cav. 4,151	Total	15,547
Scotland,	1 Reg.	"	474		"	474
Isle of Man,	3 Cos.	"	142		"	142
Ireland,	21 Regs.	"	9,815	12 " " 2,718	"	12,533
Minorca,	5 "	"	2,385		"	2,385
Gibraltar,	7 "	"	3,339		"	3,339
West Indies,	3 "	"	1,909		"	1,909
America,	18 "	"	8,580		"	8,580
Africa,	1 Corps	"	214		"	214
			38,254	6,869		45,123[4]

The regiments of the British army were of two kinds—
household regiments and regiments of the line. The
former included three regiments of Foot Guards (the 1st
or Grenadier Guards, the 2d or Coldstream, the 3d or
Scots Guards) and three regiments of Horse Guards.
These were the oldest corps in the army and constituted
a body of picked men. Ordinarily they were stationed at
London and Westminster as a bodyguard to the king.
During the American Revolution, a "brigade of Guards,"
formed by selecting fifteen men from each of the
sixty-four companies of household infantry, served in
America.[5]

The regiments of the line were simply the ordinary
regiments of the army. The infantry were numbered from
1 to 70; the cavalry, from 1 to 18; although some of the
regiments had names as well as numbers. The whole matter is set forth in detail in the appendix to this chapter.

The average strength of an infantry regiment on the

[4] This includes the 41st, Col. Wren's regiment of invalids, but does not
include the 20 independent companies of invalids doing garrison duty. The
forces in India were under the control of the East India Company. They did
not become a part of the British army until 1858. Clode, *Military Forces
of the Crown*, I, 268.

[5] W.O. 1:681, Germain to Barrington, 23 Mar. 1776; *ibid.*, 4:273, Barrington to Howe, 13 Mar. 1776. *Cf.* Trevelyan, *The American Revolution*,
II, 101.

English Establishment was 477 and on the Irish 474 men. The ordinary regiment consisted of one battalion organized into 10 companies.[6] The strength of a company varied. In a regiment of 477 men it consisted of 38 privates. Of the 10 companies in each regiment, one consisted of grenadiers and another of light infantry. When introduced into the army in 1677, the function of the grenadiers had been to hurl hand-grenades among the enemy's ranks at close quarters. The size and weight of these missiles demanded that the throwers should be tall of stature and muscular of build. By 1775 the grenades had disappeared, but the grenadiers still remained, representing in height and strength the flower of each regiment. Light infantry had been introduced, largely through the exertions of Sir William Howe, shortly before the American Revolution, to provide each regiment with a corps of skirmishers. Good marksmen of light build and active temperament were required for the service.[7] Thus the grenadiers and light infantry had come to constitute the picked men of a regiment. During an engagement they were usually placed in the flanks, and hence were known as the "flank companies." In an army it was customary to form them into one or two special battalions in order to make their united strength available for work requiring the highest courage and skill. For example, it was the flank companies of the garrison of Boston that Gage dispatched to Lexington and Concord on that memorable April night in 1775. At the battle of Bunker Hill, the grenadiers flanked the British line on the left and the light companies, on the right. When Howe

---

6 The 1st Foot and 60th Foot had two battalions in 1775.

7 The light infantry carried a special kind of musket which was lighter than used by most companies. See W.O. 1:992, Loudoun to Barrington, 28 Feb. 1776. Regarding Howe's responsibility for light infantry, see Lamb, *Memoir*, p. 89; *Dictionary National Biography*, "Sir William Howe."

landed at Staten Island in 1776, he organized the grenadiers into a reserve and grouped the light infantry into
three battalions. During Burgoyne's expedition, 1777, the
grenadier and light infantry companies were formed into
an "Advanced Corps" under General Frazer. At Freeman's Farm, 7 October, 1777, the grenadiers and light
infantry were disposed on the flanks of the British line.
Lord Rawdon set out for the relief of Ninety-Six in June,
1781, with six flank companies of the 3d, 19th, and 30th
Foot. Many other illustrations of this sort might be
given.[8]

The internal organization of an infantry regiment of
477 men may be exemplified by the 23d or Royal Welsh
Fusileers, a corps which saw much service in America.

23D ROYAL WELSH FUSILEERS (1775)[9]

Field and Staff Officers

Colonel, Lieutenant Colonel, Chaplain, Adjutant, Surgeon and
Mate.

One Company

Captain, 2 Lieutenants, 2 Sergeants, 3 Corporals, 1 Drummer, 38
Private Men. Seven companies more of the like numbers.

One Company of Grenadiers

Captain, 2 Lieutenants, 2 Sergeants, 3 Corporals, 1 Drummer, 2
Fifers, 38 Private Men.

One Company of Light Infantry

Captain, 2 Lieutenants, 2 Sergeants, 3 Corporals, 1 Drummer,
38 Private Men.

Throughout the war the strength of the cavalry regi-

[8] Fortescue, III, 149, 156; Trevelyan, IV, 177; Lamb, *Journal,* pp. 112,
159; W. Rogerson, *Historical Records of the 53d,* p. 4; Digby, *Journal,* p.
109; *London Gazette,* 10 Oct. 1779; Smythies, *Historical Records of the
40th,* p. 42.

[9] W.O. 24:480.

ments was less uniform than that of the infantry. The majority numbered 231 men. They were ordinarily divided into 6 troops each. The internal organization may be illustrated by the 17th Dragoons, the first corps of horse sent to America during the war. In April, 1775, its strength was increased to 288 sabres, and it was organized as follows:

17TH DRAGOONS (APRIL, 1775)[10]

Colonel, Lieutenant Colonel, Major, Chaplain, Adjutant, Surgeon.

One Troop

Captain, Lieutenant, Cornet, Quarter Master, Sergeants, 2 Corporals, 1 Hautbois, 37 Private Men. Five troops more of the like numbers.

At the outbreak of the war, the artillery was grouped into 1 regiment or 4 battalions, each battalion consisting of 8 companies. A single battalion was organized as follows:

Colonel, Lieutenant Colonel, Major.

One Company

1 Captain, 1 Captain Lieutenant, 2 First Lieutenants, 2 Second Lieutenants, 4 Sergeants, 4 Corporals, 9 Bombardiers, 18 Gunners, 73 Matrosses, 2 Drummers. Total 116.
Seven more companies of the same numbers.[11]

While the gunners and matrosses were enlisted men, the drivers in the artillery were hired civilians.[12] ''As

---

10 W.O. 24:481.

11 W.O. 55:373, p. 299. See also Parliamentary *Report on Ordnance Estimate for 1783.* A royal warrant of 1779 raised the number of companies per battalion from 8 to 10.

12 ''The artillery drivers are not Servants to the Crown but only Servants to the Contractors who supply Government with horses and are paid by the Contractors nine shillings a week per man.'' W.O. 1:996, Robert Clarke to Barrington, 22 Oct. 1778. *Cf.* Duncan, *Hist. of R. A.; Scott, History of the British Army,* III, 328: ''A decision was given at the Court of King's

late as 1798 field guns appearing at a Woolwich review were drawn by horses in single file and driven by plough-men on foot wearing smock frocks and armed with long whips."[13] When the army was campaigning in foreign parts, horses, wagons, and drivers were obtained from the peasantry sometimes by hire and sometimes by im-pressment. After the battle of Long Island, Howe bought a hundred horses from loyalist farmers for the artillery and hired eighty two-horse wagons with drivers for the carrying of ammunition and stores.[14] While tumbrils were usually drawn by three horses, the number of horses allotted to each gun varied with the size of the piece. In Burgoyne's army, 1777, a 6-pounder fieldpiece was drawn by four horses, a 3-pounder by three horses, a "royal howitzer" by three horses.[15] Both Howe and Burgoyne were supplied with 3-pounders mounted on light carriages, known as Congreve carriages, which made it possible to carry them on the backs of horses or mules in difficult country.[16] It was customary to allot two guns to each regiment of foot and these were known as "battalion guns."[17] The practice was criticized by some officers because it prevented concentration of artillery fire. Burgoyne seems to have abandoned it, marshaling his field guns into three "brigades" or batteries, each of which comprised four 6-pounders. One of these "bri-

Bench on the 6th of June, 1780, that the horses, conductors and drivers on contract with the Board of Ordnance for the service of the Royal Artillery, while on actual service, shall be received by Innkeepers by billet, and ac-commodated with quarters at the rate of dragoons and their horses."

[13] Vincent, *Records, of Woolwich*, II, 387.

[14] Duncan, *Hist. of R. A.*, I, 131, 303, 309.

[15] Burgoyne, *State of the Expedition*, p. 92.

[16] Duncan, *Hist. of R. A.*, I, 307, 309; Burgoyne, *State of the Expedition*, pp. 13-16.

[17] C.O. 5:164, Townshend to Germain, 15 Mar. 1778; T. Simes, *Military Guide*, II, "Field-pieces"; Duncan, *Hist. of R. A.*, I, 50, 212; Scott, *Hist. of British Army*, III, 328.

gades" was assigned to the left, another to the centre, and a third to the right. In addition, Burgoyne took with him a park of heavy guns, howitzers, mortars, 12- and 24-pounders, to reduce earthworks and blockhouses erected by the Americans and to clear away abattis.[18]

The military music which stirred the heart and quickened the step of the British redcoat was for the most part of a simple sort. Each regiment of foot had a few fifers and drummers and each regiment of horse a few trumpeters. Each regiment of the Guards enjoyed in addition a band of eight pieces, two oboes, two clarinets, two horns, two bassoons. The musicians, who are said to have been excellent performers, were civilians, hired at good pay by the month. Their chief duty was to play "from the parade on the Horse Guards to St. James's Palace, while the Kings guard was mounted, and back to the Horse Guards." The Royal Artillery Regiment also had a band composed of a master musician and eight other musicians, two trumpets, two French horns, two bassoons, and four clarinets or hautbois, ten instruments being provided for eight men. The players were ranked as matrosses and were under the Articles of War. These were apparently the only corps enjoying bands.[19]

The infantry, cavalry, and artillery constituted the three most important branches of the army. There were in addition to these a company of military artificers (the ancestors of the Royal Sappers and Miners) and a small but efficient corps of engineers. The former saw no service in America but several officers of the latter did excellent work abroad.[20] Captain John Montrésor and Lieu-

18 Burgoyne, *State of the Expedition*, pp. 13-16.
19 Farmer, *Memoirs of the Royal Artillery Band*, pp. 37, 39, 48; Kappey, *Military Music*, p. 87.
20 Porter, *History of the Royal Engineers*, I, 203-207; Chichester, *Records and Badges of the British Army*, pp. 152-153; Fortescue, IV, 915. Artificers are occasionally mentioned as participating in the American campaigns, but

tenant Page were present at Bunker Hill, where Page was wounded. Montrésor and Lieutenants Kesterman and Fyers participated in Howe's New York campaign of 1776. Lieutenant Twiss rendered capable service under Burgoyne in 1777. It was he who pointed out the fact that Sugar Hill overlooked the American works at Ticonderoga and urged its occupation, thus forcing the rebels to evacuate a strong position. Major Moncrieff won high praise for his share in the defence of Savannah in 1779 and his conduct of the siege of Charleston in 1780. Sir Henry Clinton in his dispatch of 13 May, 1780, to Germain said: "But to Maj. Moncrieff, the commanding Engineer, who planned and with the assistance of such capable officers under him, conducted the siege with so much judgment, intrepidity, and laborious attention, I wish to render a tribute of the highest applause and most permanent gratitude, persuaded that far more flattering commendations than I can bestow will not fail to crown such rare merit."[21] Of Lieutenant Sutherland, who was chief engineer at Gloucester, Cornwallis wrote at the conclusion of the Yorktown campaign, "Lieutenant Sutherland the commanding Engineer . . . merited in every respect my highest approbation."[22]

The supply and transport services were still in a crude and embryonic state. Mention is made in the Army List

they were not members of the company mentioned above. In some cases they were probably civilians, who were hired to serve for the campaign as masons or carpenters. Such apparently were the two hundred artificers engaged for Burgoyne's expedition (*State of the Expedition*, p. 93). In other cases they were doubtless privates with a knack at the building trades. Twiss recommended the formation of a corps of military artificers for American service, but no action seems to have been taken. W.O. 46:11, Townshend to Haldimand, 18 Oct. 1779. Infantry and artillery officers were sometimes detailed to serve as assistant engineers. For staff of engineers in Canada, 1776-1778, and at New York, 1774, see appendix to this chapter.

[21] Quoted by Porter, I, 207.
[22] *Ibid.*

of a Commissary General and a Waggon Master General
for the forces at home and abroad, but the nature of their
duties and the scope of their authority are uncertain. The
one, however, was the parent of the Commissariat Department and the other of the Transport Service, both
of which were later combined into the Army Service
Corps.[23]

No medical corps in the modern sense of the word existed. Ever since the time of Charles II, there had been a
Physician General and a Surgeon General, and since
1758, Inspectors of hospitals; but little is known regarding their functions. According to the regulations, a surgeon and mate were attached to each regiment of foot.
They were, however, essentially regimental officers. Although holding their commissions of the king, they were
really appointed by the colonel, whose servants they had
originally been. Sometimes the offices of captain and surgeon would be combined in one person. Many of the medical officers were Scotsmen, doubtlessly owing to the excellent facilities afforded for the study of medicine at
Glasgow and Edinburgh in the eighteenth century. In
many instances their professional knowledge must have
been slight. The surgeons were not required to hold a
medical diploma or degree, nor the mates to pass a medical examination. Sergeant Lamb, the author of the *Journal of the American War,* acted as assistant surgeon to
the 9th and 23d regiments in America, although he had
received no medical education whatsoever. Nurses were
sometimes obtained among the women who followed the
army, for it is a curious fact that the government permitted the common soldiers dispatched to America to

---

[23] Chichester, pp. 908-909. The commissary general acted under the orders
of the Treasury. He was not a military officer as was the waggon master
general.

take their "wives" with them and even rationed them from the public stores.[24] The medical service, in short, was largely extemporaneous, and the feeling seems to have been that it was cheaper "to levy a recruit than to cure a soldier."

Army doctors labored under many other disadvantages besides ignorance and inexpert assistance. They were poorly paid. In 1775 the stipend of a surgeon's mate in the 60th Foot amounted to 3s. 6d. a day. Although given a certain allowance for medicines they had to provide their own surgical outfits; were not allowed uniforms; and occupied an inferior social status among the other commissioned officers. In the matter of medicines, they were governed to a large extent by a warrant issued in 1747 whereby a certain individual had been appointed

[24] Whether the women accompanying the army were always lawfully wedded wives of the men is not certain. Sergeant Lamb states (*Memoir*, p. 75) that privates were obliged to obtain written permission of the officers of the company in order to marry, "as but few young women could be taken on board when the regiment embarked for foreign service." Lieutenant Colonel Maunsell, who was in charge of embarkations at Cork, stated on one occasion that it was necessary to allow a certain number of women to accompany the soldiers on the transports bound for America in order to prevent the men from deserting. Only a fixed number of women were tolerated in the field. Howe permitted six per company during the campaigns of 1776 and 1777; Burgoyne permitted three per company during the invasion of New York, 1777. Children as well as women connected with the army were fed and clothed out of the public stores. This must have increased the difficulty of maintaining the royal forces in America. Children were sometimes born on the march and wives are known to have accompanied their redcoated husbands upon the field of battle. *Kemble Papers*, I, 345, 374, 381-382, 386; Lamb, *Memoir*, p. 182; *ibid., Journal*, p. 143; Burgoyne, *Orderly Book*, p. 45; *ibid., State of the Expedition*, p. 116; "Minute Book of a Board of General Officers" (N. Y. Hist. Soc. *Coll.* 1916), p. 84; Wier-Robinson Correspondence, Wier to Robinson, 20 May, 1777; Stryker, *Trenton and Princeton*, p. 25, note; W.O. 1:12, Carleton to Sir Geo. Yonge, 21 Dec. 1782; *ibid.*, 1:2, Gage to Barrington, 15 Aug. 1775; *ibid.*, 1:991, "Return of Four Detachments embarked on Board Victualling Ships at Cove, 27 March, 1776."

Apothecary General with the monopoly for himself and his heirs of providing drugs for the army.[25]

If the physical welfare of the soldier was ill-cared for, his spiritual welfare was practically neglected. While there are occasional references to church parades in British orderly books of the Revolutionary period, there is little else to indicate that commanding officers took more than passing interest in the religious life of the men. There was no Chaplain's Department or Chaplain General. The regulations called for a chaplain of the Church of England for each regiment, but this was often treated as a dead letter. Like the surgeons, the chaplains were essentially regimental officers, holding commissions of the king but being nominated by the colonel. In some cases the latter pocketed their pay and dispensed with their services; in other cases they themselves drew their pay but consigned the performance of their duties to deputies. For example, the chaplains on the roster of the Royal Regiment of Artillery clubbed together and hired a curate to perform their joint duties at Woolwich while they continued to enjoy fat livings elsewhere in rural parishes. Their attendance was rarely required. In 1785 they were directed to appear at headquarters since the king intended to review the regiment. One of them begged to be excused on the ground that he was eighty-six years of age.[26] Scant mention is made of chaplains in connection with the forces in America. Their number was probably small. Carleton complains to Barrington in November, 1777: ''Not any of the Chaplains of the regiments serving in this Army are Come over, and had it not been that the Reverend Mr. Brudenell accompanied General

25 Belcher, I, 328-330; Fortescue, IV, 922-923; Chichester, p. 925; Lamb, *Journal*, pp. 388-389; Goodenough and Dalton, *Army Book of the British Empire*, p. 266; Duncan, *Hist. of the R. A.*, II, 15.

26 Duncan, *Hist. of R. A.*, II, 18-19.

Phillips to this country, and an other Gentleman who came over as deputy there would have been no person to officiate in so considerable a body of Troops.''[27] Reverend Mr. Brudenell was in fact the only chaplain to attain prominence during the war. He accompanied Burgoyne's expedition in 1777, and we have from the pen of that general a Napieresque picture of him at the burial of General Fraser after the battle of Freeman's Farm (7 October, 1777) : ''The incessant cannonade during the solemnities, the steady attitude and unaltered voice with which the chaplain officiated, though frequently covered with dust which the shot threw up on all sides of him, the mute but expressive mixture of sensibility and indignation upon every countenance,—these objects will remain to the last of life upon the mind of every man who was present.''[28] Mr. Brudenell was doubtless an exception to the ordinary run of his profession. The majority of chaplains had but a poor reputation, and were typical of an age of spiritual torpor. The only divine who took active and effective interest in the religious life of the army was John Wesley. He sought the soldiers in their camps and barracks and won many followers. Old-fashioned colonels refused to allow their men to attend church or chapel, preferring to keep them in quarters of a Sunday, on the ground that instead of going to worship they would resort to alehouses and get drunk. Religious feeling in the army was indeed at a low ebb. Dean Swift declared some years prior to the American Revolution that he had been told by prominent officers that ''in the whole compass of their acquaintance they could not recollect three of their profession who seemed to regard or believe one syllable of the gospels.'' It was observed abroad, according to the dean, that no race of mortals had so little sense of reli-

[27] W.O. 1:11, 17 Nov. 1776.
[28] *Memoirs of Madame Riedesel*, p. 122, note.

gion as the English soldiers. On the other hand, Sergeant Lamb, speaking from long experience, declared that a large proportion of the soldiery were not only moral but truly pious.[29]

The uniform of the private soldier was ill adapted for comfort and speedy movement. In the majority of regiments, it consisted of the familiar red coat (whose voluminous folds were buttoned back to form lapels), stock, waistcoat, smallclothes, gaiters reaching just above the knee, and cocked hat.[30] Ordinary regiments had facings of yellow; royal and household regiments, of blue.[31] Officers and men wore the hair "clubbed"; that is, plaited and then turned up and tied with tape or ribbon. In case

29 Trevelyan, III, 271-279; Lamb, *Memoir,* p. 70; Fortescue, IV, 925; Belcher, I, 330 ff.; Chichester, p. 916.

30 Skrine, *Fontenoy,* p. 64. Various attempts have been made to explain the origin of the red coat. Authorities concur that it was first introduced into the British army as the uniform of the New Model Army in 1644-1645. The problem is to ascertain why red was selected as the parliamentary color. It seems strange that the Puritans, who were noted for their plain and sombre attire, should have chosen to clothe their soldiery in scarlet. Stocqueler, who holds Cromwell responsible for the innovation, implies that the idea originated in the fact that the livery of the king's bodyguard was red. This would seem to be a reason against the Parliamentarians adopting the hue rather than one for their adopting it. Fortescue, however, expressly points out that red was not Cromwell's color; for when he became protector he arrayed his bodyguard in gray and silver. He traces the red coat to the troops of the Eastern Association, but confesses that "it is not clear why they should have given the pattern to the whole army; and even if it were clear, we are quite in the dark as to the ground of its predilection for that particular color." *Macmillan's Magazine,* Sept. 1893, J. W. Fortescue, "A Chapter on Red Coats."

31 For a "View of the Facings, etc. of the several Marching Regiments of Foot . . .," see appendix to this chapter. Illustrations of uniforms may be found in Belcher, I, 283, 320, 322; Chichester, pp. 167, 235; Cannon's *Regimental Records, passim; A Representation of the Cloathing of His Majesty's Household and of all the Forces upon the Establishments of Great Britain & Ireland,* 1742. Gen. Wolfe is said to have invented "a working dress to save the soldiers' clothing, which was composed of a red jacket with sleeves, over which a sleeveless redcoat could be slipped for parade or for active service." Nevill, *British Military Prints,* p. xvi.

the supply of hair on a man's head was insufficient, he was obliged to eke it out with a switch. Over his left shoulder the foot soldier wore a broad belt supporting a cartouch box, while another belt around his waist supported a bayonet and short sword. On service the infantryman also carried a knapsack containing extra clothing and brush and blackball, a blanket, a haversack with provisions, a canteen, and a fifth share of the general equipage belonging to his tent. These articles (estimating the provision to be for four days)[32] added to his accoutrements, arms, and sixty rounds of ammunition made, according to Burgoyne, a bulk totally incompatible with combat and a weight of about sixty pounds.[33]

The dragoons were armed and clad very much like the foot, except that they wore high boots and carried pistols and long swords. Being still regarded as a species of mounted infantry, they also carried firelocks and—in the case of heavy dragoons—bayonets.[34]

The uniform of the artillery consisted of a blue coat, cocked hat, white waistcoat, white breeches, and black spatterdashes. Sergeants apparently carried halberds, but corporals, bombardiers, gunners, and matrosses were armed with carbines and bayonets.[35] Bandsmen were dressed in the color of the regiment's facings.[36]

In every branch of the service the uniforms of the officers were similar to those of the men. They wore sashes of considerable length and breadth, which might serve as

[32] Cornwallis testified that each man carried three, sometimes four, days' provisions. *A View of the Evidence*, p. 16.

[33] Burgoyne, *State of the Expedition*, p. 148, note. Stedman declares that the weight of the entire equipment at Bunker Hill might be estimated at 125 lbs. *American War*, I, 128.

[34] Lamb, *Memoir*, p. 178; Fortescue, II, 592, note; III, 537; Belcher, I, 281-285.

[35] Duncan, *Hist. of the R. A.*, I, 154, 242, 265, 329.

[36] Farmer, *Memoirs of the R. A. Band*, p. 53.

a kind of ''slung stretcher'' for carrying the owner off
the field in case he were wounded. Perhaps their scarlet
hue was intended to conceal traces of blood. The most
striking feature of the officer's uniform was the gorget.
Originally this was a large steel plate designed to protect
the throat, but with the abandonment of medieval armor
it had shrunk in size until at the time of George III it
was purely ornamental, being simply a small plate—often
of gold—hung about the neck in front and bearing the
regimental device.[37]

The British regular fought the embattled farmers of
America with the ''Brown Bess.'' This was a smooth-
bore flintlock musket with a priming pan, three feet eight
inches long in the barrel, and weighing fourteen pounds.
It had an effective range of three hundred yards, but its
accuracy was unreliable at a distance greater than one
hundred. A soldier who could hit his enemy at that inter-
val must have been a first-class marksman and have possessed a Brown Bess of exceptionally good quality. At a
distance of over one hundred yards, the firing line during
an engagement relied not so much upon the shooting of
each individual as upon the general effect of the volleys
it delivered. The bayonet, which weighed over a pound
and was about fourteen inches in length, did not increase
shooting accuracy when fixed to the muzzle of the gun.
The missile used in the Brown Bess was a round leaden
bullet weighing about an ounce and made up with a stout
paper cartridge.[38] In loading, the soldier first tore the end

---

[37] Nevill, *British Military Prints*, pp. xxxii, 14.

[38] There were 14½ bullets to the pound. T. Simes, *Military Guide*, II,
''Musquet.'' Maj. Gen. Terry in L. Butler, *Annals of the King's Royal
Rifle Corps*, Appendix, p. 43, states that in 1800 the weight of the musket
was 10 lb. 2 oz. and of the bayonet 1 lb. 2 oz., length of barrel 3 ft. 4 in.,
diameter of bore .753 in., charge of powder 6 drs. F.G. with 3 flints to every
pound. *Cf.* Sawyer, *Firearms in American History*, pp. 101-103, with illustrations; plate no. 10.

off the cartridge with his teeth, then sprinkled a few grains of powder from it into the priming pan, and finally rammed the ball and cartridge down the muzzle of the barrel with an iron ramrod.[39] Although twelve separate motions were required in using the Brown Bess, it is said that a clever marksman could load and fire five times a minute. The average soldier, however, fired only two or three rounds a minute. With bayonets fixed, only one round could be fired to much purpose; since the bayonet made it difficult to ram down the charge. The men often put in powder and ball without ramming, and the effect was, of course, slight. Rapid firing was not considered by some officers as very essential. "There is no necessity," wrote Wolfe, "for firing very fast; a cool well-levelled fire with the pieces carefully loaded is more destructive and formidable than the quickest fire in confusion."[40] Burgoyne criticized his men for the impetuosity and consequent uncertainty of their fire in the action of 19 September, 1777.[41]

Another firearm in use was the fusil, which has been defined by one authority as a musket of less than ordinary length and weight, and by another as a light, rifled musket.[42] It was supplied to light companies and fusileer regiments.

[39] The ramrods were sometimes of wood, sometimes of steel. W.O. 28:7, "Report on small arms in Canada," 1 Aug. 1781.

[40] Quoted in Lloyd, *Review of the History of Infantry*, p. 155. Furthermore, the soldier did not carry more than threescore rounds as compared with the 100 that he carries to-day. At Fontenoy each man had only 24 rounds. See also *ibid.*, p. 145; Belcher, II, 59; Fortescue, III, 536; *Encyc. Brit.*, "Brown Bess"; Oman, *Wellington's Army*, pp. 301-302; T. Simes, *Military Guide*, II, "Manual of Exercise . . . in 1764."

[41] *Orderly Book*, p. 116.

[42] Fortescue, III, 536, note; Butler, *Annals of King's Royal Rifle Corps*, Appendix, p. 2. In a return of arms at Quebec, 1 Jan. 1782 (W.O. 28:7), mention is made of musquetoons. These were short muskets of large calibre used especially by cavalry. Carbines are also mentioned as used by cavalry

At this period an improved rifle was just being brought
to the attention of the military authorities. Major Pat-
rick Ferguson (of King's Mountain fame), egged on by
the boasted skill of the American marksmen, had invented a breech-loader. The breech was opened by a screw
plug to allow admission of ball and cartridge; special
arrangements were made to prevent the fouling of the
plug and the accumulation of gas, and the piece was
sighted for one hundred to three hundred yards. In June,
1776, he gave a demonstration at Woolwich before Lord
Amherst, Viscount Townshend, General Harvey, and
several other prominent officers. He astonished the be-
holders. "Notwithstanding a heavy rain and a high wind,
he fired," according to a contemporary, ". . . after the
rate of four shots per minute at a target two hundred
yards distant. He next fired six shots in one minute. He
also fired (while advancing after the rate of four miles
per hour) four times in the minute. He then poured a
bottle of water into the pan and barrel of the piece when
loaded, so as to wet every grain of powder; and in less
than half a minute, he fired with her, as well as ever,
without extracting the ball. Lastly, he hit the bull's eye,
lying on his back on the ground. Incredible as it may
seem to many, considering the variation of the wind, and
wetness of the weather, he only missed the target three
times, during the whole course of the experiment."[43]

Ferguson took out a patent for his improvements, and
was allowed to form a corps of riflemen composed of volunteers from regiments serving in America. While rifled
flintlocks were not officially adopted by the regular army

in America. Types of muskets and cartridges used by the army in 1775 may
be seen in the Museum of the Royal United Service Institution, London.

[43] Lamb, *Journal*, pp. 308-309. See also *Dict. Nat. Biog.*, XVIII, 348-350.
A picture and detailed description of Ferguson's breech-loader will be found
in W. W. Greener, *The Gun*, p. 89.

until many years later, colonels are said to have supplied them to one or two good shots in their regiments; and before the close of the war, every battalion in America had organized a rifle company for itself.[44]

Aside from their clumsiness, the firearms of the period had one very serious drawback: their efficiency was dependent upon the weather. A high wind might blow the powder out of the pans. "If a man was shooting towards the wind he had to take precautions against getting his face scorched and his eyes injured by the back blown flare from the touch-hole."[45] A rainstorm might either wash the powder out of the pans or dampen it so that it failed to ignite. If sufficiently heavy and prolonged, a downpour of rain might soak through the cartouch boxes and turn every cartridge into pulp. When Howe's army landed at the Elk River, 26 August, 1777, a heavy rain fell for thirty-six hours. The cartouch boxes were wet through and the Guards alone lost 1,600 rounds of ammunition.[46] Thus fire effects were extremely uncertain in wet weather. Not one shot in four might go off; and if the infantry were attacked by cavalry, their only reliance was the bayonet. During the siege of Louisburg in 1745, the troops were cautioned that since the air of Cape Breton was moist and foggy, they must be especially careful to keep their firearms dry. Quaintly the commander added that "the Light Infantry should fall upon some method to secure their arms from the dews and droppings of the trees when they are in search of the enemy." In the course of the Revolution, more than one

---

[44] Fortescue, *The British Army, 1783-1802*, p. 83. For some time prior to their departure for America, it is said that the Guards had been "practicing with a rifle-gun in Hyde Park, against a small target three hundred yards off." Quoted from contemporary source in Trevelyan, II, 101.

[45] Sawyer, *Firearms in American History*, p. 99.

[46] Trevelyan, IV, 224.

engagement was terminated by rain. In Pennsylvania, during the autumn of 1777, for example, the 20th Foot came to close quarters with some American troops; but, a violent wind and rainstorm arising, the firelocks were rendered useless and the two forces separated.[47]

Perhaps, after all, it made little difference whether the weather was fair or foul. Under any circumstances the marksmanship in most regiments was poor. Scant mention is made of target practice, and the inference is that there was little of it. It has been claimed that the soldiers did not aim at anything in particular. This probably accounts for the saying that it took a man's weight in bullets to kill him. An American who was taken prisoner by the 42d Highlanders during the assault on Fort Washington in 1776 relates: "Not less than ten guns were discharged with their muzzles toward us, within forty or fifty yards, and some were let off within twenty. . . . I observed that they took no aim, and the moment of presenting and firing was the same." These conditions gave rise to the sharpshooter, a man who not merely aimed his musket, but aimed it at something or somebody. During the campaign of 1777, Burgoyne formed a body of sharpshooters by selecting a group of sober, active, robust men from each regiment.[48] Officers trained in the school of European warfare, however, were prone to place more reliance upon the bayonet than upon the bullet.[49] Burgoyne in particular urged his men to use the bayonet: "Men of half [your] bodily strength and even Cowards may be [your] match in firing; but the onset of Bayonets in the hands of the Valiant is irresistible. . . . It will be

---

[47] Belcher, II, 59; Oman, *Wellington's Army*, pp. 301-302. It has been alleged that the Hessians failed to stave off defeat at Trenton because the rain fell so hard that their muskets would not go off.

[48] *Orderly Book*, 2 Sept. 1777, p. 91.

[49] Trevelyan, III, 6; IV, 158, and note; Belcher, I, 323.

our glory and preservation to storm where possible.''[50]
After the first battle at Freeman's Farm (19 September,
1777), the same commander, while complimenting the gallantry of his troops, lamented ''the mistake they are still
under, in preferring . . . [firing] to the Bayonotte
[*sic*].''[51]

In passing, it should be pointed out that the flints used
by the British soldier during the war were notoriously
poor. Colonel Lindsay of the 46th lamented that the valor
of his men was so often ''rendered vain by the badness
of the pebble stone.'' He exclaimed indignantly against
the authorities for failing to supply every musket with
the black flint which every country gentleman in England
carried in his fowling piece. In this respect the rebels
were acknowledged to be far better off than the king's
troops. A good American flint could be used to fire sixty
rounds without resharpening, which was just ten times
the amount of service that could be expected from those
used by the British forces. Among the rank and file of the
redcoats, the saying ran that a ''Yankee flint was as
good as a glass of grog.''[52]

The sword was not the weapon of the officers in all
cases. Infantry officers carried spontoons, or half-pikes,
and sergeants bore halberds. The latter were about seven
feet in length and had a crosspiece near the point to prevent overpenetration after a thrust. The woody character of the country in America induced many of the officers to discard these awkward medieval weapons and to
replace them by firelocks. Fusils were carried apparently
by all officers of the 7th and 23d (fusileer) regiments and

[50] *Orderly Book*, 20 June, 1777, p. 3.

[51] *Ibid.*, p. 116.

[52] Lindsay, *A Military Miscellany* (1796), referred to by Trevelyan, IV,
34.

by certain officers of the grenadier and light companies of some other regiments.[53]

The subject of pay is a difficult and confusing topic in the history of the army.[54] The pay of the private soldier at the time of the American Revolution amounted to 8d. a day. Of this he got little in food and drink and probably nothing in coin. His pay was divided into two parts, one known as "subsistence," the other as "gross off-reckonings." The first, amounting to 6d. a day or £9:2:6 a year, was supposed to be applied to the cost of his food and was nominally inviolable. In reality, however, several charges were made against it for items that had nothing whatsoever to do with victuals. Thus, 6d. a week was subtracted from it to pay for his shoes, stockings, gaiters, medicines, shaving, and the repair of his arms; and 1d. a week was retained as a fee by the regimental paymaster and divided between him and the surgeon.[55] From the other part of the soldier's pay, the "gross off-reckonings," amounting to 2d. a day or £3:0:10 a year, three deductions were ordinarily made: first, the "poundage" or payment of 1s. in the pound on the full pay to the paymaster general of the forces;[56] second, the "hospital,"

[53] Oman, *Wellington's Army*, p. 303; Fortescue, III, 535; Trevelyan, II, 101; W.O. 1:995, John Campbell to Barrington, 13 Mar. 1778; *ibid.*, 1:999, Ross and Gray, agents, to Barrington, 2 Mar. 1778; Butler's *Annals of King's Royal Rifle Corps*, Appendix, p. 43.

[54] The schedule of pay for all ranks is given in the appendix to this chapter.

The best and fullest account of the pay system is in the 9th Report on Public Accounts (1783) in 39 *Commons Journal*, pp. 325-344. A partial explanation relating chiefly to the net off-reckonings is in the *Report on the Land Forces and Marines* (1746). See also Fortescue, *The British Army, 1783-1802*, p. 8; *History of the British Army*, I, 318; III, 510-515; Andrews, *Guide to Materials in P.R.O.*, II, 131, 132, 134-135; J. W. Williamson, *A Treatise of Military Finance*, 1782.

[55] After 1771, the last-mentioned sum was repaid.

[56] Repaid after 1771.

or payment of one day's full pay (8d.) to Chelsea Hospital; third, the "agency" or payment of 2d. in the pound on the full pay to the regimental agent. The balance, known as the "net off-reckonings," was applied to the cost of the soldier's clothing.[57]

This brief summary affords but a faint idea of the complicated and cumbersome method of paying the troops. "The chaos of 'subsistence,' 'gross off-reckonings,' 'net off-reckonings,' 'stock purses,' and 'non-effective funds' in the financial departments of the military service," writes Fortescue, "was simply indescribable. The computation of 'off-reckonings' alone was a branch so extensive as to give title to an official in the Pay Office; and if he were truly a master of that most abstruse of sciences he must have been a very remarkable man."[58] A parliamentary commission appointed in 1780 to investigate the finances of the army is said to have abandoned its task in despair.[59]

One of the curiosities of regimental finance was the warrant men. These were six fictitious personages on the rolls of practically every regiment of foot. Their pay formed a fund to meet a variety of expenses. The pay of two of the warrant men constituted an allowance to the widows of regimental officers. The pay of the remaining four constituted an allowance to the colonel for clothing lost by deserters, an allowance to the captain for recruit-

[57] An excellent description of the system of net off-reckonings will be found in W.O. 1:1005.

Several other rather exceptional stoppages should be mentioned. A deduction of 3d. *per diem* was made from the soldier's pay when he was on board ship being transported from England to America, and a deduction of 4d. *per diem* when he was in the hospital. A fraction of his pay was sometimes deducted, also, to meet the expense of a regimental chaplain. W.O. 1:10, Howe to Barrington, 27 Mar. 1777; *ibid.*, 1:52, Edward Matthew to Richard Fitzpatrick, 31 July, 1783; Andrews, *Guide to Materials in P.R.O.*, II, 274.

[58] *History of the British Army*, III, 514.

[59] *Ibid.*, p. 514.

ing, and allowances to the colonel and the agent for their own use. Moreover, each company of foot had on its rolls several non-effectives called contingent men, whose subsistence was paid to the captain to keep the regimental arms in repair, and to defray other contingent expenses.[60]

The feeling in the army respecting pay was probably reflected in an anonymous pamphlet published in London in the same year as the battle of Bunker Hill.[61] The author, an officer, stresses the fact that since the current rate of pay was established, the prices of bread and butchers' meat had increased to four times their previous cost. Common toilers in other callings were far better remunerated than the soldiers. A tailor, weaver, or mechanic could live on his wages more respectably than an officer. As for the private in the ranks, after the usual deductions had been made in his stipend, he had not enough left to subsist himself healthfully or to enjoy any recreation costing a little money. "From the eight pence per day which is issued for the pay of a soldier, when all deductions are made, for clothing, for necessaries, for washing, for the paymaster, for the surgeon, and for the multiplied articles of useless and unmilitary fopperies, (introduced by many colonels to the oppression of the soldier for what they call the credit and appearance of the regiment) there is not sufficient overplus for healthful subsistence; and as to the little enjoyments and recreations, which even the meanest rank of men can call their own in any country, the brave, the honorable, the veteran soldier, must not aspire to."

As has been intimated, the system of buying and selling commissions was still in vogue despite repeated at-

[60] 39 *Commons Journal*, p. 330.

[61] *Observations on the Prevailing Abuses in the British Army* . . ., London, 1775. *Cf.* Fortescue, III, 41.

tempts to suppress it.[62] A commission in the cavalry was usually more expensive than one in the infantry; and a commission in the household regiments, more costly than one in the line regiments. In 1777, for example, a company of foot sold at £2,200 while a troop of horses brought 4,000 guineas. A lieutenant-colonelcy in the line cost £4,500 while one in the household brigade cost £4,800. It is not surprising that commissions in the Guards sold at higher figures than those in the line. The household troops were indeed a privileged body. Lieutenants of the Guards ranked as captains in the rest of the army; and captains, as lieutenant colonels. Officers of the Guards generally had "better birth, more money, and greater opportunities for pushing" their advancement than officers of the line. "High commands," as one writer has aptly put it, "were regarded as plums for a guardsman's consumption."[63] In fact, an officer of the line had no chance of promotion to a vacancy if there was a Guardsman anywhere in view. This came to be a sore grievance. "The rise in the Guards," so a contemporary letter runs, "is so rapid from the suppressions of the ranks of Lieutenant and Major that officers of the Line have always the mortification to find after long and painful service, a body of men who supersede them in the profession, and claim most of the elevated posts in the army. When the road seems smooth to a regiment, an inundation of captains in the Guards, by dint of Court rank and etiquette of preceding, defeat all the prospects of the actual soldier, and trample on a life of dangers and fatigue."[64]

[62] The purchasing of commissions was not allowed in the artillery. Fortescue, *The British Army, 1783-1802*, p. 34. For the prices of commissions, see appendix to this chapter.

[63] Belcher, I, 270. For sale-price of commissions as fixed by royal authority in 1766, see T. Simes, *Military Guide*, I, 348.

[64] *London Evening Post*, Feb. 1776, quoted in Trevelyan, II, 94.

Statistics seem to bear out the complaint voiced in this letter. "In 1769 out of every twelve commissioned officers, one was a Guardsman; while out of every three men commanding regiments, one had been a Guardsman."[65]

The purchase system had an amusing side. Although royal authority had forbidden it in 1711, custom still allowed infants to hold commands. This was done in order to provide support for the orphans of distinguished officers by securing to them the annual pay and allowances of a commission. Mere boys were frequently taken out of school, and placed in responsible regimental positions.[66] One of Howe's regiments was commanded by a lieutenant colonel so overcome with gout that he could barely walk. Another was nominally commanded by a lunatic. In both cases this was due to the impossibility of finding purchasers for the commissions, the gouty colonel having waited for at least three years for someone to relieve him.[67]

The purchase system had a noteworthy effect upon the character of the officers in the lower and higher grades of the army. It hampered men of moderate means from climbing very high up the ladder of rank. As a result most of the regimental officers—the lieutenants, captains, and majors—came from the middle ranks of society, that is, from the rural aristocracy in the country and the mercantile classes in the cities. The higher officers—the major generals, lieutenant generals, and generals—sprang as a rule from the nobility. Howe, Gage, Burgoyne, Clinton, and Rawdon, for example, "belonged to ancient en-

---

[65] Belcher, I, 270, 287-288.

[66] Except in the case of orphans mentioned, commissions were not as a rule granted to youths under sixteen years of age. See note appended by Barrington to a letter from William Dalrymple, 31 July, 1778, in W.O. 1:996.

[67] Belcher, I, 267-268; Clode, II, 91-92; Trevelyan, II, 93.

nobled families.'' These men were politicians as well as
soldiers, another fact which must also be considered in
accounting for their advancement. While commanding in
America, Howe, Clinton, and Burgoyne had seats in the
House of Commons. Burgoyne returned home to attend
parliament during the winter of 1775-1776. Cornwallis
was about to depart on the same errand in December,
1776, when the mishap to the Hessians at Trenton detained him in America.[68]

Many of the regimental officers were none the worse
soldiers for the purchase system. Realizing that their
lack of wealth blocked the way to high military advancement, they came to love their calling for itself. Often
forced to renounce marriage owing to the insufficiency of
their pay, they regarded ''the regiment as their home,''
and grew gray in uniform. To them the chief interest in
life came to be the efficiency and reputation of the battalion. Although perhaps a little rusty on the literature of
their own time, they were, many of them, deep students
of the older military literature, particularly the classical.
When taking up the pen to engage in any military controversy, they signed themselves ''Valerius,'' ''Postu-
mius,'' or ''Cincinnatus,'' and illustrated their views by
examples drawn from ancient warfare.[69] Off parade they
treated the subalterns as their peers and allowed nothing
to interfere with the equality which they deemed should
''exist between one gentleman and another.'' Burgoyne,
who was reputed to be the pattern of military manners,
declared, ''Any restraint upon conversation, off parade,
unless when an offence against religion, morals, or good
breeding is in question, is grating; and it ought to be the
characteristic of every gentleman neither to impose, nor
submit to, any distinction but such as propriety of con-

---

[68] Belcher, I, 271; Trevelyan, II, 95.
[69] Trevelyan, II, 96.

duct, or superiority of talent, naturally create."[70] While there were marked exceptions, many regimental officers displayed sympathetic consideration for the comfort and happiness of their men. The bond between them and the non-commissioned officers was often extremely close; and they came to regard the corporals and sergeants, who in many cases had been in the regiment as long as, if not longer than, themselves, with the same kindly feeling as a master does an old family servant.[71]

To this admirable picture there was unfortunately a dark side. Discipline was harsh. The lash was used to punish offences whether trivial or heinous. Nor was it applied either lightly or sparingly. Sergeant Lamb relates: "I well remember the first man I saw flogged. During the infliction of his punishment, I cried like a child."[72] Howe's *Orderly Book* bears testimony to the stern disciplinary methods of the day. In turning its pages, one is repeatedly confronted with such entries as the following: "Boston, 24th Nov. 1775. Thomas Bailey, Grenadier in His Majesty's Corps of Marines, tried by the General Court Martial . . . for Striking Lieut. Russell of the 4th, or King's own Regiment, and of Insolent Mutinous behaviour. The Court . . . have found him guilty of the latter, and do therefore Sentence him to receive Eight Hundred Lashes on his bare back with a Cat of nine Tails . . . 3 Jan. 1776. Thomas MacMahan, Private Soldier in His, Majesty's 43d, Regiment of Foot, and Isabella MacMahan, his wife, tried by . . . Court Martial for Receiving Sundry Stolen Goods, knowing them to be such, are found Guilty of the Crime laid to their Charge, and therefore Adjudge the said Thomas MacMahan to

[70] Quoted in Trevelyan, II, 96.
[71] Trevelyan, II, 95-99; Fortescue, *The British Army, 1783-1802*, p. 32; Lamb, *Memoir*, pp. 68, 109.
[72] *Ibid.*, p. 66.

Receive 1,000 lashes on his bare back with a Cat of nine Tails . . . and the said Isabella MacMahan, to receive 100 Lashes on her bare back, at the Cart's Tail, in Different portions and the most Conspicuous Parts of the Town, and to be imprisoned three months. Thomas Owen and Henry Johnston, Private Soldiers in His Majesty's 59th Regiment of Foot, tried by the General Court Martial . . . for having broken into and Robbed the Store of Messrs. Coffin, Storekeeper, of Sundry goods. The Court, having duly Considered the whole matter before them is of opinion that the prisoners . . . are guilty of the Crime laid to their Charge, and doth, therefore, by virtue of the Power and Authority to them given and Granted by the Second Article of War, Section 20, Adjudge that the said Thomas Owen and Henry Johnson do suffer Death by being hanged by the neck until they are Dead.''[73]

There were not wanting officers, however, who preferred an appeal to the better feelings of their men to an application of the cat. Lamb has a passage which illustrates this, and which incidentally throws light on other methods of military punishment. Referring to Major Bolton of the 9th Foot, he states: ''On the occasion of punishing a man for desertion . . . the Major attended by the officers of the regiment, came to see the sentence of law-martial enforced. After the third drummer inflicted his twenty-five lashes [*i.e.*, when the offending soldier had received seventy-five] Major Bolton, without addressing either the surgeon or officers in attendance, advanced, evidently much affected, to the halberts, in a compassionate manner expostulated with the man concerning the magnitude of his offence, and afterwards ordered him to be taken down, remitting the remainder of the intended punishment, on the soldier's promise of future good conduct. Such severe inflictions were unusual whenever he

[73] Pp. 263, 288.

commanded: he avoided flogging the men as much as possible, and only resorted to it for those great crimes which required extraordinary coercion. For the common breaches of military laws and duties, he used to send them some hours of the day to drill, sometimes making them wear the regimental coat turned inside out, in order to exhibit them as examples of ill behaviour and disgrace. They were, moreover, prevented from going on any command, or mounting the principal guards. On some occasions he confined the ill-conducted soldier to his barrack room, or the guard-house, and when his offence deserved it, the man was condemned to the blackhole, and at times obliged to live on bread and water. In short his mode of treating men showed them his unceasing strictness in preserving order and discipline, as also his fine feelings and dispassionate motives."[74]

The standard of morality in the army did not rise higher than that of the age. A passion for gambling pervaded all ranks. The author above quoted relates how private soldiers would play for the very clothes on their backs and how many of them without a stitch that they could call their own had to borrow clothes from their comrades in order to pass muster on inspection.[75] Eighteenth-century redcoats were also hard drinkers. In an age when the Foxes, Pitts, and Graftons drank to excess, it was not to be expected that the Braddocks, Howes, and Burgoynes would keep within the bounds of temperance.

[74] *Memoir*, p. 68. When it was intended to flog a man, three halberds were arranged in a triangle, across the top of which a fourth was placed "in order to make a whipping post, to which the culprit was tied." Hence arose the expression, "brought to the halberds." The cat was applied to the bare back, usually by a drummer, and from the sanguinary results, British soldiers were sometimes derisively called "bloody backs." It will be recalled that this epithet was applied to Capt. Preston's men on the night of the Boston Massacre. Nevill, *British Military Prints*, p. xvi.

[75] Lamb, *Memoir*, p. 74.

Howe must have seen many "crapulous mornings" at New York; and we have Madame Riedesel as an authority for the statement that Burgoyne nightly sought oblivion in drink towards the close of the Saratoga campaign.[76] Charges of gross immorality have also been laid against the army, but here one plunges into a fog of rumor and hearsay where the truth is difficult to ascertain. Although Burgoyne passionately denied it, some two thousand women are said to have followed the unlucky expedition from Canada in 1777.[77] Both Howe and Burgoyne are reported to have found intimacy with the wives of subordinate officers a solace to the rigors of campaigning.[78] Stedman, himself a British commissary, is authority for the statement that His Majesty's officers shocked Quaker sensibilities by sometimes bringing their mistresses with them into the houses where they were quartered during the occupation of Philadelphia.[79] The extent to which the troops were guilty of rapine and plunder is not easy to estimate. While American writers have probably tended to exaggerate the guilt of the redcoats in this particular, the fact remains that their own officers have sometimes condemned the conduct of the rank and file in strong terms.[80] Deviations from the rules of humane warfare, however, were rarely condoned by those high in command, and Howe, Burgoyne, and Cornwallis strove to stay the hand of thief and marauder.[81]

[76] *Memoirs*, p. 125.

[77] Burgoyne, *State of the Expedition*, pp. 114, 171.

[78] *Memoirs of Madame Riedesel*, p. 125; Jones, *History of New York*, I, 351; Von Elking, *Die Deutschen Hülfstruppen im Nordamerikan Befreiungskriege*, pp. 29, 316.

[79] *American War*, I, 309.

[80] *Ibid.*, pp. 241-242, 309; *Narrative of Sir William Howe*, p. 59; Kemble, *Journal*, I, 91.

[81] During Burgoyne's expedition, 1777, for example, two soldiers were sentenced to receive 1,000 lashes for robbing a man at Fort Edward. Burgoyne, *Orderly Book*, p. 74.

When one surveys as a whole the conduct of the British army in the American Revolution, comparing its deportment with that of European armies in the eighteenth century, he must come fairly to the conclusion that the forces of George III manifested unusual respect for the persons and property of noncombatants.[82]

[82] On this topic, see also Belcher, I, 274, 278-280; Fortescue, *The British Army, 1783-1802*, p. 35.

CHAPTER II

THE ADMINISTRATIVE MACHINERY OF THE ARMY

In surveying the administrative machinery of the British army at the time of the American Revolution, it will be sufficient to examine the English establishment since the Irish establishment was modelled after it on a smaller scale.

According to the constitution, the sovereign could not maintain a standing army without the consent of parliament. Hence the British army had come to have a curious legal status. Technically it was disbanded at the end of each year. That is, for more than three-quarters of a century it had been customary to pass an annual Mutiny Act which not only regulated the execution of martial law but which legalized the existence of a standing army of specified numbers for the period of a year and no longer.[1]

At the head of the army stood the king as captain general of all the forces both naval and military. It was usual, however, for him to delegate his military powers, in part at least, to some distinguished general as captain general or commander-in-chief. Marlborough, Ormonde, and Cumberland had been thus honored. From 1772 to 1778 the office remained vacant, but from the latter year until 1782, Sir Jeffrey Amherst officiated as commander-in-chief with the title of General on the Staff. He was con-

[1] Maitland, *Constitutional History*, pp. 328-329, 447-448.

sulted regarding all important questions of military policy.[2]

Next in importance to the commander-in-chief was the secretary at war. An exposition of his functions at the outbreak of the Revolution would scarcely apply to him at all times, since exceptional conditions prevailed. Not only did Lord Barrington possess more ability than the average secretary, but owing to the absence of a regular commander-in-chief, he combined many of the duties of that office with his own.

The secretary held a commission from the crown under the sign manual. Therein he was bidden "to observe and follow such Orders and Directions as he should from Time to Time receive from the King or the General of the Forces" *i.e.*, the commander-in-chief.[3] Although previous to and during the American War he had usually been a member of parliament, he was rarely a member of the Privy Council and never, it would appear, of the cabinet. Not until after 1783 did he become a minister responsible to parliament. Previous to that date he was responsible to the crown alone.

The duties of the secretary at war were so manifold that only the more important will be referred to. He was charged with framing the articles of war, issued under the sign manual, with publication of the yearly army lists, and with preparation and presentation to the House of Commons of the Army Estimates and the Mutiny Act. To that body he likewise tendered the extraordinary accounts of the paymaster general. He issued royal orders for the payment of the army, supervised the pensioning of officers' widows, and was responsible for the examina-

2 Fortescue, IV, 80. The commander-in-chief held his appointment under the great seal. See also W.O. 1:616, *passim; Cal. H.O. Papers,* II, No. 379; *Correspondence of Geo. III with Lord North, passim.*

3 W.O. 25:37, p. 1. Complete text given in appendix to this chapter.

tion of certain army accounts. Any person desiring to act as regimental agent must secure his consent. Regarding military affairs he carried on a considerable correspondence with general and field officers both at home and abroad, with the secretaries of state, and with the other departments. He furnished statistical information relative to the forces to the king, Privy Council, and parliament; and kept engineers' returns, hospital returns, and headquarters records of various kinds. He received petitions upon all sorts of subjects relating to the army; communicated to corps distinctive titles conferred upon them by the king, countersigned military commissions, orders, and warrants of one sort or another, under the sign manual; and exercised more or less control over promotions, appointments, resignations, desertions, exchanges, dismissals, leaves of absence, regimental successions, and the invaliding of soldiers. He furnished the king with special guard service, and sent muster masters upon tours of inspection. He ordered officers to repair to their posts, directed embarkations, issued orders for marching, drafting, recruiting, completing, raising, augmenting, and disbanding regiments. He had general supervision over military hospitals, courts-martial, and foreign troops in English pay. His duties were manifold and the range of his authority wide. The limits to his authority geographically were England and Scotland. Ireland possessed a separate establishment. The limits to his authority administratively were horse and foot. Artillery and engineers fell under the control of the master general of the ordnance, marines under that of the Admiralty, and the militia under that of the lord lieutenants of the counties.

The following example given by Clode, in his *Military Forces of the Crown,* admirably illustrates the functions of the secretary at war and his relations to other departments: "In 1758 Lieutenant General Bligh was selected to go on foreign service in command of a body of cavalry. Lord Barrington first wrote to him, by the command of the King, that he was appointed to that service. He then wrote to the Commissioners of the Treasury to tell them that five regiments of cavalry were to go on foreign service, that their lordships might give orders to the Victualling Board for a supply of bread and forage. He next sent orders to each regiment to hold themselves in readiness to embark. He then wrote to the Paymaster-General, signifying to him the King's pleasure, that he should issue subsistence to the men, and 12 months' off-reckonings to the Colonels; and, lastly to the Apothecary-General, desiring him to send immediately a supply of medicines for the expedition."[4]

In 1775 the personnel of the War Office, which was located in Whitehall, was as follows:[5]

Secretary at War—Viscount Barrington.

Deputy Secretary and First Clerk—Matthew Lewis.

The deputy secretary was responsible "for the execution of the detail of the office business"; and superintended the conduct of all the clerks, messengers, tradesmen, etc. There were ten or eleven clerks under him.

Paymaster of Widows' Pensions—Hon. Henry Fox.

Deputy—John Powell.

The two officials mentioned above transacted all the business relative to the pensions of the widows of army officers except the actual payment of the money.

Examiner of Army Accounts—William Smith,

Assistant—Z. R. Taylor.

The examiner of army accounts superintended the examination and settlement of all the accounts of the army that came under the cognizance of the War Office. He was

4 II, 698.
5 *Court and City Register*, 1775.

not considered subject to the directions of the deputy secretary but only of the secretary at war himself. His assistant besides examining the accounts estimated the sums to be issued on account for various services not borne on the regimental establishment, such as recruiting, extra feed, innkeepers' allowances, etc.

There were, in addition to the aforesaid departmental staff, a messenger, office-keeper, and "necessary woman."

The duties of the paymaster general are suggested by his title. He was the custodian of the moneys voted by parliament for the army, barring artillery and engineers. The office of ordnance, as will presently be shown, possessed its own treasurer and paymaster. In theory the paymaster general had no active control over the funds committed to his charge. He was not entitled to disburse them save on a warrant from the Treasury or the secretary at war.

The method of paying the army was, generally speaking, as follows: Each regiment possessed a civil agent, appointed by the colonel, with power of attorney to transact its financial affairs and under bond.[6] At the time of the Revolution, there were no regimental paymasters in the strict sense of the word. The colonel was accustomed to appoint one of the officers to act in that capacity in addition to his other duties. In the payment of the regiment, therefore, the money passed from the paymaster general to the agent, from the agent to the regimental paymaster, thence to the captains, who in turn disbursed it to the men. Thus the captains accounted with the regimental paymaster, the regimental paymaster with the agent, the agent with the secretary at war. After the latter had satisfied himself as to the correctness of the agent's accounts through the examiner of army ac-

6 H. B. Thompson, *Military Forces of Great Britain*, pp. 172-173.

counts and given the agent a certificate to that effect, the
agent was at liberty to close the account with the paymaster general.[7]

The paymaster general, however, did not confine his
attention solely to the paying of the army. He dealt with
a great variety of expenditures, ranging from the cost of
erecting a new garrison coal yard to subsidies to foreign
princes. He also assisted the secretary at war in drawing
up the army estimates, arranged with brokers for bills
of exchange for the payment of troops abroad, appointed
the clothier for the invalids under directions from the
Treasury, acted as one of the commissioners of Chelsea
Hospital, and was consulted about sundry military matters. His accounts were yearly submitted to parliament
by the secretary at war who by subscribing them acknowledged a joint responsibility.

As is well known, the office of paymaster general was
extremely lucrative, since its incumbent was accustomed
to deduct by way of fees heavy percentages from the
moneys which he disbursed. Rosebery in his *Life of Chatham* terms it "that opulent subordinate office." The paymasters were notoriously corrupt. Everyone recalls how
Henry Fox used the public moneys entrusted to him in
buying votes and how Richard Rigby, who held the office
during the Revolution, barely escaped impeachment
for his peculations. In 1781 the department was investi-
gated by a parliamentary commission. It was found that
the paymaster was accustomed to submit to the Treasury
an estimate of the sums required for the service of the
army, and that the Treasury without scrutinizing the
necessity or accuracy of the demands was accustomed to
pay the money to him. In this way he was able to ac-
cumulate large balances from which he calmly pocketed
the interest. It was discovered that the yearly balance on

---

[7] Clode, II, Ch. XXIII.

his hands amounted to £586,000 and the average monthly to £869,000. Furthermore, on quitting office the paymaster was suffered to retain the use of the balances until his accounts had been finally passed, which was a matter requiring considerable trouble and delay. Thus he enjoyed the use of the public moneys several years after he had ceased to hold office. For example, Henry Fox resigned office in 1765 but by 1780 his accounts were still unaudited. He was thus enabled for fifteen years to draw an income of £25,000 a year from moneys which were not his.[8]

Organization of the Paymaster General's Office in 1775.[9]

Paymaster General—Rt. Hon. Richard Rigby, M.P.
Deputy Paymaster General—Anthony Sawyer.
Accountant—John Powell.
Computer of Off-reckonings—Charles Bembridge.
Cashier of Half Pay—Robert Randall.
Keeper of the Stores—P. Burrell.

These officers (with the exception of John Powell), assisted by eight clerks, constituted the home pay office. There were eight subordinate paymasters abroad: *viz.*,

Gibraltar—William Sloper
Nova Scotia—G. J. Williams
New York—T. Barrow
Quebec—John Powell
Montreal—Thomas Boone
Minorca—Robert Digby
Louisburg—Peter Elwin
Boston—J. Garnier

The master general of the ordnance was chief of the

[8] See the 4th, 5th, 6th, and 9th Reports of Commissioners of Accounts in 38-39 *Commons Journal*. *Cf.* Belcher, I, 286; Fortescue, III, 511.
[9] *Court and City Register*, 1775.

department of that name. Its business was amphibious in character, pertaining both to the army and the navy. It had charge of arms, ammunition, ordnance, tents, bedding, wagons, the erection of barracks, fortifications, hospitals, and magazines. It provided military prisons, regulated the inspection of arms and accoutrements, was charged with the repair of the royal observatory at Greenwich and the preparation of maps for military purposes. It enjoyed complete control, even to the exclusion of the secretary at war, over artillery, engineers, sappers, pontoonists, and artificers. The master general enjoyed supreme control over the department. He was assisted by a board of five principal officers holding letters patent under the great seal; to wit, the lieutenant general, the clerk of the ordnance, the principal storekeeper, the clerk of the deliveries, and the treasurer-paymaster.[10] All warrants from the king, Privy Council, secretaries of state, or (in sea affairs) the board of Admiralty, were directed not to the board but to the master general; and the board carried them into execution pursuant to his orders. It was in fact subordinate to him in every respect except one. He could not order the issue of any money without a debenture signed by three members. If he did not interpose, however, the board was competent to carry on all official business, could make contracts, and direct issue of money and stores. During the absence of the master general or the vacancy of his office, the whole executive power devolved upon it.[11]

The board commonly met three times a week in winter and twice a week in summer at the Ordnance Office in Westminster. Three officers constituted a quorum. While the master general and the lieutenant general seldom

10 *Cal. H.O. Papers*, I, no. 670, 1160; III, no. 1621.
11 40 *Commons Journal*, p. 113; Farrow, *Military Encyclopedia*, ''Ordnance.''

failed to be present, some of the other officers took alternate months of attendance.[12]

The master general and the board acted in military affairs in response only to orders from the king, Privy Council, or secretaries of state. They could issue no stores, arms, ammunition, or other *matériel,* nor so much as add a storekeeper to their force of employees, without a proper warrant from one of the above sources. The board was extremely punctilious about such matters. It insisted, furthermore, that no orders for issues should be transmitted to it without previous consultation regarding their nature and amount.[13]

No department of army administration was so jealous of its prerogatives as the board of ordnance. To other branches of the service it often seemed "obnoxious and obstructive" and to its own employees painfully dilatory. The chief authority on the history of the royal artillery furnishes several homely illustrations of this: "A company in the Bahamas was ordered to be in readiness to return to England, and no clothing was sent to it for the year 1784, as the Board promised to make immediate arrangements for its transport; but 1784 passed, and also 1785, and then 1786, and no transport was forthcoming, nor was any clothing for these three years. . . . A fence happened to require repairs in front of the barracks, and its dangerous state was repeatedly pointed out by the Commandant. But not until years had passed and an officer had killed his horse, and broken his own collar-bone, did any steps occur to the Board to remedy it. Even then, while they were brooding, accidents continued, coming to a climax one night, when the Chaplain in walking home fell in and broke the principal ligament

12 *21st Report, Finance Committee,* 1797, p. 429.
13 *Cal. H.O. Papers,* 1773-1775, *passim.* For example of a royal sign manual order to the board, see the appendix to this chapter.

of his leg. . . . A temporary chapel existed in the War-
ren and . . . in 1783 the Chaplain applied for a 'cushion
& furniture for the pulpit, a surplice, Bible & prayer
books, and a few hassocks, those in use having been purchased in 1753.' After waiting patiently for *four* years,
the Chaplain again sent in a demand, stating that it was
impossible to use the old ones any longer.'"[14]

Excepting the lieutenant general, each of the principal
officers had a separate and distinct branch of business
committed to his charge.[15] The lieutenant general "acted
as a sort of adjutant to the Master General, who looked
to him for all information connected with the various
trains of artillery at the Tower & elsewhere."

The surveyor general, or master surveyor as he was
called in his patent, examined the quantity and quality
of all stores received into the storehouses and magazines
of the department, took "remains," and noted issues
and receipts.

The clerk of the ordnance, who was a kind of book-
keeper, recorded and preserved all the vouchers and instruments relative to the proceedings of the department,
kept accounts of all the cash and stores belonging thereto,
and drew up the annual estimates for parliament and the
monthly estimates for the Treasury.

The principal storekeeper was the custodian of the
ordnance stores received into and issued out of the
Tower.

The clerk of the deliveries superintended and kept an
account of the issues of the stores and ordnance. His
duties are best illustrated by indicating the process of
issuing ordnance stores. When the board proposed to
make an issue of stores, it directed the clerk to prepare

---

14 Duncan, *History of R. A.*, II, 11. *Cf. ibid.*, I, 335.

15 12th Report of Commissioners of Acts, 40 *Commons Journal*, pp. 113-
114; Duncan, *History of R. A.*, I, 17-19.

what was known as a "proportion." This was an instrument, signed by three members of the board, directed to a storekeeper, authorizing him to issue certain stores specified therein. The clerk of the deliveries delivered this warrant to the storekeeper, and on receiving the stores in question, consigned them to the person charged with their receipt. If they consisted of arms or ammunition, he caused the recipient to sign an indent whereby the latter agreed to render an account of them.

The functions of the treasurer-paymaster are implied in his title. He had "to find heavy personal securities" and was "one of the most important officers" of the board.

In addition to the aforesaid officials there were a host of minor functionaries such as clerks of the foundry, recorders, counsels to the ordnance, and "astronomical observators." Moreover, to each important garrison town was assigned a storekeeper, clerk of the survey, and clerk of the check, performing on a smaller scale no doubt the respective duties of the five principal officers.

The personnel of the ordnance department in 1775 was as follows:[16]

Civil Branch of the Office of Ordnance.

Master General—Rt. Hon. Geo. Viscount Townshend.
Lieutenant General—Sir Jeffrey Amherst, K.B.
Surveyor General—Sir C. Frederick, K.B., F.R.S.
Clerk of the Ordnance—Sir Chas. Cocks, Bart.
Storekeeper—Andrew Wilkinson.
Clerk of the Deliveries—Benjamin Langlois, Esq.
Treasurer & Paymaster—John Ross Mackye, Esq.
Secretary to the Master General—John Courtney, Esq.

[16] *Court and City Register,* 1775.

Under Secretary to Master General—T. Masterson, Esq.

Minuting Clerk—H. Simmonds.

As assistants to the above officers there were some eight clerks.

Military Branch of the Office of Ordnance.

Chief Engineer and Colonel—Lieut. Gen. W. Skinner.

Directors and Lieutenant Colonels—Col. James Montrésor, Lieut. Col. Arch. Patoun.

Sub. Directors and Majors—Four in number.

Engineers in Ord. and Captains—Twelve in number.

Engineers Extra. and Captains and Lieutenants—Twelve in number.

Practitioner Engineers and Ensigns—Sixteen in number.

It should be added that Woolwich Military Academy, established in 1741, also came within the province of the office of ordnance. The purpose of the academy being to train men for the artillery and engineering services, instruction was chiefly devoted to fortification and mathematics. There were, however, classes in arithmetic, writing, French, the classics, drawing, dancing, and fencing. Dr. Pollock was at this time professor of fortification and artillery, while the famous mathematician, Charles Hutton, taught mathematics. The direction of the institution was in the hands of a governor, lieutenant governor, and inspector.

No description of the administration of the army would be complete without reference to the judge advocate general, the apothecary general, and the comptrollers of army accounts.

The judge advocate general was appointed by letters patent under the great seal wherein he was commanded to follow the orders of the king and the commander-in-chief. The foundation of all proceedings by general court-martial was a warrant from the crown countersigned by a secretary of state and ''addressed to the Judge Advocate General for the trial of persons at home and to general officers on colonial or foreign stations for the trial of persons abroad.'' In the first class of cases, the trials were held in the great room of the Horse Guards and the judge advocate general or his deputy attended, sometimes as prosecutor for the crown or the commander-in-chief but more frequently, it seems, as a legal assessor, to observe the proceedings, to ascertain that justice was done to the prisoner, and to assist the court. In the second class of cases, the proceedings were sent home to him for examination. In either instance the judge advocate submitted the sentences with his opinion thereon to the sovereign for confirmation or rejection. He thus acted as a legal adviser to the crown in matters pertaining to military law. He also acted in the same capacity for the commander-in-chief. It was sometimes necessary for the latter to arraign officers or soldiers for offences against the rules and regulations of the army. For him ''to suffer a legal defeat'' at the hands of a subordinate would have led to an undermining of all military authority. It was consequently of the highest importance for him to have an adviser learned in military law to counsel him and in case of an arraignment to frame the charges so as to obviate the chances of any ''possible miscarriage on mere technical or legal grounds.'' The judge advocate also acted as secretary and legal adviser to the board of general officers as will be indicated later. He had chambers in the Horse Guards. During the American War the post was held by Charles Gould, afterwards known as Sir Charles Gould-Morgan.[17]

[17] Clode, II, Ch. xxvii; *36th Report, Finance Committee*, 1798; *Court and City Register*, 1775-1783.

The apothecary general, like the judge advocate general, was a noncombatant officer holding his office by appointment under the sign manual. Under directions from the secretary at war, he supplied the army with medicines, hospital stores, surgical instruments, and the like. Semi-annually he presented a bill to the Treasury, having previously submitted it for approval to the surgeon and physician generals and to the secretary at war, who certified that the medicines specified had been forwarded to their respective destinations.[18] During the Revolution the apothecary general was George Garnier.[19]

The comptrollers of army accounts were two in number. They were appointed under the great seal, and acted under the orders of the Treasury. They were assisted by a staff consisting of a secretary, four clerks, an office-keeper, and a messenger. The secretary likewise acted as secretary to the clothing board. Meeting once a week, the comptrollers audited practically all accounts relating to the army, examined the accounts for subsistence of foreign troops and of moneys paid under treaties with foreign princes, and scrutinized the pay rolls with an eye to frauds and abuses. They also arranged contracts for bread, wood, straw, and provisions for the use of troops on home service. During the greater part of the American Revolution, the comptrollers were Henry Bunbury and Thomas Bowlby and the secretary, Thomas Fauquier.[20]

In addition to the various officials above-mentioned

18 *Cal. Treas. Bks.*, 1742-1745, p. 319; *19th Report, Finance Committee*, 1797, pp. 372, 374.

19 *Court and City Register*, 1775-1783. Garnier seems to have performed the duties of the office through two deputies, John Truesdale and Joseph Partridge. T. 29:45, p. 394.

20 *19th* and *22d Reports, Finance Committee*, 1798; *Report on Land Forces*, 1746; *Report on Army Extras*, 1778; W.O. 25:37 (warrant of appointment); *Court and City Register*, 1775-1783.

there were a number of boards concerned with army administration. Regarding the Treasury and Admiralty boards, little need be said at this point, since their connection with the forces will become evident in subsequent chapters. It will be sufficient to state that the former provided the army with food, horses, blankets, camp necessaries, and certain articles of clothing while the latter furnished convoys, controlled the marines, and directed the work of the navy, victualling, and medical boards, whose functions will presently be explained.

One of the most important bodies dealing with the administration of the army was the board of general officers, which was selected by the king to advise him, the commander-in-chief, and the secretary at war upon sundry military questions. It was composed of some thirty members, five of whom constituted a quorum.[21] The eldest member present acted as president while the judge advocate general served as secretary, notifying members regarding meetings and reporting those absent, who in cases of flagrant neglect were liable to the royal displeasure. The board, which assembled in the great room of the Horse Guards, did not sit regularly but only as often as the king required. Its opinions, signed by all present affirmative as well as negative, were transmitted to the secretary at war, who laid them before the king. Until approved by a sign manual warrant they possessed no validity.[22] According to the patent creating it, the board was "to hear, examine, and determine all such information and complaints as should be brought before them by the King, the Captain-General of the Forces, or the Secretary at War, as well touching the ranks of all Regiments as the dates of all Commissions, and of the

21 Clode, II, 724.
22 Simes, *Military Guide*, I, 344.

misbehaviour or misdemeanor of any Officer, Half-pay Officer, or Soldier, or of any abuses which were or should be committed in anywise relating to the Forces, to redress Grievances, irregularities, and other ill practices that had been or should be committed amongst them, and to refer all such matters as they should think proper to Court Martial, etc., and the said General Officers are to make such observations as may be necessary in the course of their proceedings of anything that may occur to them which will tend to the advantage of the Service; . . . "[23]

Another board, which was chosen annually by the board of general officers and which was subject to the orders of the king, the commander-in-chief, and the Treasury, was the clothing board. It consisted of from fifteen to twenty general officers, three of whom constituted a quorum. Its business was to inspect and seal patterns of army clothing. At the first yearly meeting it inspected and sealed patterns for all regiments then on the establishment, excepting the artillery and engineers, whose clothing was regulated by the ordnance department. In case additional regiments were subsequently raised, it met again to perform the same service for them. It possessed no authority to make contracts for clothing—a matter for which the colonels and regimental agents were responsible—but it was charged with the duty of examining and approving such contracts and of inspecting the clothing thereby provided. In case of disputes with the contractors regarding the quality of clothing, the board and the contractors each chose a referee, and if the referees failed to agree, they (the referees) chose an umpire whose decision was final. The board possessed a president and permanent secretary, who was

23 Clode, I, 724.

also secretary to the comptrollers of army accounts. Assisted by several clerks, he made entries of the assignments and accounts and probably kept the minutes.[24]

Mention should likewise be made of the board of commissioners of Chelsea Hospital. This institution, founded by Charles II in 1682, might be called the old soldiers' home of the British army. Originally intended to accommodate all pensioned soldiers, it was soon found to be too small owing to the increasing size of the army. The question then arose as to who should have the privilege of residing there. Naturally the choice fell upon the oldest and most infirm pensioners. These so-called in-pensioners were boarded and lodged with an allowance of 8d. per week as pocket money. The out-pensioners were granted £7 12s. 6d. a year in lieu of residence at the hospital. The institution itself was maintained by a tax levied upon the pay of the army and by parliamentary supplies. The board of commissioners by which it was governed was appointed by the crown, and consisted of the president of the council, the first lord of the Treasury, the secretaries of state, the paymaster general, the comptrollers of army accounts, and the governor and lieutenant governor of the hospital. The commissioners acted under instructions issued from time to time by the crown in the form of royal warrants under the sign manual. As a rule they met monthly in the hospital chambers in Whitehall. Besides regulating the affairs of the hospital, they determined the eligibility of soldiers recommended to the Chelsea Pension. In this they were guided largely by their own judgment, since no fixed regulations regarding the qualifications necessary to secure the pension were issued by the crown until 1783. The personnel of the

[24] W.O. 7:27, *passim; 35th Report, Finance Committee*, 1797-1798, p. 669; Clode, I, 107-108.

hospital, besides the in-pensioners, consisted of a staff of doctors and numerous household servants.[25]

In addition to the aforesaid boards, there were three others which were incidentally concerned with the army. These were the navy board, the victualling board, and the board of sick and wounded seamen (later known as the medical board), each of which was subordinate to the Admiralty. The first provided transports for troops and clothing; the second stocked the transports with provisions; and the third controlled some of the military prisons.[26]

Such in outline was the administrative system—if one may call it a system—of the British army. It was characterized by overlapping, duplication, and decentralization of authority. "What a hopeless organization for war," exclaims Fortescue. If the lack of efficiency was painfully evident when the various boards and departments were called upon to administer the affairs of a small army in time of peace, the reader can imagine the situation when they were obliged to manage the business of several armies in time of war, operating at a distance of three thousand miles in the vast and sparsely settled provinces of America. No doubt the clumsy and antiquated machinery of army administration in London was partly responsible for the failure of British arms in the American Revolution.

[25] *34th Report, Finance Committee,* 1798; Clode, II, 540-544; *Court and City Register,* 1775-1783.

[26] *17th, 32d,* and *33d Reports, Finance Committee,* 1797-1798; Admiralty: Minutes of Navy, Victualling, and Medical Boards. These boards are sometimes referred to as the navy commissioners, victualling commissioners, and commissioners of sick and wounded seamen.

CHAPTER III

THE RECRUITING OF THE ARMY

WE have seen that at the outbreak of the American Revolution the total land forces of Great Britain (exclusive of militia) numbered about 48,000 men. The exigencies of the war necessitated an increase. By 1781 a force of 110,000 men had been enrolled, of which about 56,000 were located in America and the West Indies.[1] Thousands of soldiers had, in the meantime, been lost through death and the accidents of war. The question naturally arises, therefore, as to how troops were raised both to meet the increased size of the army and to make good the casualties. In a word, how was the army recruited?

Throughout the war the government experienced great difficulty in obtaining sufficient men for the ranks.[2] Again and again it was found impossible to complete the augmentation voted by parliament.[3] The correspondence of the adjutant general, Edward Harvey, is burdened with complaints about the state of the recruiting. "Sad work everywhere in recruiting," he writes in December, 1775. "In these damned times we must exert zeal."[4] The com-

[1] These were "regulars." The figures do not include a number of independent companies of somewhat irregular character. 38 *Commons Journal*, pp. 33-36.

[2] W.O. 1:992-1008, *passim*.

[3] "There is no Prospect that we shall be able to procure in time for this Campaign [1776] all that are necessary to complete the Augmentation." C.O. 5:93, Germain to Howe, 28 Mar. 1776. "We found it impossible to fill up the Augmentation voted in 1778 by obtaining Recruits sufficient for that purpose." W.O. 4:275, Jenkinson to Clinton, 5 Dec. 1780.

[4] W.O. 3:5, to Lord Gordon, 28 Dec. 1775. "In England the Government [in August, 1775] could not get above 400 recruits." H. Walpole, *Last Journals*, I, 500.

petition for recruits among the various regiments was intense.[5] Some of them, not satisfied with such able-bodied men as they could secure by hook or crook, enlisted invalids and out-pensioners.[6] Not a little ill-feeling was aroused among the militia officers by attempts to enlist their levies as well.[7] Prior to 1775 Roman Catholics as a rule had been excluded from the ranks; but now those in Connaught and Munster were gladly welcomed.[8] Recruiting parties were even sent into the American colonies.[9] As is well known the paucity of men led not merely to the hiring of the Hessians, but to the recruiting of many Germans into British regiments.[10] In 1775 bootless attempts were made to procure 20,000 mercenaries from Russia[11] and the use of a Scottish brigade in

[5] For example, see W.O. 1:996, Lieutenant Lumsden to Colonel Dalrymple, 8 Sept. 1778; *ibid.*, 1:998, Adjutant Pole to Barrington, 9 Apr. 1778.

[6] W.O. 1:998, Captain William Morris to Barrington, 20 May, 1778; *ibid.*, 1:995, W. Brown to Barrington, 29 Jan. 1778; *ibid.*, 1:997, Lord Macdonald to Barrington, 5 Feb. 1778; *ibid.*, 1:999, Lieutenant Simpson to Barrington, 9 Feb. 1778.

[7] W.O. 1:996, Sir William Codrington to Barrington, Dec. 1778; *ibid.*, 1:995, Colonel Calcraft to Barrington, 8 May, 1778.

[8] Lecky, *American Revolution* (edited by Woodburn), p. 242. Howe was strongly opposed to recruiting the army in America with Irish Roman Catholics: ''But this Army, tho' complete in the Spring, must have between 6 & 7,000 Recruits, and of the worst Kind, if chiefly composed of Irish Roman Catholics, certain to desert if put to hard Work, and from their Ignorance of Arms not intitled to the smallest confidence as Soldiers.'' C.O. 5:92, Howe to Dartmouth, 26 Nov. 1775.

[9] W.O. 1:51, Governor Dalling to Secretary at War, 31 Aug. 1781.

[10] W.O. 4:273, Barrington to Howe and Carleton, 20 May, 1776, Barrington to Howe, 31 Oct. 1776; *ibid.*, 28:7, St. Leger to Major Lernoult, 20 May, 1782; *ibid.*, 1:52, Matthew to Jenkinson, 12 July, 1782; *Correspondence of Geo. III. with Lord North*, I, 293; L. Butler, *Annals of the Kings Royal Rifle Corps*, I, 208.

[11] C.O. 5:92, Dartmouth to Howe, 5 Sept. 1775; *ibid.*, 5:93, Pownall to Howe, 5 Jan. 1776; *Dartmouth MSS.*, I, 395. As late as 7 July, 1777, Howe writes to Germain, ''A Corps of Russians of 10,000 effective fighting Men I think would ensure the Success of the War to Great Britain in another Campaign.'' C.O. 5:94.

the pay of Holland.[12] These facts strikingly illustrate the appalling scarcity of available fighting men.

Throughout the struggle, Scotland continued to be the most fertile field for recruits. "The present ardor of the Highland Gentlemen," wrote Lord John Murray, "is great to be employed in His Majesty's Service."[13] England was less productive; while Ireland was well-nigh barren, supplying recruits not only few in number but poor in quality.[14] "What can be the meaning that recruiting goes so slow in Ireland?" Harvey asks Cornwallis in July, 1775. "The regiments in Britain have 17 parties in that country and only 24 recruits are got in one week, 28 in another, and 10 more in another. This will never do. This Country [England] is but in a middling situation, if men are so scarce."[15] Political conditions account in large measure for Scotland's wealth of recruits. The military power of the chieftains had been broken in 1745; and from feudal superiors they had been converted, through the failure of the government to provide an equitable land system, into grasping landlords. Rents had indeed become so oppressive that many thrifty and industrious clansmen were leaving the country. Hence when the call for troops came, "the best fighting men of Argyllshire and Invernesshire eagerly hailed the chance of winning by their swords a settlement in America more secure than that which their progenitors had held, by the tenure of the sword in the valleys of their native Scot-

[12] Trevelyan, II, 41.

[13] W.O. 1:993, to Barrington, 20 Jan. 1776.

[14] See, for example, Duncan, *Hist. of R. A.*, I, 164, 334. *Cf.* the opinions expressed by Colonel Pattison, "Letters" (N. Y. Hist. Soc. *Coll.* 1875), pp. 81, 105.

[15] W.O. 3:5, 6 July, 1775. *Cf.* Harvey to Mackay, 6 Nov. 1775, "Recruiting as bad as ever. Ireland produces nothing worth speaking of. Something must be done if possible to correct this fundamental want."

land.''[16] Readiness to enlist was not confined in Scotland, however, merely to the clansmen. ''Many tradesmen, worth £200 to £300,'' says Stocqueler, ''forsook their business to join the army, refusing bounties. . . . A club of one hundred weavers at Glasgow draughted fourteen of their number for recruits; and made up a stock of £350 to maintain their families in their absence. Even the link boys raised 30 guineas among their number to support the war.''[17] In England widespread want of sympathy with the colonial policy of the government undoubtedly checked recruiting. No one was less wanting in such sympathy than the secretary at war himself. Lord Barrington was also opposed to the measures employed to obtain recruits, and doubted their efficacy. This must unquestionably have dampened the ardor of his military subordinates. In Ireland abundant crops seem to have made the task of the recruiting officer especially difficult at the outset of the war. The Dublin government stated in October, 1775, that the agriculturists had rarely enjoyed so prosperous a year. ''Corn of all kinds,'' wrote Lord Harcourt, ''and potatoes, the chief food of the people, are a drug.'' With their cabins overflowing with plenty, the Irish farmers were in no mood to be tempted into the ranks.[18]

A number of other circumstances tended to make recruiting difficult throughout the British Isles. Service was ordinarily for life.[19] The pay of both officers and men was inadequate to meet the rising standard of comfort and luxury.[20] Little honor was attached to military

[16] Trevelyan, II, 33-34. *Cf.* Andrews, *Journal of a Lady of Quality*, p. 38 and Appendix I.

[17] *The British Soldier*, p. 59 note.

[18] Trevelyan, II, 32-34; *Correspondence of Geo. III with Lord North*, I, 265.

[19] Wheeler, *The War Office Past and Present*, p. 90.

[20] Fortescue, III, 41.

service. In 1775 no medals or decorations were awarded for gallantry. There was nothing to correspond to the Victoria Cross. Ever since Cromwell's time, the soldier had been regarded as the natural enemy of the liberties of the people. On all sides he was held up to ridicule and contempt. The newspapers delighted in caricaturing his ignoble and unhappy life. The popular estimate of him was summed up in a saying current in the navy some thirty years later: "A messmate before a shipmate, a shipmate before a stranger, a stranger before a dog, a dog before a soldier."[21] All of these circumstances combined to make the work of the recruiting officer onerous.

Prior to 1778, the crown employed two methods of obtaining men. The first of these was voluntary enlistment. On 16 December, 1775, the War Office gave notice in the *London Gazette,* the official organ of the army, that "during the Continuance of the Rebellion now subsisting in North America, every Person, who should enlist as a soldier in any of His Majesty's Marching Regiments of Foot, should be entitled to his Discharge at the end of Three Years, or at the end of said Rebellion, at the option of His Majesty."[22] Although no mention of the fact was made in the proclamation, a bounty of one guinea and a half was offered to every volunteer.[23] A second method of obtaining soldiers was by pardoning malefactors before the law upon condition of their enlistment.

[21] Belcher, *First American Civil War,* I, 250, 258.

[22] *London Gazette,* 16 Dec. 1775. For complete text, see the appendix to this chapter.

[23] W.O. 3:5, Harvey to Elliot, 10 Mar. 1775. A rather amusing incident occurred in connection with the bounty. In 1778 the 78th was raised in the highlands of Scotland largely from the clan of Mackenzies. When the regiment had been organized, it was marched down to Edinburgh. There the men showed symptoms of dissatisfaction. Upon investigation it was found that this was due to the fact that while some of them had received no bounty, others had gotten it twice in consequence of so many having the same name. Cannon, *Historical Records 72d,* p. 4.

Vagrants, smugglers, and criminals of various kinds might thus escape such legal penalties as had been adjudged them. Even deserters, whether at large or imprisoned, were to be pardoned upon agreeing to reënter the ranks of either their former regiment or some other.[24] In this way every gaol served as a recruiting depot.

The physical requirements for men entering the ranks, whether voluntarily or perforce, seem to have been somewhat loose. No full-grown man was to be taken for the marching regiments, who was under 5 feet $6\frac{1}{2}$ inches high. Youths under that size might be enlisted, if they were well-made and promised to grow to it.[25] No doubt the recruiting officers were careful to see that the jail birds enlisted were in fairly sound physical condition. The volunteer underwent a physical examination before a surgeon, and was obliged to attest that he had "no Rupture, nor ever was troubled with Fits," and that he was in "no ways disabled by Lameness, or otherwise, but had the perfect use of his Limbs." The volunteer in Great Britain had likewise to declare that he was a Protestant.[26]

Such were the methods of recruiting the army employed during the first three years of the war. After the surrender at Saratoga, however, when hostilities with France were apprehended, they were felt to be inadequate, and additional measures were deemed necessary—measures which would not interfere with the old methods, to be sure, but which would modify them

24 *London Gazette*, 20-24 Feb. 1776, 28-31 Mar. 1778; W.O. 1:991, Grant to Christie, 6 Feb. 1776, Fenwick to Barrington, 3 Mar. 1776; *ibid.*, 1:682, 995, 997, *passim;* Clode, II, 13-14. For illustrations of enlistment of criminals, see the appendix to this chapter.

25 W.O. 1:993, Murray to Barrington, 10 Oct. 1775; *ibid.*, 1:5, Harvey to certain regimental officers, 11 Feb. 1770.

26 W.O. 1:1002, Aird to Jenkinson, 28 Dec. 1779 (enclosure).

slightly and open up new sources of recruits. Accordingly, in May, 1778, parliament passed a press act, 18 Geo. III, C. 53, "for the more easy and better recruiting of his Majesty's Land Forces."[27] It provided that every volunteer should receive a bounty of £3, and that he should be entitled to his discharge at the end of three years unless the nation were at war. It also empowered the justices of the peace and the commissioners of the land tax, who were constituted commissioners for the enforcement of the act, to levy and deliver to the recruiting officers "all able-bodied idle, and disorderly Persons, who could not, upon Examination, prove themselves to exercise and industriously follow some lawful Trade or Employment, or to have some Substance sufficient for their Support and Maintenance." They were also to raise and deliver "all Persons who should be convicted of running Goods to the Value of 40£ or under in lieu of all legal Penalties." For every man raised in either of the aforesaid ways, the recruiting officers must pay to the parish officers 20s. and to the overseers of the poor, in case the man had a wife and family chargeable upon the parish rates, not less than 10s. nor more than 40s., according to the number of children. A reward of 10s. was offered to the discoverer of any person liable to impressment within the provisions of the act. No voters and, between May 25th and October 25th, no harvest laborers were to be impressed. Impressed men might demand discharge at the end of five years, unless the nation were at war. No person should be enlisted by virtue of the act "who was not such an able-bodied Man as is fit to serve his Majesty, and was free from Ruptures, and every other Distemper, or bodily Weakness or Infirmity, which may render him unfit to perform the Duty of a Soldier." No person should be enlisted "who should appear in the

27 *Statutes at Large* (Ruffhead's Edition), XIII, 273-280.

opinion of the . . . Officers . . . to be under the Age of
seventeen Years, above the Age of forty-five Years, or
who should be under the Size of five Feet, four Inches
without Shoes.'' The act was to be put into operation in
every county on notice being given to the high sheriff by
the secretary at war; but it might be suspended at the
king's discretion throughout the whole or any part of
Great Britain.[28]

This law received the royal assent 28 May, 1778. It was
set into operation by Barrington, the secretary at war,
in the following month. Whether it was ever suspended
does not appear. Geographically its operation was confined, by direction of the secretary at war, to Scotland
and to ''the City of London, the City and Liberties of
Westminster, and such parts of the County of Middlesex
as are within the Bills of Mortality.'' Wales and other
parts of England thus escaped its action.[29] Barrington
gave as his reasons for this the fact that in the summer
of 1778 he feared to interfere with the harvesting, while
in the autumn and winter the ''Forces were not so cir-
cumstanced as to admit of a general and effectual execution of the said Act.''[30]

Apparently the statute did not prove successful, for in
January, 1779, Sir Charles Jenkinson, who had succeeded
Barrington at the War Office, begged leave in the Commons to bring in a bill for its repeal and for the substitu-
tion of a measure promising better results. He informed
the house that the chief advantages arising from acts of
this character lay in the numbers of volunteers brought
in under apprehension of being impressed. He believed,

[28] The provisions relative to the enforcement and suspension of the act
are exceedingly ambiguous. The interpretation given in the text is based
upon the actual practice.

[29] W.O. 4:965, *passim*.

[30] W.O. 4:965, Barrington to the high sheriffs of England and Wales,
8 June, 2 Dec. 1778.

therefore, that every possible encouragement should be held forth to volunteers in order to render impressment the less necessary. The law of 1778 had failed because it did not offer sufficient advantages to volunteers. This defect he hoped to remedy in the proposed measure.[31]

The result of Jenkinson's plea was the passage of a second press act, 19 Geo. III, C. 10.[32] While following in general the lines of the previous law, it met the views expressed by the secretary by holding out more attractive inducements to volunteers. The bounty offered to them was raised from £3, under the act of 1778, to £3 3s., and its payment made easier. After the expiration of their terms of service, volunteers were to be exempt from the performance of statute (highway) duty, from service as parish officers, and from service in the army, navy, or militia. They were to be allowed to set up and exercise any trade in any place in Great Britain, a concession the value of which can only be appreciated when it is realized that almost every city and corporation then possessed an exclusive system of customs and by-laws, regulating industrial pursuits within its limits in such a way as to debar any but the properly initiated. Furthermore, volunteers discharged on account of wounds, prior to the expiration of their terms, were to be entitled to the same privileges as those serving full terms; and no suspension of the act was to withhold from volunteers the benefits guaranteed therein. The new law also made less exclusive the physical requirements for both volunteers and impressed men. The act of 1778 had provided that recruits must be able-bodied men between seventeen and forty-five years of age and at least five feet four inches in height. The act of 1779 admitted able-bodied men between the ages of sixteen and fifty years. Those under

---

[31] *Parliamentary History*, XX, 112 *et seq.*
[32] *Statutes at Large* (Ruffhead's Edition), XIII, 316-317.

eighteen years were qualified if their height was at least five feet three inches. Those over eighteen years, however, were required to be at least five feet four inches. In one other important matter the new measure differed from the old. It rendered another class of malefactors available for the ranks by declaring that not only smugglers and "all able-bodied idle and disorderly persons" were liable to impressment but also "incorrigible rogues," who were defined as persons "convicted of running away from and leaving their Families chargeable upon the Parish."

This statute received the royal assent 9 February, 1779. On the same day the secretary at war directed that the act be put into execution throughout Great Britain. On 22 May, in order not to interfere with the harvesting, its operation was suspended by an order in Council in South Britain, with the exception of the "Cities of London and Westminster and such parts of Middlesex as lay within the Bill of Mortality as also some of the principal towns." On 26 November it was again put into force throughout the region of suspension. On 26 May, 1780, it was repealed, with the exception of the parts relating to volunteers.[33]

The operation of both press acts was marked by several noteworthy features. The spirit in which the earlier one was to be enforced was set forth by Barrington in two rather remarkable letters. In an age when the treatment accorded to soldiers was as a rule brutal and inhuman, and when press gangs were accustomed to seize their prey, without much regard for law or justice, he could write to the commissioners for enforcing the act, ". . . It must be confessed that to carry these good purposes into execution [i.e., the terms of the act], it has

[33] W.O. 4:966, *passim; London Gazette,* 4-8 May, 1778. For dates of passages and repeal, see 38 *Commons Journal.*

been necessary to give Powers to the Commissioners, which, if abus'd, may occasion Acts of Cruelty and Oppression. I am confident that Comm'rs will guard against every thing so disgraceful and pernicious. *Soldiers, it is true, are wanted at this juncture; but no necessity of State can authorize their being got at the Expense of Justice and Humanity . . .*"[34] At another time, writing to the magistrates with regard to certain impressed men who desired to submit proof that they did not come within the terms of the act, he manifested a similar spirit: "Frequent representations have been made to me in behalf of impressed Men who could bring evidences of their not being objects of this Act, now executing by you; but that the time of appeal being elapsed, the Commissioners do not think it proper to receive such evidence. I therefore take the liberty of acquainting you that in such cases, if you will in any instance, be pleased to admit the matter to a rehearing, *rather upon the grounds of a human indulgence than a legal claim,* I shall be very ready to concur with you in giving relief to persons, whom you shall judge aggrieved although they should not have availed themselves in due time of the appeal allowed by the legislature.'"[35]

Several nice questions of interpretation arose in connection with the acts. One was whether an impressed man might employ a substitute. It was pointed out that the latter might be a far better physical specimen than the former, and that therefore his admission would result in a greater gain for the service. Jenkinson ruled that "the practice of discharging Impressed Men upon their finding proper Substitutes is contrary to the express directions of the Act itself, and tho' the Regiment might be

---

[34] W.O. 4:965, Letters of Notice, June, 1778. The italics are mine.

[35] W.O. 4:965, Barrington to commissioners for executing the act in Kensington Gardens, 15 Aug. 1778. The italics are mine.

somewhat benefited, by getting better Men in their own room, yet the Service in general and the Public would be greatly injured thereby; for it cannot be expected that the Magistrates should proceed in the execution of the Act, if the persons impressed by their Authority are suffered to obtain their Discharge by paying a sum of money, and be left at Liberty to return to the very neighborhood where they had proved obnoxious, with minds incensed against the Magistrates and others concerned in their Commitmt.''[36]

On several occasions persons who had been taken into custody by the magistrates as liable to impressment offered to volunteer and then claimed the bounty. Was this practice allowable? Barrington, to whom the question was originally put, answered at first in the affirmative, but later, and finally, in the negative: ''Having stated in my first Circular Letter to the Commissioners, . . . that Men who come within the description of the Act and are apprehended may notwithstanding Enter as Volunteers, I think it necessary to acquaint You that on a reconsideration of the Act, It is my opinion that this Option cannot be given to persons in Custody.''[37]

Several magistrates wrote in high dudgeon to Jenkinson that men were enlisting in the militia to escape impressment. ''With regard to the practice you mention,'' answered the secretary, ''. . . I really do not think that the public suffers thereby upon the whole; for the Men, from being troublesome and obnoxious, become at once of use to their Country, to whose defence they contribute

[36] W.O. 4:967, Jenkinson to Captain Bassett, 26 Feb. 1780.

[37] W.O. 4:965, Barrington to the Commissioners, 17 Aug. 1778. *Cf. ibid.*, 1:1005, Lord Percy to Jenkinson, 8 Mar. 1779. Jenkinson concurred in Barrington's opinion in this connection, but some of the magistrates exhibited a reluctance to follow it. W.O. 1:1005, Lieutenant Mainwaring to Jenkinson, 1 May, 1779; *ibid.*, 4:966, Jenkinson to Ipswich Commissioners.

as much by voluntary Service in the Militia, as if they had been impressed into the regular Army.''[38]

In a number of instances foreigners were impressed— Hessians, Hungarians, Tuscans, Dutchmen; but, at the request of the ambassador representing their native country, were released.[39]

Apprentices were sometimes enlisted or impressed; and, although the law did not require it, were also surrendered on the masters' demand, in accordance with an opinion rendered in 1760 by Sir Charles Pratt, the attorney general.[40]

The physical requirements laid down for recruits were not to be construed too closely. Jenkinson informed one colonel that, though the impressed men "might not be such Recruits as a Battn. might choose to take in times of profound Peace, . . . in the present moment it would . . . be imprudent to part with any Man that could be made of the smallest use.''[41]

That a spirit of coöperation was often wanting between the military and civil officers engaged in enforcing the acts, there can be no doubt. Recruiting officers complained that the commissioners were negligent about levying persons liable to impressment; commissioners

[38] W.O. 4:966, Jenkinson to John Livesey and E. Brewer, 13 Apr. 1779.

[39] W.O. 1:1004; 4:965, *passim*.

[40] W.O. 1:998, "Opinion of C. Pratt," Oughton to Barrington, 6 Aug. 1778; *ibid.*, 1:1004, Lord Harrington to Jenkinson, 10 July, 1779; Clode, II, 34. Sir James Oughton warned Barrington that "Fraudulent Claims of Apprentices are so frequent and so detrimental to the Service that they ought to be guarded against with Caution." W.O. 1:998, 6 Aug. 1778. See also W.O. 1:1004, Lord Harrington to Jenkinson, 10 July, 1779.

[41] W.O. 4:966, Jenkinson to Colonel Fraser, 20 Aug. 1779. Two minor questions of interpretation should be noticed. The acts forbade any military officer to serve as a commissioner. Did this include officers on half-pay? Barrington replied in the affirmative. Were the commissioners obliged "to reduce into writing the reasons on which their decisions were grounded"? Barrington answered, No. W.O. 4:965, Matthew Lewis to Mr. Duffe, 27 Oct. 1778.

retorted that the officers were negligent about attending their meetings as required by law.[42] "I am sorry to say," wrote Jenkinson in April, 1779, "I have had more complaints of this kind from the Commissioners in Essex than from any other county."[43]

There was a similar want of harmony between military and naval officers. The competition between them for eligible recruits was bitter and, sometimes, bloody. In June, 1778, the streets of Plymouth were treated to a lively brawl between an army press gang and a navy press gang, which resulted from an attempt on the part of the sailors to rob the soldiers of an enlisted man.[44]

Such occurrences, however, were the order of the day. While the press gangs fought one another for recruits, the recruits fought the press gangs for freedom. The aversion to military service on the part of impressed men was intense. Many of them in order to incapacitate themselves cut off the thumb and forefinger of the right hand.[45] Others deserted at the first opportunity. To use the words of one officer, they were "a mighty slippery set of fellows."[46] They could not be trusted at large with the regiment while it was at home, but had to be kept under lock and key until it embarked for America or other foreign parts. "It is clear," wrote Jenkinson, "that the greater part of the Impressed Men cannot be trusted in any Regt. that is serving in Great Britain: It is doubtful

[42] See, for example, W.O. 1:1002, Lord Dunkellin to Jenkinson, 5 May, 1779; ibid., 1:1005, Colonel Peirson to Jenkinson, 15 Mar. 1779.

[43] W.O. 4:966, Jenkinson to Lindsay, 9 Apr. 1779.

[44] W.O. 1:998, Lieutenant General Parker to Barrington, 19 June, 1778.

[45] W.O. 1:1005, Oughton to Jenkinson, 27 May, 1779, Colonel Peirson to Jenkinson, 11, 15 Mar. 1779; ibid., 1:1002, Major J. Clayton to Jenkinson (undated).

[46] W.O. 1:991, Colonel Gisborne to Barrington, 29 Jan. 1776. The colonel was referring to Irish recruits, but his words were by no means inapplicable to those impressed in England. See also Andrews, *Guide to Materials for American History in P.R.O.*, II, 32 note.

whether they ought to be trusted in any Regiment serving on the Continent of America; but they may with great propriety be sent either to the Regts in the West Indies, or the Garrisons of Gibraltar and Minorca— From these places they cannot easily desert; and there are no facts to lead us to conclude that they would not serve well there."[47]

The prisons in which these men were temporarily incarcerated were often the scenes of fierce encounters between jailers and jailed. The keeper of the Savoy Prison in London, where many were confined, reported that as he and several turnkeys were locking up one evening, they were attacked by a number of impressed men "armed with short bludgeons that they had cut from the Brooms that were given them to clean their Apartments with." After a struggle the prisoners were overcome, but that night two of them threw themselves out at one of the windows. One escaped, the other fell on his head and was killed.[48]

Regarding the effectiveness of the press act of 1778, the records yield no data. Regarding the effectiveness of the act of 1779, we are fortunate in possessing a detailed report which was drawn up by Jenkinson for the benefit of Lord Amherst.[49] It shows that from March to October, 1779, no fewer than 1,463 men were impressed in South Britain; and from March to July, 61 in North

[47] W.O. 4:966, Jenkinson to Amherst, 26 Oct. 1779. Sir David Lindsay, writing to Jenkinson regarding certain recruits, stated, "116 are impressed men whom it has been absolutely necessary to keep in confinement as there is not a man of them that would stay with us twenty-four hours." W.O. 1:1004, Plymouth, 2 July, 1779. Though the fate of the impressed men was not an enviable one, they were in many instances allowed a choice of evils by being suffered to pick the regiment with which they preferred to serve. W.O. 4:967, *passim*.

[48] W.O. 1:997, William Jackson to Matthew Lewis, 22 Nov. 1778. *Cf.* W.O. 4:966, Jenkinson to Sir. J. Fielding, 31 Aug. 1779.

[49] W.O. 4:966, Jenkinson to Amherst, 26 Oct. 1779.

Britain. Considering the demands for soldiers, these can hardly be considered large figures. The report points out, however, that the act had greatly stimulated voluntary enlistment. The apprehension of impressment had induced many reluctant persons to volunteer. This was especially true as regards the navy and the militia, both of which had gained increased numbers of voluntary recruits since the passage of the law. The regular army, while profiting less, had secured by voluntary enlistment about 2,200 more men than would have been the case without the stimulus of the press act. This represented an increase of more than one-third upon the ordinary recruiting.

On 1 October, 1779, the 1,463 men impressed in South Britain were disposed as follows:

Embarked for foreign Stations, or serving on board the Fleet as Marines	236
Incorporated in the Regts. and additional Camps at home	726
Discharged as absolutely incapable of service	178
Discharged upon the Certificate of the Commrs. on a Rehearing, or by order of the Court of King's Bench, as not being Objects of the Act	138
Discharged upon the Claim of Foreign Ministers, or as belonging to old Corps	29
Dead	17
Remain at Chatham and in the Savoy, not yet appropriated	139
Total	1,463

We have seen that between 1775 and 1781, the regular army was increased from 48,000 to 110,000 men. Having examined the methods by which these men were obtained, we have now to examine the manner in which the organization of the army was expanded to receive them; for it is obvious that, in enrolling 60,000 more men, either the regiments existing at the outbreak of the war must have been enormously increased in size or new regiments must have been added. In point of fact the expansion was affected in two ways: (1) by enlarging regiments existing in 1775, and (2) by creating new regiments.[50]

(1) Regiments existing in 1775 were enlarged by adding new companies or battalions, by increasing the numbers in the existing companies or battalions, or by a combination of both methods. For example, in 1775 the 60th Foot was augmented by the addition of two battalions, the 21st Foot by raising each company from thirty-eight to fifty-six men, and the 4th Foot by raising each company from thirty-eight to fifty-six men and adding two companies of fifty-six men each.[51] These seem to have been the methods employed at the beginning of the war. Prior to 1778 only one new regiment was raised—the 71st Foot, in 1775.[52]

(2) The surrender of Burgoyne and the Franco-American alliance led to a change. In the spring of 1778, while the old methods of augmentation were retained, no less than twelve new regiments of foot were raised.[53] In the spring of 1779 still another[54] was added, together with three regiments of light dragoons.[55] The latter were formed out of light troops from other dragoon regiments. The declaration of war by Spain in June led to further activity. In the summer and autumn, thirteen

---

[50] The merits of the two methods were debated in two contemporary pamphlets: T. Cadell: *Considerations upon the Different Modes of Finding Recruits for the Army*, London, 1775; J. Bew: *A Letter to the Author of a Pamphlet entitled Considerations upon the Different Modes of Finding Recruits for the Army*, London, 1776.

[51] W.O. 24:481.

[52] W.O. 24:481.

[53] To wit, 72d, 73d, 74th, 75th, 76th, 77th, 78th, 79th, 80th, 81st, 82d, 83d. W.O. 24:494. *Cf.* Fortescue, III, 245. Six of these regiments were Highland: *viz.*, 73d, 74th, 76th, 77th, 78th, 81st.

[54] 84th. W.O. 24:499. *Cf.* Fortescue, III, 289.

[55] 19th, 20th, 21st. W.O. 24:499. *Cf.* Fortescue, III, 289.

regiments of foot and one of light dragoons were raised.[56] To these were added three regiments of foot, which were raised during the winter of 1779-1780.[57] Adding two more regiments of foot which appear on the list for 1781,[58] we find that no fewer than thirty-one independent regiments of foot and four regiments of light dragoons were created between 1778 and 1781. This does not include a large number of fencible[59] and volunteer corps of a somewhat irregular character for home service. Most of the newly raised regiments, whether regular or irregular, were disbanded at the close of the war.[60]

Not a few of these corps were raised by noblemen or gentlemen, partly at their own trouble and expense. This was done, of course, only with the king's permission. The precise nature of the agreement entered into in every case by the crown on the one hand and the raiser of the regiment on the other cannot be ascertained. In most instances, probably, the nobleman or gentleman, in return for the trouble entailed in recruiting the men, was granted the command of the regiment and the privilege of nominating some or all of the officers. The officers doubtless bought their commissions from the nobleman and shared both the work and the expense of the recruiting. The permission to raise a regiment and the conditions attached thereto were embodied in what was known as a "letter of service," addressed to the prospective colonel by the secretary at war. The enlistment was

[56] 85th, 86th, 87th, 88th, 89th, 90th, 91st, 92d, 93d, 94th, 95th, 96th, 97th, and 22d Dragoons formed from drafts from light troops of other regiments. W.O. 24:499, 504. *Cf.* Fortescue, III, 290.

[57] 98th, 99th, 100th. W.O. 24:504. *Cf.* Fortescue, III, 293.

[58] 101st, 102d. W.O. 24:512. In addition to these the *Army List* for 1782 gives regiments 103 and 104, and for 1782, regiment 105.

[59] The fencible corps were "a species of militia, raised for the defence of particular districts, from which several of them could not by the conditions of their enlistment, be detached." Grose, *Military Antiquities*, I, 164.

[60] Fortescue, III, 290, 498.

carried on under authority of a "beating order,"[61] which was likewise issued under the hand of that official. When several corps were being raised at the same time, the seniority (regimental number) of each in the army was usually determined by the date of completion.[62]

A concrete illustration may serve to make this clear. On 19 December, 1777, Barrington issued a letter of service to John Campbell of Barbreck, a Scottish gentleman, stating that the king had given him permission to raise a Highland regiment of foot, 1,082 strong.[63] The conditions were to be as follows: Campbell was to have the colonelcy and the nomination of the officers. In case he nominated as major an officer who had served less than five years in the army as captain, that officer was to pay £300 for his commission, which sum was to be used in helping to defray the cost of recruiting. The seniority of captains and subalterns in the regiment was to be determined by the date at which they completed their respective companies. The officers of the first company completed would be senior to the officers of the company next completed, and so on through the entire ten companies of which the corps was to be composed. The officers

61 For example of beating order, see the appendix to this chapter.

62 There was no little rivalry among colonels for numerical precedence as regards regimental title. In 1778, for example, the Duke of Atholl and William Gordon were engaged each in raising a regiment in Scotland. Each longed to have his corps numbered the 73d, which appears to have been the lowest vacant title at the time. Atholl wrote to Barrington in high dudgeon, 8 February, that Gordon had been publishing notices in the Edinburgh papers referring to his regiment as the 73d, although he had absolutely no authority for so doing and had raised only a few hundred men. W.O. 1:995.

63 There were to be 8 battalion companies, 1 company of grenadiers, and 1 company of light infantry. The battalion companies were to consist each of 1 captain, 2 lieutenants, 1 ensign, 5 sergeants, 5 corporals, 2 drummers, 100 private men. The flank companies were to consist each of 1 captain, 3 lieutenants, 5 sergeants, 5 corporals, 2 drummers, 2 pipers, 100 private men. The field officers were to include 1 lieutenant colonel and 2 majors.

were to be entitled to half-pay in case the regiment should be disbanded at the close of war. To help meet the cost of recruiting, the government allowed Campbell: (1) £3 bounty money per man; (2) the pay (barring "subsistence") of the entire regiment from the date of the beating order (19 December); (3) 5 guineas for every man reviewed and approved; (4) the subsistence money of every non-commissioned officer and private man from the date of his attestation (enlistment). Recruits had to be at least five feet four inches in height and between eighteen and thirty years of age. The regiment was to be raised and approved within four months from the date of the letter of service. It later became the 74th Foot, serving in America during the war.[64]

This entire system, known as "raising men for rank," was by no means peculiar to the American Revolution, but had been utilized in previous wars.[65] George III, however, adopted it with extreme reluctance. He feared that the formation of new corps would interfere with

[64] 36 *Commons Journal*, p. 613; *ibid.*, vol. 37, p. 45. Letters of service for several of the regiments raised in 1777-1778 will be found in *ibid.*, vol. 36, pp. 612-617. Some examples are given in the appendix to this chapter. In January, 1778, the king commissioned nine gentlemen as captains, each of whom was to raise an independent company of 100 private men in Wales. They were allowed to nominate the subalterns, and were subject to practically the same conditions as if each had been raising a regiment. The companies were subsequently united to form the 75th (Prince of Wales').

[65] Clode, II, 5-6; Chichester, *passim;* W.O. 1:997-998, *passim.* During the war the War Office was fairly flooded with offers to raise regiments on terms similar to the above. Lord Dunmore in December, 1777, for example, offered to recruit a Highland regiment among the Campbells, Gordons, Macdonalds, and Murrays. *Correspondence of Geo. III with Lord North*, II, 101. See also 37 *Commons Journal*, pp. 523-529. In some cases commissions were granted to men who would raise a company of 100 men. *Correspondence of Geo. III with Lord North*, I, 265; II, 95. *Cf.* Fortescue, II, 576. The author of a pamphlet entitled *Reflections on the Pernicious Custom of Recruiting by Crimps* (undated but apparently of 18th century origin) alleges that many persons who engaged to raise men for rank procured their recruits by means of crimps.

completing the old regiments to a war footing; that it would, as he put it, "only perplex and totally annihilate all chances of compleating the regular forces, which alone in time of need can be depended upon; particularly in England, the raising new corps would be total destruction to the army."[66] He preferred increasing the strength of the old regiments to raising new ones. "A new raised corps," he stated, "will from time of being compleated require at least a year before it can be properly trained for actual service; an [old] regiment composed of good officers and non-commissioned officers will bear a great augmentation, and three months fit them for service."[67] He suspected, furthermore, that every nobleman who raised a regiment would have in view not the service of the country but the procuring of commissions for relatives. In other words, the thing might be turned into a job. This could not fail to arouse disgust among the officers of existing corps. They would be obliged to witness men securing commissions equal to or higher than their own, not through merit, experience, or seniority, but through favor. "By an unwearied attention to the services of officers," wrote the king to North, "I flatter myself I have their goodwill, which would be totally destroyed if I was giving away to every job that noblemen are wishing for their relations, not the service of the country."[68] Nevertheless, the difficulty of obtaining recruits by the ordinary methods forced His Majesty to adopt a policy which he could not at heart approve.

[66] *Correspondence of Geo. III with Lord North,* II, 120.

[67] *Ibid.,* I, 265.

[68] *Ibid.,* II, 108 (29 Dec. 1777). *Cf. ibid.,* I, 265, 300. In 1781 Jenkinson also expressed himself as opposed to raising new regiments, *ibid.,* II, 366-367. The king laid down this rule regarding appointments in the new regiments: "I ever objected to a corps almost entirely composed of men that had never been in the service; the Captains of these companies must have been Lieutenants, the Lieutenants ensigns." *Ibid.,* II, 115.

Of the regiments thus raised for rank, the following served in America and the West Indies during the war, and are therefore of especial interest:

71st. This regiment of two battalions was raised in the latter part of 1775 by Simon Fraser, Master of Lovat. Fraser's father, a Scottish nobleman, had been compelled to forfeit his estates for participation in the rebellion of 1745. After his death, in February, 1775, the son besought the king to restore the estates to him. George III consented, and out of gratitude Fraser proceeded to raise the regiment in question. During the Seven Years' War he had raised a Highland regiment, the 78th, which had been disbanded in 1763. The new regiment contained many officers and privates of the old ''Fraser's.'' It was formed at Glasgow, and served under Cornwallis in the Carolinas. The greater part of the regiment was included in the troops surrendered at Yorktown. It was disbanded in 1783.[69]

74th. This regiment, commonly referred to as the ''Argyle Highlanders,'' was raised by Colonel John Campbell of Barbreck in 1777-1778, as previously explained. He was a veteran of the old 78th above-mentioned. The regiment served in Nova Scotia, and distinguished itself in the defence of Penobscot Bay against an American squadron under command of Commodore Saltonstall. The flank companies saw service in Canada. It was disbanded in 1783.[70]

76th. This regiment was raised by Lord McDonnel in the Highlands and Isles in 1777-1778. When inspected in May, 1778, it was found to consist of 683 Highlanders, 118 Lowlanders, 114 Irish, and 9 English. It was sent to the

---

[69] Chichester, p. 731; Cannon, *Historical Record 71st; Correspondence of Geo. III with Lord North*, I, 275, 292.

[70] Chichester, p. 734; 36 *Commons Journal*, p. 613.

relief of Jersey, when that island was attacked by the French, and subsequently to America, where it served under Cornwallis in North Carolina and at Yorktown. During the campaign, 400 of the Highlanders were horsed in rough and ready fashion, and served as mounted infantry. The regiment was disbanded in 1784.[71]

82d. Raised in the Scottish Lowlands by the Duke of Hamilton in 1779, this regiment served in Nova Scotia and Antigua. The uniform was red faced with black. Sir John Moore of Peninsula fame obtained his company in it. The flank companies were lost at sea off the coast of New Jersey. The remainder of the corps was disbanded in 1783.[72]

84th. This regiment, consisting of two battalions and known as the "Royal Highland Emigrants," deserves special mention. It was raised in 1779 by Colonel Allan Maclean out of the families of soldiers of the 42d, 77th, and 78th Highlanders, who had settled in Canada at the close of the Seven Years' War. Recruits were also obtained from Scottish emigrants in New York and North Carolina. Maclean drove a hard bargain with the king. He was to receive not merely the lieutenant-colonelcy of the corps, but in case of his death, his wife was to have a pension and his children a grant of lands in America. Grants were likewise to be given to the officers. The uniform consisted of the full highland garb with the facings and regimental tartan of the Black Watch (42d). The 1st battalion served in Canada, the 2d in the Carolinas and Virginia. One detachment of the latter was present with Cornwallis at Yorktown, while another fought un-

[71] Chichester, p. 463; 36 Commons Journal, p. 613; 37 ibid., p. 45; W.O. 1:997-999, passim. Beating order dated 25 Dec. 1777. Regiment returned complete on 1 July, 1778.

[72] Chichester, p. 527; 36 Commons Journal, p. 613.

der Lord Rawdon in South Carolina. The regiment was disbanded in 1784.[73]

85th. Two noblemen, Lords Harrington and Chesterfield, raised this regiment in London in 1778. Unofficially it was known as the "Westminster Volunteers." The uniform was red faced with bright yellow. For some years the corps was located in Jamaica. The greater part of it was lost on board the *Ville de Paris* and other French prizes taken in Rodney's action with Comte de Grasse, which were swept away by a cyclone off the Banks of Newfoundland, when homeward bound in 1783. The remainder of the regiment was disbanded at Dover Castle in the same year.[74]

86th. Charles, 5th Duke of Rutland, raised this regiment under an order dated 2 July, 1779, the recruiting rendezvous being at Newark and Grantham. It was commanded by Colonel St. Leger, and served in the West Indies. Detachments were also employed as marines on the West India and American stations. The regiment was disbanded at York in April, 1783.[75]

87th. Formed at Bromsgrove, Worcestershire, in 1778 by George Lord Chewton, afterwards Earl of Waldegrave, this regiment served in the West Indies, and was disbanded at Coventry in April, 1783.[76]

[73] Chichester, pp. 712-713; W.O. 1:681, Dartmouth to Gage, 15 Apr. 1775; *Correspondence of Geo. III with Lord North*, I, 240.

[74] Chichester, p. 647. The king wrote to North, 15 Jan. 1778, "I hope care will therefore be taken to turn the idea of a Westminster regiment into a subscription for compleating the army at large." His hopes were not realized as the context indicates. Later (24 June, 1779) he writes, "The E. of Harrington will raise at his own expense and without any unreasonable jobs for officers." *Correspondence of Geo. III with Lord North*, II, 120, 265.

[75] Chichester, p. 782. The duke was rewarded with a lord-lieutenancy. As in the case of the Earl of Harrington, the king expressed pleasure that the 86th was to be raised "without any unreasonable jobs for officers." *Correspondence of Geo. III with Lord North*, II, 265-266.

[76] Chichester, p. 791.

105th. This regiment was raised by Lord Rawdon at Philadelphia in 1777 during the British occupation under the title of the "Volunteers of Ireland." It was not placed upon the establishment, however, until 1782 or 1783, when it was brought into line as the King's Irish Regiment of Foot. It saw much active service in America, and was disbanded in 1783.[77]

The foregoing regiments were infantry. One cavalry regiment, the 22d Dragoons, was raised in like manner (*i.e.*, by a nobleman) but saw no service in America.

The raising of new regiments was not confined, however, to a few gentlemen or noblemen. In the latter part of 1777 and beginning of 1778, the towns of Manchester, Edinburgh, Glasgow, Aberdeen, Birmingham, Warwick, and Coventry volunteered to perform a like service. These offers, excepting the last four, were accepted. As in the case of an individual raising a regiment, the town was allowed to nominate some or all of the officers.[78] The only difference lay in the fact that the town bore practically the entire expense of the recruiting. The funds were realized by public subscription among the townspeople. Thus in 1779 the 72d (Royal Manchester Volunteers), the 79th (Royal Liverpool Volunteers), the 80th (Royal Edinburgh Volunteers), and the 83d (Royal Glasgow Volunteers) were formed.[79]

It cannot be said that the king was any more pleased with this method of raising regiments than with the method of raising them through noblemen. Again he

[77] Chichester, p. 638.

[78] In the case of the Liverpool regiment (79th), for example, the corporation nominated no officer above the rank of captain. *Correspondence of Geo. III with Lord North*, II, 100.

[79] Fortescue, III, 245; 36 *Commons Journal*, pp. 613-615. The king made a point of appointing as colonels of these regiments officers who had distinguished themselves on American service. W.O. 4:274, Barrington to Howe, 3 Feb. 1778.

feared that the appointments might be turned into a job for the benefit of some man or some family. In the case of the Edinburgh regiment, he stated that although he appreciated the zeal manifested by the citizens, he preferred to have them devote their subscription to completing one of the old Scottish regiments rather than to raising a new one.[80]

The first of the so-called "loyalty regiments," the 72d, saw no service in America. The 79th, popularly known as the "Royal Liverpool Blues," cost the town £2,951. Sent to Jamaica in 1780, it returned home in 1784 and was disbanded.[81] The 80th did good service under Cornwallis; while the 83d, after serving in Jersey at the time of the French descent upon that island in 1781, was sent to New York. Both regiments were disbanded at the close of the war.[82]

Subscriptions were also started in some of the towns and counties to stimulate enlistment by offering to each man a sum of bounty money (varying from one to six guineas) in addition to that granted by the crown. Such was the case in Bath, Bristol, Birmingham, Warwick, Coventry, Leeds, and Lancaster. In Ireland, Cork exhibited its loyalty in this way; while the Roman Catholic inhabitants of Limerick offered a guinea per head to the first five hundred men who should there enlist. As regards the counties, Oxfordshire alone assisted in supplying ten regiments by offering a bounty of six guineas to

[80] *Correspondence of Geo. III with Lord North,* II, 120.

[81] Chichester, p. 771. The town did not recommend to commissions higher than the rank of captain. *Correspondence of Geo. III with Lord North,* II, 100.

[82] Chichester, pp. 504, 780. In a letter to North (24 Jan. 1778) the king intimates that he is displeased because the people of Edinburgh insist on recommending part of the officers, whereas the Glasgow people had acted handsomely in leaving the appointments to the crown. *Correspondence of Geo. III with Lord North,* II, 124.

every volunteer; while Nottinghamshire devoted itself to the 45th Foot with the king's promise that it should be called the Nottinghamshire regiment as soon as the county had raised three hundred recruits. This was accomplished without difficulty, and in this manner the so-called "territorial system" is said to have been initiated. At the same time the nobility of Norfolk resolved to start a subscription to complete one or more regiments and begged the king to send recruiting parties into the county.

Thus in 1778 about 15,000 men, of whom two-thirds came from Scotland, were raised through the efforts of towns and individuals for the service of the state;[83] and in January of that year it was necessary to appoint an inspector general and superintendent of recruiting of the forces on foreign service.[84]

No treatment of the methods of recruiting the army would be complete without an explanation of the system known as "drafting." When a regiment in America, or in fact on any foreign station, had become much reduced in strength, it was customary to draft (*i.e.*, to transfer) the remaining privates into some other regiment whose ranks needed replenishment. The first regiment would thus be reduced to a mere skeleton, consisting of the commissioned and non-commissioned officers and the drummers. These would be sent home to fill up the *cadre* by recruiting.[85] Drafting was also used in other cases. When

---

[83] W.O. 1:682. "Resolution of Nobility of Norfolk"; *ibid.*, 1:996-998, *passim;* Fortescue, III, 290; Chichester, p. 583; Cannon, *Historical Record 73d*, p. 1. Referring to the number of corps raised in Scotland, the king seemed inclined to complain because so much opportunity for promotion had been give to one part of his kingdom in preference to the rest. *Correspondence of Geo. III with Lord North,* II, 120.

[84] Lieutenant Colonel Samuel Townshend. See commission in W.O. 25:33.

[85] W.O. 1:616, Carleton to Lord Robert Bertie, 21 May, 1776.

it was desired to send a regiment to America and it was
found that the numbers were not equal to a war footing,
the deficiency would sometimes be made good by drafting
men from corps on home service. Similarly regiments already stationed in America would have the gaps in their
ranks filled by drafts from regiments at home.[86] A regiment receiving drafted men compensated the regiment
delivering them at the rate of £5 per man.[87] Frequently a
regiment in America would keep its ranks full by leaving
one or two companies at home to serve as a kind of recruiting depot for the collection, training, and shipment
of new levies.[88]

In spite of the fact that drafted men were each allowed
a bounty of a guinea and a half, the practice was bitterly
disliked, as was only natural.[89] A man who had expressed
a preference for a particular regiment by enlisting in it
was bound to feel resentment on being transferred to
some other regiment in which he had no interest, senti-
mental or otherwise. Transference to regiments under
orders for the West Indies evoked especial indignation.
Men went to that quarter of the globe only to die of dis-
ease or neglect or both.

The wrath aroused by drafting is well illustrated in
two letters addressed to the secretary at war by Major
Cochrane of the 69th.[90] Writing from Bedford, 26 April,
1776, he states: "I acquainted your Lordship that last
Wednesday twenty Draughts from the Regiment for the

86 W.O. 1:680, Lord Rochford to Barrington, 23 January, 1775.

87 W.O. 4:273, Barrington to Gage, 31 Jan., 31 Aug. 1775, Barrington
to Carleton, 18 Apr. 1776.

88 Numerous examples of drafting methods are to be found scattered
through the records of the colonial and war offices for 1775-1783. See Lamb,
Memoir, p. 107.

89 W.O. 4:273, Barrington to Gage, 31 Jan., 31 Aug. 1775; *ibid.*, 1:52,
Edward Matthew to Thomas Townsend, 12 July, 1782.

90 W.O. 1:991, Cochrane to Barrington, 26, 28 April, 1776.

Regts in America march'd from this [place] for Chatham, under the care of a Serjeant and two Corporals; and at the same time expressed my fear of the Serjeant's being able to manage them on the march. This morning I had Accounts from Hitching, which is only 16 miles from this, and I was told they were extremely riotous and not to be governed—indeed I suspected it, nor do I think it will be in the power of the Serjeant to get them on; and much mischief may happen.'' Two days later, the Major writes again: ''Serjeant H—— who commands the escort writes me of yesterday's date from Highgate; acquaints me that three have deserted and the rest will do nothing but what they please, and he is obliged to put up with every affront.'' Whether the unfortunate sergeant ever got his irate charges to Chatham, we are not told.

A much more striking and serious illustration of the trouble caused by drafting occurred at Leith in April, 1779. It chanced that the 83d was about to sail from that port to America when orders were issued to complete its ranks with drafts from the 31st, 42d, and 71st regiments. The men from the 31st and part of those from the 42d submitted without trouble. The rest, however, obstinately refused to embark. Being mainly Highlanders, they were reluctant to join the 83d, since they would be compelled to abandon their native costume, the kilt. A detachment of two hundred men under Major Sir James Johnstone was dispatched to seize the mutineers. He found forty or fifty of them drawn up near the quay at Leith with backs against a wall and with bayonets fixed. Johnstone vainly remonstrated with them. One of the mutineers while trying to escape was seized by the collar by one of Johnstone's men and dragged from the wall. This precipitated a fight. Both sides opened fire. Thirty mutineers were killed or wounded. The rest were overpowered and

taken prisoners to Edinburgh Castle.[91] Frays of this sort
with drafted men were not an uncommon occurrence in
the life of the army officer during the war.[92]

[91] W.O. 1:616, Buccleugh to Oughton, April, 1779; Oughton to Amherst,
22 April, 1779. Lord John Murray had previously warned Barrington in a
letter of 11 Mar. 1778 that it would not be wise to draft Highlanders. ''By
reason of the difference of their dress and language it has not been usual
to draught them into other Regiments, which if now done might be detrimental to recruiting.'' W.O. 1:997. The officers objected to drafting no
less than the men, but on different grounds. A board of field officers at
New York in 1780 reported: ''There has been great confusion made and
apparent hardship done both to Regiments and to the Individuals themselves, by numbers of men that were enlisted and cloath'd by one Regiment having been drafted into another just previous to their embarkation,
and in many cases without any settlement of their accounts.'' C.O. 5:100,
report dated 25 Oct. 1780.

[92] Clode states (II, 4) that after 1765 drafting ceased except with the
soldier's consent. In most cases his consent was evidently taken for granted.
There are plenty of cases, however, to show that it was not freely given,
if given at all.

CHAPTER IV

THE PROVISIONING OF THE ARMY

THROUGHOUT the Revolution, the British army in America derived its provisions from two sources—from the British Isles and from America. In dealing with the subject of food supply, therefore, it seems advisable for the sake of clearness to treat the two sources separately, considering, first, how and what provisions were obtained from the home country and, secondly, how and what provisions were secured in America.

1. *The British Isles as a Source of Provisions*

To begin with, it must be realized that the forces in America derived the bulk of their provisions from the British Isles.[1] They did not ordinarily live off the enemy's country as did a Napoleonic army. As one parliamentary orator aptly expressed it, they were fed from Leadenhall. At the outbreak of the struggle, to be sure, the authorities flattered themselves that the troops could obtain most, if not all, their provisions in the colonies.[2] The futility of such hopes, however, soon became manifest. America was too sparsely populated to yield large and certain quantities of provisions in the immediate vicinity of the army; the inhabitants, if not actually hostile, were often indifferent; the roads and bridges

[1] For statistics relative to the provisions shipped to America during the war, see the appendix to this chapter.

[2] T. 64:106, Robinson to Howe, Apr., June, 22 Oct. 1776, 14 Jan. 1777; *ibid.*, 64:102, Robinson to Day, 27 Mar. 1777; *Correspondence of Geo. III with Lord North*, II, 51.

were few and poor; and the area controlled by the British forces so limited that foraging parties wandering far from the main body were in danger of being cut off.[3] Howe's commissary general bluntly but truthfully summed up the situation when he declared, "There is no dependence for supplies for the Army from this Continent."[4] To the very close of the war, the government acted on the truth of this statement, and year after year contracts were concluded for the furnishing of a complete daily ration to every soldier in America.[5] After 1778, to be sure, when France declared war upon England, there was difficulty in transporting supplies from Great Britain to the forces in New York, and provisions had sometimes to be purchased in America at high prices, but nevertheless the British Isles continued to be the principal source of foodstuffs.[6]

Let us examine, in the first place, the system by which the troops were victualled. The responsibility for provisioning them rested with the commissioners of the Treasury.[7] It was they who determined the quantity and quality of the provisions and until 1779, when the Navy board undertook the business, engaged transports for their shipment to America.

The provisions were first brought from all parts of the British Isles to Cork, which constituted a kind of food *dépôt* for the forces in America. In the latter part of the war, Cowes and, for a very brief period, Deptford served

[3] *Correspondence of Geo. III with Lord North*, II, 7, 52.

[4] T. 64:118, Chamier to Robinson, 31 Mar. 1777. *Cf.* statements made by Wier in letters to Robinson, 20 May, 1777, 8 June, 1777, 29 Nov. 1777, in Wier-Robinson Correspondence.

[5] T. 29:44-53, *passim*.

[6] "Minute Book of a Board of General Officers" (N. Y. Hist. Soc. *Coll.* 1916), p. 81.

[7] The victualling commissioners were chiefly concerned with the navy and subsisted the troops only on shipboard during passage from England to America.

in like capacity for provisions destined for the West Indies and certain parts of America.[8] Neither, however, compared in consequence with Cork, which was in effect the ultimate base of the army in America. The importance of Cork was due to several reasons. It was the largest western port of the British Isles; it lay on the route of ships bound for the colonies; it possessed a good and capacious harbor with facilities for loading and unloading vessels; and it constituted the natural outlet of a region whence the contractors drew large supplies of beef, pork, and butter.[9] Furthermore, it was an important recruiting center for southern Ireland, and troops assembled at the town could conveniently be embarked aboard the victuallers and thus be transported to the seat of the war.

At Cork the provisions were carefully inspected and then loaded on transports bound for the colonies. To take charge of this work, the Treasury in 1776 appointed Robert Gordon, the surveyor general of Munster, as commissary of provisions, at a salary of 20s. *per diem.* In 1779 he was succeeded by John Marsh, who held office of the Navy board, with the title of agent victualler.[10] Both of these officials were assisted by a number of subordinates.[11] At Deptford and Cowes, there was likewise an

[8] T. 64:200, Navy Board to Treasury, 15 July, 3 Aug., 18, 22 Sept. 1779; *ibid.,* 64:201, Robinson to Navy Board, 5 Apr., 27 June, 1780.

[9] T. 64:200, p. 64.

[10] T. 64:106, Robinson to Howe, 12 Apr. 1776; *ibid.,* 64:200, Navy Board to Lieutenant Harris, 11 Aug. 1779; *ibid.,* 29:48, pp. 335, 380, 397; *ibid.,* 29:49, p. 7; *ibid.,* 29:45, pp. 40-41, 117, 207-208.

[11] Gordon had as subordinates an assistant commissary, Mr. Younger, appointed by him, and a superintendent of shipping, Joseph Graham, appointed by the Treasury board. Both officials retired with their chief in 1779 upon the appointment of Marsh as agent victualler. Graham was succeeded by Lieutenant Harris, appointed agent for transports by the Navy board. For further details, see chapter on "Army Transport" and also, T. 1:519, Robinson to Gordon, 7 Feb. 1777; *ibid.,* 29:49, Minutes, 4 Nov. 1779.

agent victualler, appointed by the Navy board, in the person of George Cherry.[12]

From Cork the provisions were carried to what might be termed sub-*dépôts* in America. These were Montreal, Quebec, and Halifax for Canada, New York and Philadelphia for the Middle colonies, Charleston and Savannah for the Southern, and St. Lucia for the West Indies.[13] From these points they were in turn distributed by the commissariat to the various portions of the army.[14]

The Treasury board obtained provisions by contract; and since the business of victualling the troops was of such vital importance, the method of contracting and the nature of the contracts deserve somewhat detailed study.

The board entered upon the work of contracting on direction from the secretary of state for the colonies. The latter was accustomed to signify the king's pleasure that the lords commissioners arrange provision contracts for a specified number of men during a specified period.[15]

---

[12] T. 64:200, Navy Board to Treasury, 3 Aug. 1779, 18 Sept. 1780.

[13] T. 64:201, Robinson to Navy Board, 23 Jan. 1781; *ibid.*, 64:102, Day to Robinson, 15 May, 1777; C.O. 5:101, Germain to Clinton, 3 Jan. 1781. See also evidence in W.O. 60:11, 16; *ibid.*, 4:333, Robinson to Secretary at War, 5 May, 1780.

[14] An entire year's supply was rarely sent out at once, but was divided into thirds or quarters and shipped at intervals of from three to four months. For example: ''The Provisions contracted for, deliverable at Cork for the Year 1779, or under consideration to be contracted for, are as follows:

One third in January ⎫
 ''   ''   '' April   ⎬ With a view of their being despatched from Cork
 ''   ''   '' June   ⎭ in February, May, and July.'' T. 64:201.

See also T. 1:519, Robinson to Gordon, 24 June, 31 July, 1776, 20 Mar. 1777; *ibid.*, 64:201, Robinson to Navy Board, 26 Feb. 1781.

[15] For example, see T. 29:47, Minutes, 18 Feb. 1778: ''Read letter from Lord George Germain dated the 16th Instant: acquainting my lords that the King has directed a Reinforcement of 4,000 new troops to be sent out to the army under Sir Wm. Howe—of 2,670 to N. S. and 2,000 to St. Augustine and signifying his Majesty's pleasure that a sufficient quantity of Pro-

Thereupon the board would summon the heads of several firms, known as the army contractors, to attend it in meeting.[16] Here terms and proposals would be fully discussed, and actual samples of biscuit and flour would be examined. Whether there was any competitive bidding between the contractors is not clear. It sometimes happened that the board would settle the terms of a contract with one firm alone, and then require the others to accept the same arrangement.[17] There does not seem to have been any public advertising for bids as there is to-day and as was the practice of the victualling board at that time.[18]

In framing contracts, the Treasury board received recommendations from various sources—from the prime minister (who was of course the first lord of the Treasury), from the secretary and under secretary of state for the colonies, and from the secretary at war. The commanders and commissaries in America were also in constant correspondence with the board and their letters constituted a body of helpful information. The advice of officers familiar with the needs of the army and with conditions in America was sometimes sought. Considerable reliance was placed upon the views of the adjutant general, Edward Harvey. He was sometimes invited to confer with the board in formal meeting. Expert advice respecting the price and quality of foodstuffs was secured from the victualling commissioners; and after 1779, when the Navy board assumed responsibility for transporting

visions for the Supply of the said troops should be sent out to the Places of their respective destinations . . .

My Lords give Directions accordingly . . .''

[16] The following contractors are most frequently mentioned: Messrs. Nesbitt, Drummond, & Franks; Mure, Son, & Atkinson; Anthony Bacon, Esq.; John Amyand, Esq.; Henneker, Wheeler, Wombwell, & Devaynes; James Bogle French, Esq.; John Durand, Esq. See A. O. Bundles, 197-208.

[17] T. 29:45, Minutes, 1776, *passim.*

[18] The *London Gazette* contains the advertisements for bids authorized by the victualling board.

provisions to America, it likewise was consulted in regard to problems of package and delivery. Respecting the purely financial aspect of the contracts, the commissioners of the Treasury received estimates from the comptrollers of army accounts. Thus data were acquired from a number of sources, official and unofficial. As soon as the terms of a contract had been agreed upon, the solicitor to the board was directed to embody them in a formal agreement for signature.[19]

In spite of the fact that copies of the contracts must have been lodged in the Treasury and were regularly transmitted to various officials, few of them are now to be found in the archives.[20] Information regarding them is therefore somewhat fragmentary, and is mainly confined to the correspondence and minutes of the Treasury board. Fortunately, the contracts in their main features seem to have been much alike from year to year. They usually ran for a period of twelve or sixteen months, during which the contractor agreed to furnish complete daily rations for so many thousand men at so much per ration.[21] The provisions were deliverable at the contractor's risk and expense, sometimes in America, but usually at

[19] For data regarding methods of making contracts, see T. 29:44-54, Minutes, 1774-1783, and *Report on Army Extras*, 1778.

[20] Among the officials receiving copies of the contracts were the commissary at Cork, the comptrollers of army accounts, and the commissary generals and commanders in America.

[21] For example, in 1776 the contractors agreed to provision 48,000 men in America for a period of 16 months at 5¼d. per ration, according to the following division:

	No. men
Messrs. Nesbitt, Drummond, & Franks	12,000
" Henneker, Wombwell, Devaynes, & Wheeler	12,000
Mr. Amyand	3,000
Mr. Durand	3,000
Messrs. Bacon & Mayne	6,000
Messrs. Jones, Smith, Baynes, & Atkinson	12,000

The rate per ration in 1777 was 5¼d.; in 1778, 5¾d.

Cork. Such of them as upon inspection should prove bad and unfit for consumption were to be replaced.[22] The lords commissioners agreed to refund to the contractor such import or export duties as he might be called upon to pay and to settle for the provisions upon presentation of a certificate, signed by the proper officials, stating that they had been received in good condition.[23]

A concrete example may make the nature of the contracts clear. On 2 April, 1776, the board concluded a contract with Messrs. Nesbitt, Drummond, & Franks.[24] By its terms the contractors were to deliver at their own cost and risk into the army storehouses at Cork daily rations for 12,000 men for a period of sixteen months beginning January 1, 1776. The provisions were to be delivered in such quantities and at such times as the board should direct. They were to be "good wholesome and sound . . . of a Quality and condition fit for the purpose of export-

[22] At the beginning of the war, it appears that the contractors warranted provisions good upon delivery at the designated *dépôt* in Great Britain or Ireland. Later, however, owing to the fact that many of the provisions were found to be in bad condition upon arrival in America, apparently they were obliged to warrant them good upon delivery in the colonies. T. 1:519, Robinson to Gordon, 7 Feb. 1777; *ibid.*, 64:106, Robinson to Howe, 12 Apr. 1776, 14 Jan. 1777; *ibid.*, 64:200, Lieutenant Harris to Navy Board, 23 Oct. 1779; Wier-Robinson Correspondence, Robinson to Wier, 6 Dec. 1777.

[23] *Report on Army Extras*, 1778. The contractor upon delivering his supplies to the army in America was given a receipt signed by the commander-in-chief and the commissary general. This instrument upon being presented to the Treasury board was referred to the comptrollers of army accounts. They, upon finding the certificate satisfactory, so reported to the board, which thereupon ordered a warrant for payment to be prepared. The latter, drawn up under the sign manual and countersigned by the lords of the Treasury, directed the paymaster general to pay to the contractor the sums due. In case the comptrollers reported any deficiency in the certificate, the board sometimes referred the report back to the comptrollers with further directions; sometimes directed one of the comptrollers to attend and, after hearing him, issued such orders as the case demanded.

[24] T. 64:106, pp. 64-67. For complete text of this contract, see appendix to this chapter.

ing to America for the use of his Majesty's Troops.''
They were to be ''packed·in the best Manner and most
suitable for the intended Service.'' The contractors were
allowed 5¼d. per ration. In case any of the provisions
should ''be found bad in their kind or unfit for the purpose'' upon delivery at Cork, they were to be replaced;
but the contractors were not to be held answerable for
any provisions damaged after delivery. The lords commissioners agreed to remit any custom duties laid upon
the provisions and to render payment upon presentation
of a ''Certificate, signed by the Commanding Officer and
Commissary of Stores at Corke,'' specifying that the provisions had been received ''in good Order and Condition.''[25]

A list of all the various kinds of provisions supplied to
the army would be lengthy. The most important were
beef, pork, bread,[26] flour, oatmeal, rice, pease, butter, and
salt. Of somewhat less importance were cheese, bacon,
suet, fish, raisins, and molasses.[27] Numerous kinds of
vegetables were shipped occasionally, such as potatoes,
parsnips, carrots, turnips, cabbages, and onions.[28] These
were intended mainly for the hospitals. Onions, sauerkraut, porter, claret, spruce beer, malt, vinegar, celery
seed, and brown mustard seed were used as anti-scorbutics. The contractors averred that celery seed boiled in
soup, and the seeds of brown mustard when dried,

[25] In theory the contractors were not to receive payment for provisions
until actual delivery had taken place. In practice, however, the board often
granted them imprests in advance for the purpose of facilitating their work.
A willingness to construe the terms of the contracts rather loosely was also
shown in times of haste or emergency when the lords commissioners modi-
fied or dispensed with obstructive requirements. T. 29:47, pp. 75, 83.

[26] The troops often baked their bread on the march. See Burgoyne's
Orderly Book, pp. 7, 120; *A View of the Evidence*, p. 13.

[27] For lists of provisions, see W.O. 60:11, 19, 20, 21, *passim;* T. 1:519,
passim; ibid., 64:200, *passim.*

[28] T. 64:106, Robinson to Gage, 9 Sept. 1775; C.O. 5:93, p. 265.

bruised, and eaten with meat were potent antidotes for scurvy.[29] Sauerkraut, spruce beer, and vinegar, however, seem to have been the most successful anti-scorbutics.[30] Vegetable seeds were also sent out for the soldiers to plant.[31] During the siege of Boston the Treasury board informed Gage: "A good quantity of the small Salled Seed will be sent out, as it will grow, on being sown, almost anywhere on a little earth, and may be raised by the Soldiers on a little Space by each Mess, in sufficient quantities for their refreshment and use."[32]

It is difficult to describe the composition of the soldier's ration during the war, since it varied from week to week, if not from day to day, and according as service was by land or by sea.[33] Only examples of it can be given. Although the yearly provision contracts were not all alike, they varied but slightly, and the Canada contract for 1778-1779 may be considered as typical. It provided that seven rations per man were to consist of:

> "7 lbs of Flour, of the first Quality, made from wholly
>   Kilndried Wheat
> 7 lbs of Beef, or in lieu thereof 4 lbs of Pork
> 6 oz. of Butter, or in lieu thereof 8 oz. of Cheese
> 3 Pints of Pease
> ½ lb of Oatmeal."[34]

[29] T. 64:106, Robinson to Gage, 9 Sept. 1775; Mure, Son, & Atkinson to Howe, 25 Sept. 1775; *ibid.*, 64:103, Day to Robinson, 22 Aug. 1777; *Report on Army Extras*, 1778.

[30] The allowance of sauerkraut in Howe's army in 1776 was ¼ lb. per man *per diem. Report on Army Extras*, 1778. *Cf.* T. 64:103, Phillips to Day, 6 Sept. 1777; *ibid.*, 64:103, Mure, Son, & Atkinson to Howe, 14 Sept. 1776; T. 29:45, p. 259.

[31] T. 64:106, Mure, Son, & Atkinson to Howe, 14 Sept., 21 Oct. 1776; *Report on Army Extras*, 1778.

[32] T. 64:106, Robinson to Gage, 9 Sept. 1775. See also Wier-Robinson Correspondence, Robinson to Wier, 26 Sept. 1777.

[33] At sea the troops were usually put on two-thirds allowance. W.O. 60:11, Ross to Crawford, 1 Apr. 1779; *Kemble Papers*, I, 379.

[34] T. 29:48. In the contracts for 1776-1777, seven rations were to consist of "7 Pounds of Flour, or in lieu thereof 7 Pounds of Bread; 4 Pounds

It seems doubtful whether provisions were often distributed according to such specifications, owing to the fact that the victuallers arrived irregularly and the amounts of the different provisions in store fluctuated greatly. Garrison orders issued at Three Rivers at the beginning of the war regulated the allowance of provisions as follows:

"A compleat Ration for one Man for one day in every Species

Flour or Bread	1½ Pounds
Beef	1 Pound
or Pork	½ Pound
Pease	¼ Pint
Butter	1 Ounce
Rice	1 Ounce

Whenever the situation of the Army prevents this Distribution of Provisions, it will be delivered in the following manner which is to be the Compleat Ration,

Flour or Bread	1½ Pounds
Beef	1½ Pounds
or Pork	10 Ounces

Should it happen that no provisions except Flour or Bread or Rice can be issued, a Compleat Ration is

Flour or Bread	3 Pounds
or Rice	1½ Pounds

Whenever fresh Provisions can be procured for the Army, the Rations to be the same Allowance. . . ."[35]

of Pork, or in lieu thereof 7 Pounds of Beef; 6 Ounces of Butter; 3 Pints of Pease; ½ Pound of Rice, or in lieu thereof ½ Pound of Oatmeal." T. 29:45. Nathaniel Day writes to Burgoyne from Montreal, 31 May, 1777, that the contracts made by the Treasury board for 1777 are proportioned for one man's allowance *per diem* as follows:

"1 lb Bread or Flour
1 lb Beef or 9¼ oz. pork
¾ pints pease
6/7 oz. Butter or in lieu 1¼ oz. Cheese
2²/₇ oz. flour or in lieu 1¼ oz. Rice or 1¼ oz. Oatmeal."

T. 64:103.

[35] T. 64:102, Garrison Orders, Three Rivers, 11 June, 1776.

Masters of victuallers were charged to victual every six men at full allowance according to the following table:

	Bread or Flour Pounds	Beef Pounds	Pork Pounds	Butter Pounds	Pease Pints	Rice or Oatmeal Pounds	Rum Jills
Sunday	6		6		3		8
Monday	6			¾	4½		8
Tuesday	6	10½				1½	8
Wednesday	6			¾	2		8
Thursday	6		6		2		8
Friday	6			¾	4½		8
Saturday	6	10½				1½	8
	—	—	—	—	—	—	—
Total	42	21	12	2¼	16	3	56

When the commanding Officer orders Vinegar to be issued, a Quart per Week to six Men is the Allowance. . . .''[36]

Provisions for a certain colonial garrison were to be rationed as follows:

"1 lb good Salt Beef per Man per Day
1 lb Flour per Man per Day
6 oz Butter per Man per Week
1½ [lb] Rice per Man per Week
1 Pint Teneriffe or other Strong wine per Man per day."[37]

Rum was a regular and very important part of the soldier's ration.[38] Before being given to him, it was usually diluted with water. The ordinary allowance was a gill

[36] W.O. 60:22, ''Rules to be observed by Masters and Commanders of Transport Ships in victualling Land Forces,'' issued by John Morrison, deputy commissary general. The above seems to have been the regular allowance of vinegar on land, but see T. 64:106, Mure, Son, & Atkinson to Howe, 21 Oct. 1776.

[37] T. 64:201, Robinson to Navy Board, 4 Apr. 1781.

[38] There was no regular allowance of rum in Howe's army, according to Commissary General Wier, until June, 1776. ''Minute Book of a Board of General Officers,'' 1781 (N. Y. Hist. Soc. *Coll.* 1916), p. 81.

and a half or a gill and a third *per diem* except during in-
clement weather or especially hard duty, when an additional gill was allowed.[39] The troops were occasionally
permitted to have small quantities of claret, spruce beer,
or porter. In 1775 the secretary to the Treasury board
wrote to Gage that he was sending 375,000 gallons of
porter to Boston. "This quantity," he stated, "is on a
calculation of allowing to each man, a Pot of Porter per
day, and . . . is to be used at the discretion of the Commander-in-Chief."[40] In the following year, spruce beer as
more healthful was substituted for porter.[41] Like other
beverages excepting rum, it was issued at the discretion
of the general in command.[42] Burgoyne ordinarily allowed each man two quarts in the field and three pints
in quarters a day.[43] It seems to have been a popular drink
with the soldiers, owing partly to the fact that it involved
no stoppages in pay.[44] In 1777 an army brewery for the
manufacture of spruce beer was established at New
York.[45]

Some conception of the fare of the sick soldier may be
gained from the following regulations, drawn up by the
inspector general of hospitals in North America. Surely
there could have been little temptation to malinger.

---

[39] *Report on Army Extras,* 1778. Rum was supplied to the Indians with
Burgoyne's army "without any Rule or Ration." A supply of 125,000
gallons was shipped to America for them in 1776.

[40] T. 64:106, Robinson to Gage, 9 Sept. 1775.

[41] T. 64:106, Robinson to Howe, 22 Oct. 1776, Mure, Son, & Atkinson to
Howe, 21 Oct. 1776.

[42] *Report on Army Extras,* 1778. There was an assistant commissary of
beer attached to Burgoyne's army in 1777. *Orderly Book,* p. 179.

[43] T. 64:103, Day to Robinson, 22 Aug. 1777.

[44] Stryker, *Trenton and Princeton,* p. 71.

[45] T. 64:118, Chamier to Robinson, 31 Mar. 1777. Breweries were also
established in the rear of Burgoyne's army during the invasion of New
York, 1777. T. 64:103, Day to Robinson, 22 Aug. 1777; Phillips to Day, 6
Sept. 1777.

"Concerning the full and low Diets of the Hosp'l,

Full Diet

Rice Gruel, or Water Gruel, with Sugar or Butter

Dinner

One Pound of Fresh Meat: Viz: Beef, Mutton, or Veal, with Greens

Supper

Two Ounces of Butter, or Cheese

Half Diet

Dinner

Rice, and Pudding, and half a Pound of Fresh Meat; four times a week

Breakfast & Supper, as full Diet

Low Diet

Breakfast, and Supper, Rice or Water Gruel; Milk; Porridge, Sago or Salop

Dinner

Broth & Pudding

One Pound of Bread; each Man per Diem, with three pints of Spruce Beer in Summer and a Quart in Winter.

Rice Water; for common drink in Fluxes; and Barley in Fevers. . . ."[46]

No fact stands out more clearly and prominently in the records than the defectiveness of the army's food supply. Provisions were frequently so poor in quality as to be absolutely inedible even by hungry redcoats. The commissary generals complained again and again of mouldy bread, weevily biscuit, rancid butter, sour flour, worm-eaten pease, and maggoty beef. In November, 1776, despite repeated protests to the Treasury board, the commissary general at New York asserted that the bread

[46] W.O. 28:6, Hospitals, 1778-1781.

supplied to General Howe's army continued to be "very bad in quality mixt with old bread, musty and much broken."[47] Surveyors, appointed to examine the cargo of one victualler at New York, reported that it consisted of "very old Bread, Weavile Eaten, full of Maggots, Mouldy, musty and rotten and entirely unfit for men to eat." The cargo of another victualler was found to be composed of "very old Flour of different sorts and very inferior qualities, and in general musty and rotten."[48] On one occasion, the agent victualler at Cork stated that he had been obliged to condemn over five hundred casks of pease, "several Casks promiscuously taken being found all more or less to have live Maggots in them, some quite rotten and those that were the best with a great mixture of Green Pea, which on boiling proves to have no Substance and leaves little more than the Husk." He also declared that he had been compelled to reject four hundred barrels of the same article "for having a live Worm and being otherwise of a very inferior Quality."[49] On another occasion, he complained: "It is with the utmost Difficulty I can keep any exact Accounts from the Irregularities of the Contractors, and the little Assistance they give as well as the Confusion that is caused by the Provisions coming in such bad order principally with respect to the Casks, and the Damages they sustain, which renders the closest Inspection necessary, particularly with regard to wet Provisions which I am obliged to examine very minutely from having discovered Impositions that are at-

47 T. 64:118, Chamier to Robinson, 9 Nov. 1776.

48 T. 64:118. Surveys of the cargoes of the *Providence, Increase,* and *Valiant,* victuallers, in Chamier's letter to Robinson, 20 Apr. 1777. "It is highly unpleasant," writes the king to Lord North, 1 Jan. 1777, "to see the contractors have continued delivering such bad biscuit and flour after the repeated directions given by the Board of Treasury." *Correspondence of Geo. III with Lord North,* II, 51.

49 T. 64:200, Marsh to Navy Board, 2 Jan. 1780.

tempted and been under the Necessity of rejecting some large Supplies of Beef and Butter, finding the former to be for the most part lean Cow beef, and the Butter of an inferior Quality.''[50] A private aboard a troop transport bound for America humorously described the fare of his unhappy fellow soldiers as follows: ''Pork and pease were the chief of their diet. The pork seemed to be four or five years old. It was streaked with black towards the outside and was yellow farther in, with a little white in the middle. The salt beef was in much the same condition. The ship biscuit was so hard that they sometimes broke it up with a cannonball, and the story ran that it had been taken from the French in the Seven Years' War and lain in Portsmouth ever since. . . . Sometimes they had groats and barley, or, by way of a treat a pudding made of flour mixed half with salt water and half with fresh water, and with old mutton fat.''[51]

The records abound with reports and statements like the foregoing.[52] Those quoted will serve to illustrate the kind of food often supplied to the British soldier in America. Nor must it be assumed that bad provisions were small in amount. There is ample testimony to show that large quantities had to be condemned.[53] For example, Howe, on quitting Boston in March, 1776, left behind as

[50] T. 64:200, Marsh to Navy Board, 12 Feb. 1780.

[51] Seume, *Mein Leben*, quoted in Lowell's *Hessians in the Revolution*, p. 56.

[52] T. 64:200, Marsh to Navy Board, 12 Feb. 1780, Cherry to Navy Board, 20 July, 1780, Harris to Navy Board, 23 Oct. 1779; *ibid.*, 29:45, Minutes, 14 Aug. 1776; C.O. 5:93. ''Returns of Provisions in Store at Boston,'' 2 Oct., 16 Nov. 1775, 22 Jan. 1776; W.O. 1:50, Petition of the Four Companies of the Royal American Regiment at Antigua; *Kemble Papers*, I, 157; Wier-Robinson Correspondence, *passim*.

[53] C.O. 5:93. ''Memo. of Failure on the part of the Contractors for Victualling His Majesty's Troops at Boston''; ''Returns of Provisions in Store at Boston,'' 16 Nov. 1775, 22 Jan. 1776; T. 64:200, Cherry to Navy Board, 20 July, 1780, Harris to Navy Board, 23 Oct. 1779, Marsh to Navy Board, 12 Feb. 1779; T. 29:45, Minutes, 14 Aug. 1776.

"unfit for His Majesty's Troops to eat" 61 barrels of pork, 32 firkins of butter, 1,000 pounds of cheese, 12 casks of raisins, 393 bags of bread, and "A Quantity of Mutton in Puncheons . . . spoiled in curing and unfit for Use." These were in addition to 4,000 barrels of flour which he had condemned in the preceding October.[54] Of 2,000 bags of bread landed at the head of the Elk River in the campaign of 1777, "300 were condemned as unfit for Men to eat and of the 254 Bags carried on the March 50 or 60 were left on the way on the same Account."[55]

Much food was damaged or destroyed by rats and other vermin,[56] much through careless stowage aboard the victuallers,[57] much through being packed in bags and barrels too flimsy to sustain the shocks of an ocean voyage and the rough usage of a campaign.[58] The commissary general at New York declared that "the bags that contained the Bread and part of those with the Pease were so thin and Rotten they wd. scarce bear Removing

[54] C.O. 5:93, "Provisions and Stores left at Boston."
C.O. 5:93, "Memo. of Failure on the part of the Contractors for Victualling His Majesty's Troops at Boston."
[55] Wier-Robinson Correspondence, Wier to Robinson, 25 Oct. 1777.
[56] T. 64:103, Day to Robinson, 22 Aug. 1777; ibid., 64:120, Paumier to Robinson, 7 Aug. 1779; ibid., 64:106, Gordon to Robinson, 21 Jan. 1777. Mure, Son, & Atkinson, writing to Howe 21 Oct. 1776, stated in reference to a fleet of oat ships: "Each ship will receive at Cork one piece of Canvas and a parcell of Needles and thread to enable them to mend the Bags [of Oats] when unloading as the Rats will pretty certainly make that precaution necessary." T. 64:106.
[57] T. 64:118, Chamier to Robinson, 20 April, 1777. Referring to certain damaged provisions in victuallers, Chamier wrote: "For want of Dunnage between the Flour and Coals, the flour by the motion of the ship have partly buried themselves amongst the Coals whereby the flour acquired much Damp." See also W.O. 60:16, Ross to Wier, 24 Mar. 1778; T. 1:528, Howe to Robinson, 5 June, 1777.
[58] T. 64:200, Marsh to Navy Board, 17 Dec. 1779, 12 Feb. 1780, Cherry to Navy Board, 20 July, 1780; ibid., 64:103, Day to Robinson, 22 Aug. 1777; ibid., 64:106, Robinson to Howe, 14 Jan. 1777, Gordon to Robinson, 21 Jan. 1777; ibid., 64:120, Paumier to Robinson, 7 Aug. 1779; Wier-Robinson Correspondence, Paumier to Wier, 28 Sept. 1777.

from the vessells in which they came without much
Waste. The Casks in which part of the Flour was packed
were so slight that they wou'd not admit of being removed far by Land Carriage.''[59] Casks and barrels were
not only ill-adapted to the service in strength but also in
size. ''Great inconvenience,'' wrote the commissary general in Canada, ''has happened through the enormous
size of Provision Casks, puncheons being sent out with
Beef and Pork whereas no Cask should come here larger
than a Barrel which are calculated for our Carts and
Batteaux, for the want of which many of the puncheons
have been stove.''[60] Much food was damaged because no
proper covering had been provided to protect it from the
inclemencies of the weather. To remedy this defect one
commissary humbly prayed the Treasury board to be
''supplied with Twelve Large Provision Tents similar in
size with those of the Hospitals, and two Hundred Oil
Cloaths made of Russia sheeting.''[61] Climatic conditions
also played havoc with army foodstuffs. This was especially true in the Southern colonies where the summer
heat melted the butter to oil, turned the flour sour, and
caused the sauerkraut to spoil.[62] In Canada, however, it
was not the temperature which robbed the army of its
provisions. Thieving inhabitants must bear the blame.
The commissary general in that country complained that
he was compelled to employ in the transport service Canadians ''whose propensity for pilfering is such that it
obliges me to send Conductors to protect the provisions.
Notwithstanding all my efforts to protect it, I have had
the Mortification to see the Butter taken out of Firkins
and Stones etc. put in lieu to compleat the Weight; and

[59] T. 64:118, Chamier to Robinson, 11 Aug. 1776.

[60] T. 64:102, Day to Robinson, 26 Oct. 1776.

[61] T. 64:102, Day to Robinson, 26 Oct. 1776; *ibid.*, 64:106, Gordon to
Robinson, 21 Jan. 1777.

[62] T. 64:120, Paumier to Robinson, 20 June, 7 Aug. 1779.

so dextrously headed that the best Eye could not perceive the deception, which theft has not been confined to butter only but at large without exceptions of Species; and the Losses sustained . . . is [*sic*] very considerable.'"[63]

The process of victualling the army was, furthermore, characterized by careless, dilatory, and sometimes dishonest, business methods. The supply of provisions was often ill-proportioned, there being too much of one species and too little of another, too much bread and flour and too little beef and pork. In July, 1777, Commissary General Wier complained to the Treasury board that the amount of pease shipped to New York was so much in excess of the needs of the army that the stuff was perishing on his hands. He was only restrained from shipping it back to England by the fear that the rascally contractors would promptly repurchase it and send it back to America again.[64] One of the chief reasons for the defectiveness of the supply at certain times was the failure of the commissaries to make prompt and accurate returns of the numbers to be victualled. "On careful perusal of the dispatches . . . of Sir H. Clinton," writes the king to John Robinson on one occasion, "it appears very clearly that any deficiency of Provisions doth arise from the old complaint—a want of clearly stating in N.A. the numbers to be victualled."[65] Contractors were tardy in filling orders, and occasionally resorted to frauds in order to cheat the government, such as mixing sand with the flour or sending over barrels of rum, flour, or beef short in

[63] T. 64:102, Day to Robinson, 20 June, 1777.

[64] Wier-Robinson Correspondence, Wier to Robinson, 12 July, 1777, 25 Oct. 1777; T. 64:118, Chamier to Robinson, 11 Aug. 1776; *ibid.*, 64:106, Robinson to Howe, 22 Oct. 1776; *ibid.*, 64:201, Robinson to Navy Board, 30 Mar. 1781; *ibid.*, 29:46, Minutes, 2 Dec. 1777; W.O. 4:274, Jenkinson to Clinton, 5 Apr. 1779; *ibid.*, 4:275, Jenkinson to Clinton, 5 Feb. 1781.

[65] Addit. MSS. 37,833, fo. 43, George III to Robinson, 29 Nov. 1778. *Cf.* Addit. MSS. 37,833, fo. 1, 5 Sept. 1778.

weight.[66] The shortage would sometimes be slyly concealed by weighting cask or barrel with stones. The deputy commissary general at New York complained that of the beef shipped to Howe's army in 1777 some barrels were "deficient upwards of 40 lb. Weight and in general they run 15 to 20 lb. short of their customary and Invoice Weight. The Pork likewise is deficient from 8 to 10 lb. per Barrel, . . ."[67] In some instances, owing to the connivance or carelessness of the commissaries in failing to report the marks on the packages, it was impossible to detect the guilty contractor. "The peculation in every profitable branch of the [military] service," wrote Wedderburn to a confidential friend, "is represented to be enormous, and, as usual, it is attended with a shocking neglect of every comfort to the troops. The hospitals are pest-houses, and the provisions served out are poison; those that are to be bought are sold at the highest prices of a monopoly."[68]

In this connection, however, it is only fair to state that the contractors did not enjoy a monopoly of dishonesty and inefficiency. More than one commissary general fell under suspicion of being engaged in doubtful transactions at the expense of the government. During the autumn and winter of 1776, foi example, a fleet of seventeen victuallers arrived at New York. Both Howe and Com-

---

66 T. 64:120, Paumier to Robinson, 7 Aug. 1779; *ibid.*, 64:106, Gordon to Robinson, 20 Aug. 1776; *ibid.*, 64:200, George Cherry to Navy Board, 14 Feb. 1780, Navy Board to Treasury, 14 Feb., 4 Aug. 1780; *ibid.*, 64:201, Robinson to Navy Board, 11 Nov. 1779, 13 Mar. 1781; T. 1:519, Robinson to Gordon, 21 June, 1776.

67 Wier-Robinson Correspondence, Paumier to Wier, 6 Nov. 1777.

68 Quoted in *Correspondence of Geo. III with Lord North*, I, 299. Burke summed up the situation rather strikingly, "The merchants begin to snuff the cadaverous *haut goût* of lucrative war; the freighting business never was so lively on account of the prodigious taking up for transport-service; great orders for provisions of all kinds, new clothing for troops, puts life into the woolen manufactures."

missary General Chamier complained of the condition of
the bread and flour with which it was freighted. The
Treasury board instituted an investigation. Fourteen of
the transport masters took oath that they had delivered
the provisions in good condition at New York; and ten of
them furthermore swore that large quantities of flour,
bread, and pease were left by the commissary for days on
the wharves, exposed to the snow and rain. One witness
offered to assert on oath that after the bread and flour
had thus got thoroughly soaked, it was sold by the commissary and then bought back again and served out to
the troops, the implication being that at some stage of the
transaction the commissary had managed to make a
profit on his own account. There seems to be no evidence
that Chamier ever successfully denied these allegations.
Further suspicion was cast upon him by the fact that his
complaints were dated prior to his certificates of inspection and by the fact that although the barrels and packages were all marked by the names of the respective contractors, he failed to specify whose provisions were at
fault. It was not long after this that he ceased to hold
office as commissary general.[69]

This entire state of affairs frequently resulted in a
dearth of provisions that was very alarming to the generals in America and that seriously affected the conduct
of the war. Howe was repeatedly hampered in his campaigns by insufficiency of provisions. Writing to the
Treasury board from Boston in December, 1775, he declared, "I am in great Pain from the small Quantity of
Provisions now in Store." In the same month, he informed Lord Dartmouth, "The small Quantities of Provisions in Store . . . fill me with Alarms. . . . If Victual-

[69] T. 64:106, *passim*. See also T. 64:106, Robinson to Howe, 8 Apr. 1777;
ibid., 1:519, Robinson to Gordon, 20 Mar. 1777; W.O. 1:10, Clinton to
Germain, 18 Dec. 1778.

ling Ships should not arrive before the latter End of this Month, nor the Navy be able to afford Assistance, I shall be obliged to put the Troops upon short Allowance."[70]

Howe has sometimes been blamed for not starting his campaign in the Middle Colonies in 1776 more promptly. It will be recalled that his troops did not land at Staten Island until midsummer. Had he put them in the field a month or two earlier, it has been pointed out that he might have succeeded in conquering Pennsylvania as well as New York and New Jersey. This would have been a far more serious blow to the Americans than the occupation of New York and New Jersey alone. Indeed, it might have sufficed to terminate the war. The advent of winter compelled him to suspend operations with the conquest of New Jersey. Howe's tardiness, however, was not entirely of his own making. His army was delayed at Halifax and much valuable time lost owing to insufficiency of provisions. "I tremble," he wrote Germain from that place on 7 May, "when I think of our present State of Provisions, having now Meat for no more than thirteen Days in Store."[71] In short, Howe was compelled to await the arrival of a tardy fleet of victuallers before he could embark for New York.[72] The partial success of the campaign may be traced in a measure to this circumstance.

Howe has likewise been censured for failure to pursue Washington more vigorously during the latter's retreat

[70] C.O. 5:93, Howe to Dartmouth, 1 Dec. 1775; *Report on Army Extras, 1778*, appendix no. 4. The plight of the garrison was well put in a contemporary ballad:

> "And what have you got with all your designing
> But a town without dinner to sit down and dine in."
> *Memorial History of Boston,* III, 91.

[71] C.O. 5:93, Howe to Germain, 7 May, 1776.

[72] C.O. 5:93, Howe to Germain, 7 June, 7 July, 1776. *Cf.* Channing, *History of United States,* III, 232.

across New Jersey in November, 1776.[73] If we may accept the statement of Cornwallis, who was in direct charge of the pursuit, this was not due solely to want of initiative. ''We subsisted only on the flour we found in the country; and as the troops had been constantly marching ever since their first entrance into the Jerseys, they had no time to bake their flour . . .''[74] The necessity of stopping to bake flour collected from the countryside, the only form of breadstuff obtainable by the troops, helped to delay the pursuit and enabled Washington to withdraw unmolested across the Delaware.

Strictures have also been passed upon Howe for placing a portion of his army in scattered cantonments in New Jersey during the winter of 1776-1777, and thus allowing Washington to strike isolated detachments at Trenton and Princeton.[75] Once more, however, a scarcity of supplies forced him to adopt measures of which under normal circumstances he would scarcely have approved. The provisions at New York were too limited to feed his entire army during the winter. The only alternative was to place a portion of the troops in cantonments so widely separated that the various detachments could live off the countryside without mutual interference.[76]

Again, Howe has been condemned for not taking the field earlier in 1777. He did not receive the camp equipage necessary for the campaign until the 24th of May, however; and inasmuch as the government compelled him to obtain his hay and oats in America, and would not supply him to any extent with those articles from England, he was forced to wait until the green forage was on the ground. His difficulties during the ensuing campaign

---

[73] Smith, *Wars between England and America*, p. 85; Stryker, *Trenton and Princeton*, p. 36.

[74] *A View of the Evidence*, p. 13.

[75] *Correspondence of Geo. III with Lord North*, II, 57.

[76] C.O. 5:93, Howe to Germain, 30 Nov. 1776.

were greatly augmented by the deficiency in quality and quantity of the provisions supplied to his forces.[77]

Clinton labored under similar disadvantages. Writing from New York in September, 1778, he informed Germain: "You will perceive how low we are in a Stock of that very essential Article [food] notwithstanding the arrival of Six Ships lately from Cork."[78] Conditions had not improved by winter. "Your Lordship will be startled," he wrote in December, "when I inform you that this Army has now but a fortnight's Flour left. . . . Our Meat with the Assistance of Cattle purchased here will last about forty days beyond Xmas, and a Bread composed of Peas, Indian Corn and Oatmeal can be furnished for about the same time. After that I do not know how we shall subsist."[79] Clinton's inactivity at New York in 1779 was due partly to a shortage of provisions. In that year Haldimand had planned to seize Oswego and create a diversion along the Canadian frontier for such operations as Clinton might undertake but was balked owing to a scarcity of food supplies.[80] Meantime, General Augustine Prevost was writing to the commander-in-chief that the same cause had become a capital obstacle to the adoption of any active measures in the South.[81] By 1780 Clinton's patience regarding the subject of provisions seems to have become well-nigh exhausted. "Your Lordship well knows," he wrote to Germain, "how often this army has been on the Eve of being reduced to the greatest distress for Want of Provisions . . . The same melancholy Prospect (notwithstanding the many Representations

---

[77] *Correspondence of Geo. III with Lord North*, II, 77; *A View of the Evidence*, p. 18; Stedman, *American War*, I, 287; Wier-Robinson Correspondence, *passim*.

[78] C.O. 5:96, Clinton to Germain, 15 Sept. 1778.

[79] C.O. 5:97, Clinton to Germain, 15 December, 1778.

[80] C.O. 5:98, Haldimand to Clinton, 19 July, 29 Aug. 1779.

[81] C.O. 5:98, Prevost to Clinton, 15 Mar., 30 July, 1779.

that have been made heretofore on this Subject) again appears in a very alarming Degree. It becomes therefore highly necessary for me to represent to Your Lordship, as the Commissary General has frequently done to the Treasury Board, that unless some Measures are speedily adopted to supply us more effectually than we have hitherto been, I have the greatest Reason to apprehend that the most fatal Consequence will ensue. We have not as yet received one ounce of this Year's Supply."[82]

If provisions were scarce at New York, they were yet scarcer in the West Indies. No words can paint the distress of the troops in that quarter for want not merely of food but everything essential to an army's welfare. "The situation of the Troops in this Island," wrote Lieutenant Governor Graham of Tobago to Jenkinson in September, 1779, "must be Dreadful if a Vessel does not arrive soon with Provisions from Government. Salt Provisions and Flour cannot be got at any price. I hope some Measures are already taken for that purpose." Two months later no relief had come. "I took the Liberty," he wrote in November, "to represent to you in my last Letter, the great necessity there was to have provisions immediately sent out by Government for this Island. I cannot purchase any more provisions in this Island— my sole dependence is on St. Lucia. Sir Henry Calder has sent me supplies at different times, but the provisions there begin to be bad in quality and the expense of the freight enormous."[83] In the same month a year later, General Vaughan, who was stationed at Barbadoes, informed the secretary at war: "The distress we are in will I trust make the measure of sending us some immediate assistance appear to you as necessary as I feel it to be.

[82] C.O. 5:100, Clinton to Germain, 31st Oct., 1780. *Cf. Kemble Papers,* I, 167, 170, 173.

[83] W.O. 1:51. Graham to Jenkinson, 13 Sept., 23 Nov. 1779.

Therefore, I do beg and intreat [sic] that some provisions, and a reenforcement of troops may be sent out as sickness and death have reduced our effective numbers very low.''[84] Pathetic testimony regarding conditions in the West Indies is borne by ''The humble Petition of the Non-Commissioned Officers and Privates of the Four Companies [of the 60th Regiment] . . . stationed in Antigua.'' Therein they complain of ''the miseries we have endured ever since our Arrival in this Island for want of wholesome Provisions, as what we have been able to buy for our Support from time to time was not fit for men to eat; and also at the time we presented our humble Petition to you, Provisions of the very worst kind, bore such exorbitant Prices, that our pay was not sufficient, to purchase enough to Support Nature.''[85]

Examples of this sort might be multiplied.[86] The records abound with them. That the generals, whether in the island colonies or on the continent, were seriously handicapped by want of provisions, there is ample evidence. It is no exaggeration to affirm that the British forces in America were sometimes on the verge of starvation.[87]

2. *America as a Source of Provisions*

From the foregoing account, the reader is likely to gain the impression that the army in America was provisioned solely from the British Isles. While it is true that the bulk of the supplies were derived from that source, a considerable quantity were obtained directly in America. Before enumerating these and explaining the

84 W.O. 1:51, Vaughan to Jenkinson, 2 Nov. 1780.
85 W.O. 1:51, undated.
86 C.O. 5:98, Prevost to Clinton, 15, 28 Mar., 16 Apr. 1779; *ibid.*, Haldimand to Clinton, 19 July, 20 Aug. 1779; W.O. 1:51, Vaughan to Jenkinson, 22 Jan. 1781; T. 64:201, Robinson to Navy Board, 30 Sept. 1780; *Kemble Papers*, I, 167, 170; Carrington, *Battles of the American Revolution*, p. 190.
87 T. 64:201, Wier to Robinson, 14 Sept. 1780.

methods by which they were acquired, an examination of the officers engaged both in securing victuals in the field of operations and in distributing those shipped from abroad is necessary. In short, a word should be said regarding the organization of the commissariat—"the department," as one of its officers remarked, "that is of greatest Consequence to the Army. It goes with every Plan and without its unfailing Assistance no Operation can have Action or Success."[88]

There were two commissary generals of provisions attached to the forces in America—one to those in Canada, the other to those in the region between Nova Scotia and West Florida.[89] Each was a civilian and each held an identical commission under the sign manual wherein his duties were broadly outlined. He was authorized "to inspect the buying and delivering of Stores, Provisions, and Forage for the use of the . . . Forces, whether the same be done by Contractors or others, and likewise to settle and adjust all accounts relating thereunto; And . . . to observe and follow such Orders and directions from time to time as he shall receive from . . . the Commander in Chief of the . . . Forces [in America], or any other superior Officer, according to the Rules and Discipline of War." While no mention is made of the fact in his commission, each commissary general was also subject to the orders of the Treasury board to which he constantly reported.[90]

[88] T. 64:102, Day to Robinson, 14 Jan. 1777.

[89] April 14, 1778, Colonel William Roy was commissioned commissary general of all the forces at home and abroad. His exact status in the British military hierarchy is not clear. He does not seem, however, to have exercised any direct control over the commissariat in America. W.O. 25:34, commission. See also Andrews, *Guide to Materials for American History in P.R.O.*, II, 91.

[90] A detailed description of the commissary general's duties will be found in "instructions" drawn up for Nathaniel Day in T. 64:104 (undated). These are quoted in full in appendix to this chapter.

As far as can be ascertained, the office of commissary general to the forces in Canada was held by one man only, Nathaniel Day, who was commissioned 20 March, 1776, and apparently occupied the post until the latter part of 1777.[91] As regards the commissaries general to the forces south of the St. Lawrence, it is regrettable that while the date of commission can be fixed with exactitude, the date of resignation or removal can in some cases be given only approximately.[92] The list is as follows:

Daniel Chamier, 7 Feb. 1774-Feb. 1777.[93]

Daniel Wier, 1 Feb. 1777-Sept. 1781.[94]

Brook Watson, 14 Mar. 1782-5 Dec. 1783.[95]

[91] Date of commission given with "instructions" in T. 64:104. The last record of Day's activities in Canada is a letter to John Robinson dated Montreal, 6 Oct. 1777. T. 64:103. He may have remained longer in America.

[92] See W.O. 60:32, 33, 36 for commissions. In the list given above the first date after each name is the date of the commission.

[93] The commissions of Wier and Watson made them each a commissary general to the forces "serving within Our Colonies in North America; lying upon the Atlantic Ocean from Nova Scotia on the North to West Florida on the South, both inclusive." Chamier's commission differed in that he was appointed commissary general "for all Our Forces employed or to be employed in North America"; but like Wier and Watson he seems to have served only those troops in the region extending from Nova Scotia to West Florida. On 4 Mar. 1777, Robinson informed Chamier that he was to be succeeded in the commissariat department by Wier and that he (Chamier) had been appointed comptroller of accounts to the forces in America. That he ever exercised the duties of the office—whatever they may have been—Howe declared that he did not know or believe. At the time of his death, 27 Nov. 1778, Chamier was still recorded on the staff returns as comptroller. *Report on Army Extras*, 1778; T. 64:118, Robinson to Chamier, 4 Mar. 1777, Chamier to Robinson, 19 May, 1777.

[94] Wier left England for America in the latter part of March or beginning of April, 1777. Robinson informed Clinton, 4 Sept. 1781, that he was to be given leave of absence. T. 64:107; C.O. 5:126, William Knox to Philip Stephens, 3 Mar. 1777; Admiralty Board to Germain, 22 Mar. 1777. For Wier's commission, see appendix to this chapter.

[95] Brook Watson took charge of the department in New York, 27 May, 1782. His charge terminated 5 Dec. 1783, when the army sailed from the port of New York. W.O. 60:20; Andrews, *Guide to Materials for American History in P.R.O.*, II, 110.

As subordinates each commissary general had a number of deputies and assistants (usually civilians), who were sometimes appointed by him, sometimes by the commander-in-chief in America, sometimes by the Treasury board; while a very few held commissions under the sign manual from the crown.[96] Thus, in April, 1776, the commissariat department at New York included the following officers:[97]

Daniel Chamier, Esqr., Commissary General
Major John Morrison ⎫
Peter Paumier   ⎬ Deputies
George Brinley   ⎭
James Christie   ⎫
James Porteous   ⎬ Assistants
John Crawford   ⎭

In addition to the deputies and assistants, two other species of commissary require mention. At the time of his expedition to South Carolina in 1781, Clinton appointed what were referred to as commissaries of captures, "for the purpose of preserving the property of his Maj[s] loyal Subjects in that Country or making them recompense for the losses or damages they might sustain and for the purpose of converting to the good of his Maj[s] Service and to the use, conveniency, and benefit of the Army, all Cattle and moveable property which might be captured from his Majesty's enemies."[98] In the same year, Clinton made Colonel Beverley Robinson commissary of captured

---

96 *Report on Army Extras*, 1778; W.O. 1:12, Alexander Ross to Townshend, 10 Aug. 1782; T. 64:102, Day to Robinson, 27, 30 Mar., 15 May, 20 June, 1777; *ibid.*, 64:104, Instructions to Day (undated); *ibid.*, 64:105, Burke to Haldimand, 26 Apr. 1782; *ibid.*, 64:106; Robinson to Howe, 12 Apr. 1776.

97 T. 64:106, Robinson to Howe, 12 Apr. 1776.

98 T. 64:107, Robinson to Clinton, 19 Dec. 1781.

cattle in North America, but the nature of his duties and the scope of his authority are uncertain.[99]

Sometimes the commissary general followed the army into the field, sometimes he remained at his headquarters, which were located at either Montreal or Quebec for Canada and at New York for the provinces to the southward. In 1777, for example, Nathaniel Day remained at Montreal while his deputy, Fleetwood Parkhurst, and Jonathan Clarke, assistant commissary general, accompanied Burgoyne on his march southward.[100] In the same year, on the other hand, Daniel Wier went with Howe to Philadelphia, leaving his deputies, Robert Ross and Peter Paumier, to manage affairs at New York.[101]

Some conception of the work and organization of the commissariat may be gained from the arrangement made by Brook Watson at New York.[102] A number of departments, or branches, as they were sometimes called, were established as follows:

Commissary General's Office

Robert Ross, Comptroller of Transport Accounts.
Frederick W. Hecht, Assistant Commissary and several assistants, clerks, and porters.

Provision Department

Gregory Townsend and Roger Johnson, Assistant Com-

---

[99] C.O. 5:102, Clinton to Germain, 7 July, 1781; *ibid.*, 5:105, Clinton to Germain, 10 Oct. 1781. Among some of the very minor officials connected with the commissariat, we find mention of John Buxton, inspector of the king's bakeries, and Joseph Orchard, superintendent of the same, at New York in 1777. Here and there mention is made of regimental bakers and inspectors and provers of rum. In many instances regimental officers acted as commissaries. T. 64:103, 107, 118, *passim*.

[100] T. 64:200, "List of commissaries with the Army under Burgoyne," June, 1777. Parkhurst remained at Sorel. Clarke went on to Saratoga where he was captured.

[101] W.O. 60:11, *passim*; Wier-Robinson Correspondence.

[102] W.O. 60:12, *passim*. The scheme of organization given above is for June, 1782.

missaries and several coopers, carpenters, laborers, assistants, and clerks.

Fleming Pinkstan, Surgeon to the Department.

Forage Department

George Brinley, Deputy Commissary and several assistants, clerks, laborers, collectors and issuers of forage.

Cattle Department

Abijah Willard, Assistant Commissary, and a clerk, issuer, and butchers.

Fuel Department

Joseph Chew, Superintendent, and several clerks and negro laborers.

His Majesty's Brewery

Edward G. Lutwyche, Superintendent, and a clerk and several laborers.

That the life of the average commissary general was no sinecure, we have the testimony of Nathaniel Day, who wrote at one time, "Since my return to Montreal . . . I have been a slave and prisoner to Business . . . Writing late at Night has hurt my sight and my close Application and Attention to every part of my department since my Arrival in Canada to this day has greatly impaired my Memory."[103] Nor was it easy for the commissary general in Canada to procure able assistants to relieve him: "The proper people for my department is not to be had in this Province. Such as could assist me should be active, sober, honest People, who must have the good of the service at Heart, and make no difficulties, and not Young People who think so much of their dear selves as to attend to the Fopperys and Neglect the Essentials."[104] Then there were certain financial inconven-

[103] T. 64:102, Day to Robinson, 15 May, 1777.
[104] T. 64:102, Day to Robinson, 20 June, 1777.

iences in being a commissary general: "I hope my Lords will take under their Consideration the many expences I have been subject to since my Arrival in this province to the present Time and the losses I must sustain by advancing Money to different people in Order to engage their Attention to Manufacturing Flour and procure [sic] other Necessarys [sic] so Essential to the Comfort and Health of the Army in Canada; that since my commencement in this extensive and weighty department, I have received no allowance other than my daily pay which has Obliged me to draw upon my Private Fortune to make up for losses, pay House and Office rent, Postage of letters, Expresses, travelling Charges, Books and Stationary [sic]; and many other expenses Attending the Chief Commissary which do not affect the Deputys or Assistants . . . "[105] In a sense, too, the commissary general was a kind of caterer to the army, and like most caterers and cooks since time immemorial found it difficult to concoct a bill of fare acceptable to everybody's taste. Day grumbled that "the Canadians employed in the Upper Country will not use English Biscuit. I am obliged to procure for them Canadian." And again: "Neither Indians nor Canadians will eat salt Beef tho' exceeding good."[106] "Mr. Day," wrote the Treasury to Haldimand, "having stated that the Troops do not like Oatmeal, that will be left out of the Ration to be supplied

[105] It has not been possible to determine the pay of the commissaries in all instances. Wier received £3 *per diem*. Chamier's deputies were paid 30s. and his assistants 20s. *per diem*. A request of the deputies and assistants to be placed on half pay after the war was denied by the Treasury board on the ground that there was no precedent for it and that "most if not all of the Commissaries were positively told at the time of their appointment that half pay could not be granted to them." T. 64:118, Robinson to Chamier, 12 Apr. 1776; W.O. 1:824, Grey Cooper to Barrington, 25 Feb. 1777; T. 64:107, Sheridan to Clinton, 28 Aug. 1783.

[106] T. 64:102, Day to Robinson, 20 June, 1777.

in future.''[107] Veritably the way of the commissary was sometimes hard.

Turning to the articles of food obtained in America, we find that one of the most important was flour, or, in its original form, grain. In the latter part of 1774, just as the war clouds were gathering, Gage, commanding in Boston, received a considerable quantity from Maryland.[108] In November, 1776, Chamier was planning to bake bread at New York for next year's campaign from ''Flour purchased out of Prizes or Ground from a large Cargo of Wheat from a prize,'' although he was experiencing some trouble in finding bakers.[109] At the same time, Day in Canada was obtaining grain and flour from the inhabitants for Carleton's army but only with considerable difficulty.[110] He was much hampered by the scarcity of mills throughout the country, the people being accustomed to sell their grain to the merchants without grinding it into flour. Day proposed to meet the situation by constructing a mill on the rapids of Chambly, which would grind summer and winter, for the use of the commissariat. In the spring of 1777, when preparations were being made for Burgoyne's expedition up the lakes, there was an added difficulty. The preceding winter had been one of the mildest known in Canada, with very little snow. As a result the rivers were low, and for some months the mills were prevented from grinding even enough flour for the na-

---

[107] T. 64:105, Robinson to Haldimand, 30 July, 1779.

[108] C.O. 5:92, Gage to Dartmouth, 15 Nov. 1774.

[109] T. 64:118, Chamier to Robinson, 9 Nov. 1776.

[110] Between 25 May and 24 Dec. 1776, Day purchased from the inhabitants breadstuffs in the following amounts:

Baked Bread	522,482 lbs.
Flour	3,686,551 ''
Biscuit	119,952 ''

T. 64:102.

tives.[111] To take another example, Cornwallis in his invasion of North Carolina in 1781 halted for two days at "Ramsour's Mills" to collect flour from the countryside.[112]

Another important article of food obtained in America was rice. In 1776 Howe dispatched an expedition to Georgia under Major General Grant, which seized no less than 31,083 tierces.[113] From the same province Clinton in 1779 likewise received large quantities.[114]

The provisions obtained in the theatre of operations were sometimes curious. When General Augustine Prevost marched from St. Augustine upon Savannah in 1778-1779, his supplies were transported in boats along the shore and his troops were often separated from them. As a result the men were frequently hard pressed for food. At one time they lived on oysters found in inlets of the sea; at another, on alligator and some Madeira wine salvaged from a wreck.[115]

Outranking either rice or flour as a foodstuff obtained in America was fresh meat. At the outbreak of the war a small quantity of live stock was shipped from England; for in 1775-1776 the Treasury board contracted with Anthony Merry, merchant, to supply live stock to the troops in Boston and New York.[116] Such shipments, however, were exceptional; and the policy of the Board, in general, was to compel the army to find fresh meat in America. This was only natural. The freightage of live

[111] T. 64:102, Day to Robinson, 25 May, 1777.

[112] *London Gazette*, 2 June, 1781.

[113] T. 29:45, Minutes, 13 June, 18 July, 1776.

[114] T. 64:120, *passim*.

[115] Butler, *Annals of King's Royal Rifle Corps*, I, 210.

[116] T. 29:45, pp. 137, 151, 158, 198-199; *ibid.*, 1:519, Cooper to Merry, 26 Jan. 1776, Grey Cooper to Howe, 19 Apr. 1776; *ibid.*, 64-106, Robinson to Howe, 24 June, 1776. It appears that Merry intended to obtain sheep and oxen from Mogador (Morocco).

stock was expensive and in spite of great care many of the cattle were likely to perish in transit.[117] Thus we find the commissariat at all times zealously engaged in searching for live stock in the theatre of operations. During the siege of Boston, Gage sent out transports manned by soldiers to search the shores and bays of New England for live stock and succeeded in obtaining one hundred oxen and eighteen hundred sheep.[118] "In regard to live stock," wrote Chamier from New York in November, 1776, "we have been able to purchase, or receive from Long Island, or this neighborhood a number sufficient to give the Army meat for two days in Seven, and to supply the Hospital fully."[119] Later, he might have added that bullocks, cows, sheep, and hogs were being shipped to Howe's army from Halifax.[120] Expeditions similar to those dispatched by Gage from Boston were sent out by Clinton from New York to Martha's Vineyard and the eastern end of Long Island. One of these, under Major General Grey, secured from Martha's Vineyard, in September, 1778, no less than three hundred oxen and ten thousand sheep.[121] During Burgoyne's invasion, Tory "cowboys" robbed the people on either side of the Hudson of their cattle, sheep, hogs, and poultry; and sold them to the British.[122] Nor were the forces in the South less active in searching for live stock in the field of operations. Lieutenant Colonel Campbell, commanding the expedition dispatched to Savannah in December, 1778, reported: "All the Rebel Cattle within reach of our

[117] *Report on Army Extras*, 1778.

[118] C.O. 5:92, Gage to Dartmouth, 20 Aug. 1775; Kemble, *Journal*, I, 55-56.

[119] T. 64:118, Chamier to Robinson, 9 Nov. 1776.

[120] T. 64:118, "Return of Live Stock," 19 Nov. 1776.

[121] C.O. 5:98, Clinton to Germain, 15 Sept. 1778; *London Gazette*, 24 Oct. 1778.

[122] Stone, *Burgoyne's Campaign*, p. 238, from the "Personal Reminiscences of the late Charles Neilson."

Posts have been ordered for Slaughter, and to be salted up, for the use of the Navy and Army. We have also given encouragement to the Farmers, to bring in their Bullocks, Hogs, Sheep, Poultry, etc. as cannot fail of establishing good and reasonable Markets at each of our Posts.''[123] Subsequently Peter Paumier, the deputy commissary, collected numbers of cattle, branded them, and placed them in ranges for the use of the troops.[124]

Although occasional shipments of forage continued to be made to the army during the war, the Treasury board was averse to the practice, representing that the bulkiness of hay and oats made the freightage expensive and the difficulty of obtaining sufficient tonnage, great. The commanders and the commissaries were therefore repeatedly urged to obtain the necessary forage in America: ''Hay you must provide yourselves,'' wrote the Treasury to Wier, ''and the same is much wished in regard to Oats, for the Tonnage they require, and the Freight of them is a grievous burden.''[125] How these instructions were fulfilled will be illustrated.

During the occupation of Boston, the want of sufficient forage was keenly felt.[126] While the meadows about the town yielded a certain amount of hay,[127] they failed to

123 C.O. 5:97, Campbell to Clinton, 19 Jan. 1779.

124 T. 64:120, Paumier to Robinson, 20 June, 1779. See also T. 64:107, Robinson to Clinton, 13 Mar. 1781.

125 *Report on Army Extras*, 1778, Robinson to Wier, 26 Sept. 1777. See also T. 64:106, Robinson to Howe, 12 Apr., 26 Sept. 1776; *ibid.*, 64:201, Robinson to Navy Board, 27 Mar. 1781.

A ration of forage consisted of 18 lbs. of hay and 1 peck of oats (W.O. 1:823, J. Irwine to Barrington, 19 May, 1778). It is also stated that each horse should be allowed 10 lbs. of oats per day (T. 64:118, ''Return of Oats . . . N. Y. April 10, 1777.'' Signed by Chamier). Another statement is to the effect that horses should be allowed 12 lbs. of hay *per diem* (C.O. 5:254, Germain to Admiralty, 19 Apr. 1776).

126 C.O. 5:92, Howe to Dartmouth, 26 Nov. 1775.

127 Howe's *Orderly Book, passim.*

satisfy the needs of the garrison, and recourse was therefore had to distant quarters. Vessels were dispatched to the Bay of Fundy and other parts of Nova Scotia for hay and to the Province of Quebec for hay and oats.[128] In October, 1775, Gage reported that no less than thirty-eight transports had been sent out from Boston in search of fuel and forage.[129] When Howe's army landed at Staten Island in July, 1776, Chamier proceeded to secure all the hay, wheat, oats, rye, and straw on the island.[130] After the capture of New York, he evidently found the amount of forage in the vicinity inadequate to the needs of the troops. Accordingly, he directed one[131] of his subordinate officers to purchase forage in Quebec and another[132] the same article in Nova Scotia.[133] The latter succeeded in procuring 760 tons of hay and 3,400 bushels of oats. This record was broken by a third commissary,[134] who accompanied the expedition sent to Rhode Island under Clinton in December, where 1,500 tons of hay, 5,000 bushels of Indian corn, and 3,000 bushels of oats were purchased.[135] In the meantime, Howe had determined that it would be necessary to quarter a large body of troops in East Jersey during the winter in order to obtain a sufficient amount of covering, forage, and supplies of fresh provisions.[136] Accordingly, detachments were

[128] C.O. 5:92, Gage to Dartmouth, 12 June, 20 Sept. 1775; Kemble, *Journal*, I, 45.

[129] C.O. 5:92, Gage to Dartmouth, 7 Oct. 1775.

[130] T. 64:118, Chamier to Robinson, 11 Aug. 1776.

[131] James Porteous, assistant commissary.

[132] Isaac Deschamps, deputy commissary.

[133] T. 64:118, Chamier to Robinson, 24 Sept. 1776. See Howe's "Remarks on Horse Provisions Necessary for the Campaign of 1776" in the appendix to this chapter.

[134] Major John Morrison, deputy commissary.

[135] T. 64:118, Chamier to Robinson, 28 Dec. 1776.

[136] C.O. 5:93, Howe to Germain, 30 Nov. 1776.

posted at Newark, Brunswick, Trenton, Bordentown, Whitehorse, and Burlington; and instructions were issued that cattle, grain, and forage were to be secured from the farmers in the region and placed in magazines for the subsistence of the army.[137] These measures were not unlike those pursued by Clinton two years later while confined in New York by Washington. In October, 1778, with a view to procuring forage, he directed Cornwallis and Knyphausen to take advanced positions to the north of the town—the former between the Hackensack and the Hudson, the latter between the Hudson and the Bronx.[138] Similarly, in December, 1777, during the occupation of Philadelphia, Howe posted a considerable detachment on the heights of Derby, across the Schuylkill, to cover the collecting of forage. "About 1,000 Tons," he wrote, "were brought in, a Quantity judged to be nearly sufficient for the Winter Consumption."[139] This supply was supplemented by a considerable quantity brought from Rhode Island by the navy and without which Howe would have been much distressed.[140] In the following spring (1778), foraging parties ranged the country for many miles around the city and in New Jersey with unexpected success. One detachment in particular made a descent upon the shores of the Delaware near Salem and secured a very seasonable supply.[141] When Burgoyne set out on his ill-starred expedition from Canada, he brought a quantity of oats with him. The rest of his forage, he strove to collect along the line of march. Whenever he encamped, parties were sent out to scour the neighborhood for hay, grass, and Indian corn. In the closing stages of the cam-

137 Stryker, *Trenton and Princeton*, p. 317.
138 *London Gazette*, 28 Nov. 1778.
139 *London Gazette*, 14 Mar. 1778.
140 *Narrative of Sir William Howe*, pp. 48-49.
141 *London Gazette*, 9 June, 1778.

paign, he was much hampered by the difficulty of feeding his horses and cattle.[142]

Fuel was yet another article obtained in considerable quantities in America. Wood was procured by foraging parties in the vicinity of the troops. The garrison of Boston in 1775-1776 was hard pressed for it, and houses, fences, and wharves were confiscated to meet the need.[143] The troops in New York obtained supplies of fuel, not only from Manhattan Island but from Long Island, a number of vessels being dispatched in search of it as far as Lloyd's Neck, some fifty miles from New York. The regiments wintering in New Jersey, 1776-1777, and Pennsylvania, 1777-1778, were supplied with fuel by the inhabitants at slight expense.[144] Large quantities of coal appear to have been sent out from England, although the Treasury board made the usual complaints about expense of freightage and dearth of tonnage.[145] The chief source of coal in America was the Island of Cape Breton. The mines there were constantly drawn upon throughout the war.[146] The attention of the authorities was first brought to them by Governor Legge of Nova Scotia, who pro-

[142] Burgoyne, *State of the Expedition*, p. 92; *Orderly Book, passim;* Digby, *Journal*, pp. 266, 276, 284, 286.

For other examples of methods of obtaining forage, see C.O. 5:98, Prevost to Clinton, 11 June, 1779; *ibid.*, 5:101, Arnold to Clinton, 13 Feb. 1781.

[143] C.O. 5:93, Howe to Dartmouth, 14 Dec. 1775. According to Frothingham, the few houses in Charlestown that escaped the conflagration were divided into lots and a portion assigned to each regiment. *Siege of Boston*, p. 281.

[144] "Minute Book of a Board of General Officers" (N. Y. Hist. Soc. *Coll.* 1916), pp. 97-98.

[145] T. 64:106, Robinson to Howe, 14 Sept. 1775, 12 Apr. 1776, 26 Sept. 1777; *ibid.*, 64:107, Robinson to Clinton, 31 Oct. 1778.

[146] There is an excellent report on the coal mine at Cape Breton, dated 9 July, 1777, by Anthony Bacon in T. 1:528. Relative to this subject, see also T. 64:107, Robinson to Clinton, 15 July, 1779; W.O. 60:15, Watson to John Crawford, 19 July, 1783; T. 29:45, Minutes, 14 Aug. 1776.

posed to Dartmouth in December, 1775, that the garrison
of Boston should be supplied thence.[147] In September,
1775, Gage reported that the barrack master had sent
"people" to work the mines, and by December the latter
was able to state that "Six thousand Chaldrons of Coals
were then digging and would be ready in the Spring to be
Shipped at Spanish River."[148] The supply, however,
seems never to have been wholly adequate to the wants
of the army, and had constantly to be supplemented by
shipments from England, coals sometimes being utilized
as ballast aboard the victuallers.

One other matter relating to the subject of obtaining
provisions in America deserves note. One of the chief
difficulties in buying food supplies lay in the practice of
the inhabitants in some quarters of artificially raising
prices. People in Canada, for example, formed combinations for raising the price of flour so that in 1779 the
Treasury board resolved to rely no longer upon a supply
from that region.[149] The same thing occurred in the Southern colonies. The planters raised the price of Indian corn
and clean and rough rice to an exorbitant figure.[150] After
the siege of Savannah in October, 1779, Commissary
Paumier reported that four of the townsmen had en-
grossed all the rum and raised the price to 2s. per gallon,
which was nothing less than an imposition.[151] It was in
the face of such difficulties as these that the commissariat
strove to secure provisions in America.

[147] C.O. 5:92, Dartmouth to Gage, 28 Jan. 1775.

[148] T. 64:106, Robinson to Howe, 12 Apr. 1776.

[149] T. 64:105, Robinson to the commander-in-chief in Canada (un-
named), 30 July, 1779.

[150] T. 64:120, Paumier to Robinson, 7 Aug. 1779.

[151] T. 64:120, Paumier to Robinson, 4 Nov. 1779.

CHAPTER V

THE PROBLEM OF TRANSPORTATION

THE subject of army transport is conveniently divisible into two parts—first, transport between Great Britain and America, that is, *ocean transport;* second, transport between points in America, that is, *land transport.* Under the first topic, we should expect to find an answer to the question as to how men and *matériel* were brought over to America from the mother country; under the second, as to how they were conveyed from one place to another in the theatre of operations.

1. *Ocean Transport*

At the outbreak of the war (1775), the direct responsibility for ocean transport was divided among three boards—the Ordnance, Navy, and Treasury boards. Roughly speaking, the first was responsible for the transport of artillery, engineers, guns, and ordnance stores;[1] the second (subject to the orders of the Admiralty board) for that of infantry, cavalry, clothing, hospital stores, tents, and camp equipage; the third for that of provisions. In 1779 the system was slightly altered. Until that year the Treasury employed, as agents for hiring provision transports, the firm of Mure, Son, & Atkinson. That is, for a certain commission these contractors agreed to provide such tonnage as the board should require.[2] The arrangement, however, was found to be ex-

[1] For statistics relative to tonnage employed by the ordnance department, see appendix to this chapter.

[2] It would seem that the commission received by Mure, Son, & Atkinson up to August, 1777, was 2½% on the sums expended in purchasing or hiring

pensive, and in November, 1777, the Treasury proposed that the Navy board should undertake the work. It declined. In January or February, 1779, the offer was renewed. This time the Navy board, with the approbation of the Admiralty board, consented. The Navy commissioners were to be subject to the directions of the Treasury board in matters relating to provision transport; and, as a compensation for the additional labor involved, the Treasury board agreed to an increase in their salaries.[3] Thus, from 1779 onwards, they were responsible for the transportation not only of cavalry, infantry, clothing, etc., but also of provisions. This change was strongly opposed by Germain, and was the cause of much friction between him on the one hand and the Treasury and Navy boards on the other.[4]

The division of labor among the three boards was not rigidly maintained. Thus, an Ordnance transport might bear clothing, a Navy transport artillery, and a Treasury transport troops. In fact, it was usual to convey troops to America on provision and clothing ships, both as a matter of economy and convenience and to increase the fight-

craft. In June, 1777, the Treasury took the fairness of this allowance into consideration. Mr. Atkinson attended the board by order on the 24th. He represented that 2½% was the common commission and constant allowance between merchant and merchant, but that being ''sensible of their Ldps. favor to his house in employing it to transact the business of the Treasury,'' he was ready in the future to ''submit to and accept such allowance and Commission as their Ldps. shall think fit.'' The board then proposed a commission of 1½%; T. 29:46, Minutes, 24 June, 16 Aug. 1777; ibid., 64:105, Robinson to Haldimand, 30 July, 1779.

[3] For an account of this, see T. 29:46-48, passim; ibid., 64:200, passim.

[4] The cause of the trouble seems to have been in the fact that the Navy board sent the victuallers to America unarmed and under convoy, whereas the Treasury board had sent them armed and without convoy. Germain considered that by the former method the army was not supplied with provisions as regularly and promptly as by the latter. A warm controversy arose relative to this question. See T. 64:200, Germain to Treasury Board, 4 Aug. 1780; ibid., 64:201, Robinson to Stephens, 27 Mar. 1779; ibid., 29:49, p. 316.

ing strength in case of attack. On her trip back to England, a ship would often bring wounded men and recruiting parties. Officers of high rank and specie for the army paymasters were usually transported by men-of-war.[5] It should be added that the business of stocking the transports with food for crew and passengers fell to the victualling commissioners.

As subordinates to the foregoing boards there were a number of minor officials concerning whom we unfortunately have scant knowledge yet who nevertheless deserve mention. Thus, the Ordnance board had in its employ a Captain John Dickinson as superintendent of the Ordnance transports. He was a capable and zealous officer. His duty consisted in procuring adequate ships and crews for the conveyance of ordnance stores.[6] Major George Carleton is mentioned as agent for embarkations (of troops) at Cork in 1776.[7] His functions are not entirely clear. In 1777-1778 Colonel Maunsell seems to have acted in a similar (if not in the same) capacity. He was stationed at Charles Fort, about twelve miles from Cork, where recruits bound for America were brought. He saw that they were properly quartered until the time for embarkation, provided them with clothing, and assigned them to the respective transports. His letters testify to his zeal and ability.[8] We have seen that in February, 1776,

[5] For example, the Admiralty was requested to receive Commissary General Wier on the H. M. S. *Albion*, when he went out to America in the spring of 1777. C.O. 5:126, William Knox to Philip Stephens, 3 Mar. 1777.

[6] C.O. 5:163-4, *passim*.

[7] W.O. 1:824, certificate dated Cork, 24 Feb. 1776, and signed by Robert Cunningham; T. 29:45, Minutes, 27 June, 1776.

[8] W.O. 1:992, *passim;* T. 1:519, Robinson to Gordon, 20 Mar. 1777. "The Col. resides at Charles Fort, about 12 miles from Corke where he has excellent Quarters and a Hospital and a Surgeon. When Invalids arrive, they can in general be conveyed to Charles Fort at a trifling expense either by land or water, where every Case will be taken care of. No troops can go to Corke without being embarked by me or without my knowledge. Whenever

the Treasury board appointed Robert Gordon Commissary of Provisions at Cork. His chief duty was "to inspect and survey all Provisions that the Contractors for supplying his Majesty's Troops in America . . . shall from time to time put on board any Vessels appointed to carry the same to America; and . . . after having examined such Provisions . . . to sign Certificates of the Quantities thereof, and of the Provisions so shipped being good, wholesome, proper, and fitting for the Use of His Majesty's Troops agreeably to the Contracts . . .'"[9] In the following year Joseph Graham was made his subordinate as superintendent of shipping. He was instructed "to superintend, inspect, and examine the arming, fitting, and lading of Victuallers at Cork.'"[10] When the Navy board took charge of provision transport in 1779, it replaced Gordon by John Marsh with the title of agent victualler and Graham by Lieutenant Harris with the title of agent of transports.[11]

that has happened, I have always put the officer who had charge of ye Men, under ye Command of Col. Maunsell who has given them every assistance." W.O. 1:825, Samuel Townshend, inspector general of recruiting, to William Smith, 4 Nov. 1778.

[9] T. 29:45, Minutes, 9 Feb. 1776.

[10] T. 1:519, Robinson to Gordon, 7 Feb. 1777.

[11] T. 29:48, Minutes, 7, 22, 27 July, 4 Nov., 21 Dec. 1779. This displacement in the officials at Cork was due partly to dissensions which arose between Gordon and Harris. When Harris was appointed transport agent by the Navy board, it was apparently intended to retain Gordon as inspector or commissary of provisions. The two officials, however, seem to have had somewhat conflicting duties, and one of them (Harris) being under the orders of the Navy board and the other (Gordon) being under those of the Treasury board, they were soon at loggerheads. The specific form that the dispute took was as to whether the victuallers should be loaded at Cove or Passage, Harris advocating the latter and Gordon the former. Writing to the Navy commissioners, 16 July, 1779, Harris declared that without their interposition it would be absolutely impossible for him to carry on the service. He complained that he had not sufficient weight with Gordon to get any requisitions complied with two days in succession, and that much of his time was wasted in attending the commissary's office. "Nothing but positive Orders from the Treasury will have any effect, for those I receive from

While a few transports were owned or bought by the government, the majority were hired. Most of them were naturally English-built, though a few may have been of Dutch or German construction.[12] The offer of a vessel of French build was received with characteristic British scorn: "A French ship is not fit for His Majesty's service."[13] In size the transports ranged from one hundred to eight hundred tons, the tents and camp equipage of a single regiment requiring from twelve to eighteen tons.[14] Many of them were old and unseaworthy—the refuse of the trading fleet.[15] Manned by ordinary merchant crews, they made the voyage from England to America in six or eight weeks. With the exception of the victuallers, they generally went armed and under convoy, in fleets of from two to twelve sail or even more. Prior to 1779, the victuallers usually sailed armed and without convoy. After that date, however, when the Navy board took charge of them, the reverse was true: they proceeded unarmed but under convoy.[16] Although the transports were apparently ordered to carry six guns, some of them carried more, the pieces ranging from six- to twelve-pounders and many of

you have no weight with him." The Navy board repeated this complaint to the Treasury commissioners, and the upshot of the matter was that Gordon was removed and John Marsh substituted, with the title of agent victualler, subject to the orders of the Navy board. T. 64:200, *passim*.

[12] Adm. Vict. Out-Letters, 27, to Philip Stephens, 21 Feb. 1776; W.O. 1:992, Maunsell to Barrington, 26 Aug. 1776.

[13] W.O. 1:824, *passim; ibid.*, 55:371, "Account of Ordnance Transports 1775-1777"; *ibid.*, 55:374, "Account of Ordnance Transports 1779"; *ibid.*, 1:890, pp. 26, 32, 185, 191; *ibid.*, 1:825, Robinson to Barrington, 16 Oct. 1778.

[14] Adm. Navy Bd. In-Letters, 280, from Walter Cope, etc., received 11 Mar. 1779. See note on back.

[15] Trevelyan, II, 99. *Cf.* Belcher, I, 255; *Clinton-Cornwallis Controversy.* I, 490, Cornwallis to Clinton, 26 May, 1781.

[16] T. 29:49, Minutes, 26 July, 1780; *ibid.*, 64:200, Germain to Treasury, 4 Aug. 1780; T. 64:105, Robinson to Carleton, 8 Apr. 1779; *ibid.*, 64:200. Navy Board to Treasury, 11 Feb. 1779.

them being swivels.[17] Each fleet was under general charge of a lieutenant of the navy, known as the agent, or superintendent, of transports, and subject in American waters to the orders of the commander-in-chief.[18] One of these officers, Lieutenant Bourmaster, won high encomiums from Gage and Howe for his zeal at Boston in 1775.[19] Usually a petty naval officer (often a midshipman) was assigned to each troop ship to superintend the navigation, to explain to the captain the signals made by the convoy, to direct affairs in case of separation, and in event of attack to assist in conducting the defence.[20]

The picture suggested by the records of life aboard the transports is not a pretty one. Conditions were often fatal both to man and beast. The situation was truthfully, if rhetorically, summed up by an officer of the Guards, who was going with a detachment to join Howe at New York, when he wrote: ''There was continued destruction in the foretops, the pox above-board, the plague between decks, hell in the forecastle, the devil at the helm.''[21] Scores of soldiers, if they did not die of scurvy or other diseases, at least landed in a sickly and much weakened state. Captain Jacobs, in charge of some transports bringing German mercenaries to Quebec in September, 1776, reported that no less than twenty-eight had died,

[17] T. 64:106, Mure, Son, & Atkinson to Howe, 21 Oct. 1776; *ibid.*, 64:106, Robinson to Howe, 24 June, 1776. Germain instructed the Ordnance board, 29 Aug. 1776, that their ships were to be ''provided with at least 12 Carriage Guns, 9- and 6- pounders, and a Complement of Men equal in number to three to each Gun.'' C.O. 5:163, Germain to Townshend.

[18] C.O. 5:163, *passim;* C.O. 5:102, Mure, Son, & Atkinson to masters of oat ships, 11 July, 1781; Adm. Navy Bd. 3526, ''Allowance to Agent Victuallers to 31 Dec. 1779''; Adm. Navy Bd. In-Letters, 279-280, *passim;* Adm. 2:244-50, *passim.*

[19] C.O. 5:92, Gage to Dartmouth, 13 May, 1775; *ibid.*, Howe to Dartmouth, 27 Nov. 1775.

[20] Adm. 2:244, Admiralty to Navy Board, 22 Apr. 1776; T. 29:45, Minutes, 3, 30 Apr. 1776.

[21] Quoted in Belcher, I, 255. *Cf.* Trevelyan, II, 100.

mainly of scurvy.[22] Clinton, announcing the arrival of a
contingent of recruits at New York in September, 1779,
lamented that "many of the Troops are very Sickly, owing to the extreme Length of the Voyage."[23] Out of
twenty-four hundred Germans coming to that port in August, 1781, he recorded that four hundred and ten were
sick on landing, while sixty-six had perished from
scurvy.[24] On one occasion the transport *Lyon,* homeward
bound with British wounded, struck foul weather. An officer aboard wrote that "the Invalids growing very sickly,
Ten of them died on the passage, and I do imagine some
of them would have shared the same fate, had we not been
so lucky as to get in here [Scilly Islands]."[25]

The same unhappy fate that befell men aboard the
transports also befell horses: many of these poor beasts
perished. Quartermaster Kemble of Howe's army notes
in his *Journal* on one occasion that "Horses to compleat
the 17th Light Dragoons and a number for the General
Service were embarked [in England] . . . but the length
of their passage makes it very much to be apprehended
that most of them have Perished."[26] In transporting his
army from New York to Philadelphia in June-July, 1777,
Howe lost many of the mounts belonging to his dragoons.
For a voyage that lasted forty days, only three weeks'
forage had been shipped. Many of the unfortunate beasts
were thrown overboard as a humane alternative to allowing them to perish of hunger and thirst. This had a serious bearing upon subsequent operations. Had Howe
possessed a well-mounted corps of light cavalry at
Brandywine (11 September, 1777), Sullivan's division

22 C.O. 5:125, "Report of Capt. Jacobs," Quebec, 24 Sept. 1776.

23 C.O. 5:98, Clinton to Germain, 4 Sept. 1779.

24 C.O. 5:103, Clinton to Germain, 20 Aug. 1781. See also W. O. 1:12,
"Return of Recruits," New York, 27 June, 1781.

25 W.O. 1:991. Capt. Herbert to Barrington, 14 Jan. 1776.

26 *Kemble Papers,* I, 91 (3 Oct. 1776).

would doubtless have been cut to pieces and the battle converted from a defeat into a disaster for the Americans.[27] Clinton affirmed that in his expedition to South Carolina in 1779-1780, he lost every horse in the passage from New York to Charleston for want of proper transports.[28] Benedict Arnold (in the British service), referring to the voyage of his troops from New York to Virginia in January, 1781, stated that about one-half of the cavalry horses were lost.[29]

Numerous other difficulties attended the transport service. Ships containing much-needed food were often delayed for weeks by fogs, contrary winds, and foul weather.[30] Victuallers bound from Cork to New York were sometimes blown off their course as far south as the West Indies.[31] The failure of the Cape Fear expedition in the spring of 1776 must be ascribed largely to the fact that the armament intended for it was delayed at Cork by bad weather.[32] Many ships were lost through storms or capture.[33] The presence of the combined French and

[27] Trevelyan, IV, 214; Belcher, II, 240.

[28] C.O. 5:100, Clinton to Germain, 14 Sept. 1780.

[29] C.O. 5:101, Arnold to Clinton, 21 Jan. 1781. See also W.O. 1:10, Howe to Barrington, 1 June, 1777.

[30] T. 64:106, Robinson to Howe, 12 Apr. 1776; C.O. 5:101, Germain to Clinton, 7 Feb. 1781; *ibid.*, 5:97, Clinton to Germain, 15 Dec. 1778; *ibid.*, 5:93, Germain to Howe, 1 Feb. 1776.

[31] T. 64:106, Robinson to Howe, 2 May, 1776; C.O. 5:93, Captain Payne to Germain, 1 Mar. 1776.

[32] T. 64:201, Navy Board to Treasury, 12 Oct. 1780; C.O. 5:93, Germain to Clinton, 1 Feb., 3 Mar. 1776, Clinton to Germain, 3 May, 1776, Cornwallis to Germain, 16 May, 1776.

[33] T. 64:201, Robinson to Navy Board, 24 June, 1780; *ibid.*, 64:200, Robinson to Navy Board, 24, 28 Aug. 1780; W.O. 1:273, Barrington to Carleton, 24 Mar. 1777; Stedman, I, 166, note. In the West Indies hurricanes often played havoc with the transports. In September, 1780, General Vaughan wrote from Barbadoes that a most violent hurricane had swept over the island, driving away the victualling, store, and hospital ships, "which I wholly despair of seeing any more." W.O. 1:51, Vaughan to Jenkinson, 21 Sept. 1780.

Spanish fleets in the Channel in the summer of 1779 seriously threatened communications with America, and delayed the departure of the victuallers. For a time it was thought that, instead of sailing due west from Cork to New York, they would have to be sent up St. George's Channel and around the north coast of Ireland.[34] The replacing of provisions condemned by the inspectors at Cork was a fruitful source of delays, since it was sometimes necessary to send afar to make good the deficiency.[35] Labor troubles also played their part in retarding shipments. In October, 1776, the hands engaged to load and man the victuallers at Cork entered into combination and struck for higher wages. Disorder and rioting ensued with the result that the ships were detained long after the date originally fixed for their departure.[36] Even under normal conditions seamen were frequently scarce.[37] In March, 1778, John Dickinson, in charge of the Ordnance shipping, reported that he was having much trouble in manning the store-ship *Brilliant* at London.[38] Navy press gangs had frightened all the seamen into the country, and he had been compelled to send as far away as Scarborough, Ipswich, and Yarmouth for men. In Janu-

34 T. 64:200, Navy Board to Treasury, 24 Aug. 1780; *ibid.*, 64:201, Robinson to Navy Board, 20 Aug. 1779, Navy Board to Treasury Board, 9 Nov. 1780, Anthony Bacon to Treasury Board, 16 Nov. 1780.

35 T. 64:200, Marsh to Navy Board, 12 Feb. 1780, Cherry to Navy Board, 27 Mar. 1780.

36 T. 64:106, Mure, Son, & Atkinson to Howe, 21 Oct. 1776; *ibid.*, Robinson to Howe, 22 Oct. 1776, 14 Jan. 1777; *ibid.*, 1:519, Robinson to Gordon, 23 Oct., 2 Dec. 1776, 7 Feb. 1777. It is a curious and interesting coincidence that, contemporaneously with these disturbances, firms engaged in making clothing for the army in America were also being troubled by combinations among the employees. See W.O. 1:681, George Nixon to William Montgomery, 11 June, 1776; T. 64:102, Mure, Son, & Atkinson to Howe, 21 Oct. 1776.

37 T. 64:201, Gordon to Robinson, 23 Aug. 1779.

38 C.O. 5:164, Dickinson to Townshend, 22 Mar. 1778.

ary, 1779, Clinton was informed that a fleet of transports had been tied up at Cork for a month "from the unfortunate Circumstances of the Want of Seamen." In order to attract sailors to the victuallers, it was necessary to hold out the lure of prize money and masters of these craft were granted letters of marque. This proved to be an expedient of doubtful value, however, since the ships sometimes departed from their courses in search of prizes and thus delayed the arrival in America of provisions much needed by the army.[39]

Throughout the war, moreover, there was an unfortunate scarcity of available tonnage.[40] Merchants were reluctant to lease ships to the government. The reasons were explained at length in a letter addressed to Howe by Mure, Son, & Atkinson during the siege of Boston.[41] It will be recalled that the firm was employed by the Treasury board from 1775-1779 as agents for the hiring of transports. The writers declared that merchants engaged in an established course of European trade found an insurmountable objection to leasing vessels to the government in the fact that their ships after delivering an outward bound cargo to the army could find no further employment. Loyal American merchants did not dare to enter the service for fear that the rebels in revenge would commit depredations upon their property at home. There remained no other class of shipping except that employed in the West Indies trade. Here, too, the merchants were

[39] T. 64:107, Robinson to Clinton, 19 Jan. 1779; *Wier-Robinson Correspondence*, Wier to Robinson, 25 Oct. 1777, Robinson to Wier, 6 Dec. 1777.
[40] T. 64:106, 25 Sept. 1775.
[41] T. 64:106, Mure, Son, & Atkinson to Howe, 21 Oct. 1776, Robinson to Howe, 12 Apr., 24 June, 1776; *ibid.*, 64:200, Navy Board to Treasury Board, 18 Sept. 1780; *ibid.*, 64:107, Treasury Board to Navy Board, 30 Mar. 1781; C.O. 5:93, Germain to Howe, 28 Mar. 1776; *ibid.*, 5:98, Clinton to Prevost, 2 May, 1779.

averse "because of the great Expense their ships sail at and the too frequent instances of detention [by the army], whereby the main object of their Voyage, the loading home in due time from the West Indies, has been frustrated, a disappointment for which the payment of demurrage is no Compensation." However, by setting a good example in the transfer of four of its own West India vessels to the government service, the firm had finally induced others to engage at very reasonable rates. This was effected, however, only when the most positive assurances had been given that the cargoes would be promptly taken over by the army and that the vessels would not be detained an hour afterwards.

The words cited above were written in 1775. In 1776 every harbor in England was searched for available ships and recourse was had even to the ports of Holland and later to those of Germany. "The Extensions of the different Transport Services," wrote the Treasury to Howe, "and the immense Quantity of Tonnage employed and wanted, have drained this Country of Ships so that without raising the price much higher or distressing the Commerce of the Kingdoms, Transports are not to be had . . . The Distress for Want of Transports is so great that it would be of the utmost Benefit . . . if it should be possible for you . . . to spare some of your largest Ships and return them home to be employed as Victuallers."[42] Nothing proves the scarcity of tonnage so eloquently as the rise in freight rates. In 1775 the government had paid 10s. per ton on the tonnage of the vessel. In June, 1776, the Treasury informed Howe: "This Country is so exhausted of Ships which can be spared from the Commerce and Trade otherways essential to be carried on, that it is with the utmost difficulty a sufficiency of Tonnage can be

42 T. 64:106, Robinson to Howe, 12 April, 1776.

got, and we have been obliged to raise the price to 12:6 per Ton."[43] By 1779 the rate had jumped to 14s.[44]

Undoubtedly the pressing demand for shipping might have been relieved to a considerable extent had the commanders in America seen fit to unload promptly and send back the transports. This they failed to do despite repeated remonstrances on the part of the home authorities.[45] "I must remark," Germain writes to Clinton on one occasion, "the very great difficulty we labor under for want of Transports, occasioned, in great measure, by so many of them being detained in North America . . . I must entreat you to encourage the returning as many Transports as possible to this Country, that we may be enabled with greater facility to reinforce you with Troops, and supply you more regularly with Provisions."[46] Hasten the return of the transports came to be the burden of the letters directed by the departments to the commanders in America.[47]

[43] T. 64:106, Robinson to Howe, 24 June, 1776. "All expedition," writes Adjutant General Harvey to Lieutenant General Irwine, "is using to Transport. You know full well that Spurring will not always do with Shipping." W.O. 3:5, 12 Aug. 1775.

[44] W.O. 55:371, Account of Ordnance Transports 1775-1777; *ibid.,* 55:374, Account of Ordnance Transports 1779. For statistics relative to the expense of ocean transport, see appendix to this chapter.

[45] C.O. 5:96, Germain to Clinton, 15 Sept. 1778; *ibid.,* 5:101, Clinton to Germain, 27 Feb. 1781; T. 64:107, Robinson to Clinton, 31 Oct. 1778, 19 Jan. 1779, 23 May, 1781; *ibid.,* 64:107, Rose to Clinton, 26 Sept., 31 Dec. 1782; *ibid.,* 64:200, Navy Board to Treasury, 27 June, Sept. (date of month omitted) 1780.

[46] C.O. 5:100, Germain to Clinton, 13 Oct. 1780.

[47] The home authorities urgently desired to have the transports sent back as quickly as possible not merely because of the scarcity of shipping but as a measure of economy. As far as possible they wished to circumscribe the number of transports in government pay. The enormous expense of ocean transport service was constantly emphasized in the letters from the home departments to the generals. See, for example, C.O. 5:97, Germain to Clinton, 3 Mar. 1779; *ibid.,* 5:93, Germain to Howe, 21 June, 1776; T. 64:107, Robinson to Clinton, 19 Jan. 1779.

The transport service was crippled by other forms of mismanagement. If contractors were tardy in filling orders,[48] masters of transports were guilty of stowing the cargoes carelessly and thereby using up a great deal more than the necessary tonnage.[49] That victuallers failed to bring a lading suitable to their tonnage thus became an oft-repeated complaint. At the risk of the army's success and contrary to regulations, the masters sometimes tried to carry goods for trading in America on their own account. Thus, it was reported that the ''Masters of the Transports, which carried the 17th Regiment of Light Dragoons to Boston last Year [1775], had filled part of the lower Tier of their Casks with Porter, on their own private Account, which might have been the Cause of the Loss of the Horses had they been longer at Sea.''[50] Small wonder that army officers were accustomed to refer to transport masters as ''doubtful characters.''[51]

Added to such practices were an inertia and want of comity and coöperation among the several departments concerned with the transport service, which were fatal to efficiency. Many pages of records are filled with the mutual recrimination of departmental officers. In particular there was constant bickering between the Admiralty and

[48] T. 64:201, Anthony Bacon to Treasury, 16 Nov. 1780, Robinson to Navy Board, 11 Nov. 1779; *ibid.*, 64:200, Navy Board to Treasury, 14 Feb. 1780, Cherry to Navy Board, 14 Feb. 1780; *ibid.*, 29:48, Minutes, 7 July, 1779; Adm. 3:81, Minutes, 1 Dec. 1775; Adm. Navy Bd. In-Letters, 280, from Anthony Richardson, 23 Dec. 1779.

[49] T. 1:519, Robinson to Gordon, 26 June, 1776; *ibid.*, 64:118, Chamier to Robinson, 9 Nov. 1776; *ibid.*, 64:106, Gordon to Robinson, 21 Jan. 1777.

[50] C.O. 5:254, John Pownall to George Jackson, 27 Jan. 1776.

[51] W.O. 60:16, *passim.* If the transport masters were sometimes wanting in honesty, the crews were sometimes wanting in courage. In 1776, 3,000 Highlanders were sent to reinforce General Howe. The transports bearing them were attacked by American privateers, and one-quarter of the force was captured. This was due to the fact that the crews refused to defend the ships, and went below. The clansmen made a gallant, but hopeless, fight. Trevelyan, II, 92, footnote.

the Treasury and between the Treasury and the secretary
of state for the colonies—the latter trouble originating
perhaps in the ill-feeling that existed between North and
Germain. The Admiralty showed itself far from zealous
in providing convoys promptly,[52] and repeatedly allowed
its press gangs to rob army transports of their crews.[53]
This resulted in numerous delays and became the subject
of much warm correspondence between the Treasury and
Admiralty boards. On one occasion the former protested
that unless the practice were stopped, it would be utterly
impossible to victual the army.[54] Despite such remonstrances, however, navy press gangs continued to retard
the service in this manner. Nor were such disputes and
differences confined solely to the upper strata of officialdom. In the lower as well they were unfortunately evident.

Such being the circumstances under which the ocean
transport service was conducted, is it any wonder that
the army was often lamentably wanting in men, food, and
equipment? That some of the obstacles were beyond the
power of man to prevent must be admitted; but that
others might have been obviated must also be admitted.
Whether the British army would have triumphed even
with an efficient transport service is debatable; but certainly some of the disasters that it encountered would
have been lessened or avoided, had there been good man-

[52] Adm. 3:82, Minutes, 3 May, 1777, and *passim;* T. 64:201, *passim;*
ibid., 64:200, Navy Board to Treasury, 4 Aug. 1780; *ibid.*, 29:48, Minutes,
27 July, 1779; *ibid.*, 29:46, Minutes, 24 Jan. 1778; C.O. 5:100, Clinton to
Germain, 31 Oct. 1780.

[53] T. 29:45-50, *passim;* C.O. 5:258, Robinson to [D'Oyley?]; W.O.
47:90, Minutes, 3 Sept., 9 Oct. 1777; *ibid.*, 47:89, Minutes, 18 Apr. 1777.
In March, 1778, Major Skene, who was busily engaged in embarking troops
for America, reported to Barrington that everything was at a standstill,
owing to the navy's "pressing the Sailors of transports." W.O. 1:999, 24
Mar. 1778.

[54] Adm. 1:4288, Robinson to Admiralty, 6 Feb. 1779.

agement and hearty coöperation among the departments at home.

2.   *Land Transport*[55]

The responsibility for land transport in America rested ultimately with the commander-in-chief. Howe testified that he "settled what number of Waggons, Horses, and Drivers should be employed for a Campaign, and the Distribution of them among the several Regiments, Corps, and Departments. He settled the Price of the Hire of the Waggons, Horses, and Drivers, and the Tonnage of the small Craft employed."[56] The actual procuring of the horses, drivers, and wagons, however, fell mainly to the quartermaster general, although the commissary general, the barrack master general, and the chief engineer sometimes hired means of transportation on their own account.[57]

During the course of the war a number of transport officers were appointed. In June, 1776, Francis Rush Clarke, Gent., was appointed inspector and superintendent of the provisions train of horses and wagons attending Howe's army. He was subject not only to the orders of the commander-in-chief in America but to those of the Treasury as well.[58] The train under his charge consisted

[55] For a very complete and informing analysis of the land transport service, see the "Seventh Report of Commissioners of Public Accounts" in 38 *Commons Journal*, pp. 1066-1111. Many interesting data are also to be found in "Minute Book of a Board of General Officers" (N. Y. Hist. Soc. *Coll.* 1916).

[56] *Report on Army Extras*, 1778.

[57] "Minute Book of a Board of General Officers" (N. Y. Hist. Soc. *Coll.* 1916), pp. 74-75, 227-229. The train used by Howe in the campaigns of 1777 was organized on his orders by Sir William Erskine, the quartermaster general. *Ibid.*, 75. See appendix to this chapter for the number of vessels and wagons employed by the quartermaster general in North America, 1776-1780.

[58] T. 64:106, Robinson to Howe, 20 June, 1776; "Minute Book of a Board of General Officers" (N. Y. Hist. Soc. *Coll.* 1916), p. 75.

of a few horses and wagons sent from England. During Howe's operations in the Middle Colonies (1777-1778), the quartermaster general became so overburdened with the business of providing wheeled transport that it was found necessary to detail someone to take charge of the river craft. Accordingly, a naval officer, Captain David Laird, was appointed (1 January, 1777) superintendent of vessels. He was authorized "to charter or hire vessels for inland Navigation, to see that they were properly manned and equipped, and justly rated as to their Tonnage."[59] Three similar officials existed in Clinton's army at New York towards the close of the war—an agent to the army small craft, an inspector of small craft, and a comptroller of transports.[60] In July, 1782, Major Robert Molleson received an appointment under the sign manual as waggon master general to the army in America. He was the first officer of the kind to be appointed. He assisted the commissary general of Clinton's army in the transport service, and had charge of the military wagon yard at New York.[61] Attached to Burgoyne's forces in 1777, were a commissary of the waggons or waggon master general and a commissary of horse. The duty of the former was to buy or hire ox-teams wherever they could be found; of the latter, to take charge of the horses and drivers furnished by contract for the purpose of "transporting provisions and stores brought to Fort George for the use of the army."[62]

[59] *Report on Army Extras*, 1778; 38 *Commons Journal*, pp. 1068, 1095-1096. Laird served as superintendent until Dec. 1780. *Ibid.*, 1070.

[60] W.O. 60:12, 21, *passim*. In 1781 there were an agent for transports and agent for armed vessels on the pay roll at New York. "Minute Book of a Board of General Officers" (N. Y. Hist. Soc. *Coll.* 1916), pp. 60, 62.

[61] W.O. 25:37, p. 94; *ibid.*, 60:12, *passim*. A waggon master general existed in England, but he seems to have had little to do directly with the forces in America. For complete text of Molleson's commission, see the appendix to this chapter.

[62] Burgoyne, *State of the Expedition*, p. 56.

For land transport the ordinary conveyances were carts, wagons, and trucks, of various sizes and kinds. In Canada and New York sleighs and sledges were extensively used during the winter.[63] Of the wheeled vehicles, some were brought over from England. In the spring of 1776, three hundred four-horse wagons were sent to the forces under Howe and Carleton. These were built under the directions of the Ordnance board by a Mr. Fitzherbert at a contract price of £31: 11: 6 apiece.[64] The majority of the wagons, however, were procured in America through capture, purchase, or hire.[65] A few were built at the army wagon yard in New York.[66] Of the total number of vehicles employed by the army, it is safe to state that about two-thirds were hired in America by the month or day.[67] Hiring was judged by Howe and other commanders to be a more efficient and economical method of obtaining carriages than purchasing. In the first place, the vehicles could be discharged when no longer needed. In the second place, the owners were concerned to keep them in good condition whereas the loss of a vehicle owned by the government concerned nobody in particular. Lastly, there was less opportunity for fraud and imposition.[68]

The hire by the day of a small wagon with one driver and two horses varied from 6s. 9d. to 7s. 6d.; of a large

63 T. 1:528, Day to Robinson, 12 June, 1777; *ibid.*, 64:102, Day to Robinson, 15 May, 1777; *London Gazette*, 25 Apr. 1780; C.O. 5:100, Norton to Matthew, 6 Feb. 1780.

64 T. 29:45, Minutes, 19 Jan., 27 Jan., 3 Apr. 1776; C.O. 5:250, Knox to Robinson, 14 Feb. 1776; W.O. 47:87, Minutes, 16 Feb. 1776.

65 W.O. 47:89, Minutes, 28 Feb. 1777; W.O. 60:12, 21, *passim;* C.O. 5:98, Prevost to Clinton, 15 Mar. 1779; ''Minute Book of a Board of General Officers'' (N. Y. Hist. Soc. *Coll.* 1916), pp. 75-76.

66 W.O. 60:12, 21, *passim.*

67 38 *Commons Journal*, p. 1068.

68 38 *Commons Journal*, pp. 1074-1075; ''Minute Book of a Board of General Officers'' (N. Y. Hist. Soc. *Coll.* 1916), p. 197; Burgoyne, *State of the Expedition*, App., p. liii.

wagon with one driver and four horses, from 11s. 9d. to 12s.; of a single horse, from 1s. 6d. to 1s. 9d.[69]

There were vehicles for every purpose. A number of ammunition carts or caissons—sometimes small enough to be drawn by men—usually accompanied the artillery; forge carts "compleat with anvils and bellows" for horse-shoeing attended the cavalry; and wagons for carrying bread and baggage were attached to each regiment of horse and foot.[70] Mention is also made in the records of pontoon and hospital wagons and bat-horses for carrying medicine chests.[71] Officers were usually allowed a certain number of bat-horses varying with their rank.[72] Clinton stated that in his march across New Jersey in 1777, the bat-horses and train of provision and baggage carriages following the army extended for about twelve miles.[73]

Of the horses used by the army some were brought over from England; while others were obtained through hire, purchase, or capture in the colonies.[74] In January, 1776,

[69] 38 *Commons Journal*, p. 1068; "Minute Book of a Board of General Officers" (N. Y. Hist. Soc. *Coll.* 1916), pp. 229, 253.

[70] C.O. 5:165, p. 183; *ibid.*, 5:161, Germain to Townshend, 4 Dec. 1775; *ibid.*, 5:93, Howe to Dartmouth, 2 Dec. 1775 (enclosure); 38 *Commons Journal*, pp. 1106-1107.

[71] W.O. 55:369, p. 250.

[72] W.O. 1:890, Account of 17th Light Dragoons, 16 July, 1775; C.O. 5:93, Howe to Dartmouth, 2 Dec. 1775 (enclosure). A common abuse was for officers to use horses and wagons of the provision train for their baggage. Burgoyne was obliged to issue an order forbidding this. *State of the Expedition*, p. 55; Burgoyne, *Orderly Book*, p. 85. See appendix to this chapter for proportion of bat-horses in Burgoyne's expedition.

[73] *London Gazette*, 24 Aug. 1778. As illustrating the amount of provisions carried in the army wagons, Howe's statement is interesting: "I think in Pennsylvania [in 1777] we carried about 22 days rum, about 6 days pork, and 12 or 14 days bread." *A View of the Evidence*, p. 16.

[74] W.O. 60:12, 21, *passim;* C.O. 5:98, Prevost to Clinton, 15 Mar. 1779; *ibid.*, 5:162, Amherst to Germain, 20 June, 1776; C.O. 5:163, Boddington to Knox, 21 June, 1777; T. 64:106, Robinson to Howe, 20, 24 June, 1776. Simcoe, *Journal*, pp. 46, 61. This statement applies also to cavalry and artillery horses.

no less than one thousand draught and bat-horses were sent over by the Treasury for the troops under Howe and Carleton.[75] On the other hand, in July, 1782, the commissary general of Clinton's forces purchased some nine hundred horses in America.[76] Viscount Townshend, the master general of the ordnance, at one time strongly advocated the use of mules, pointing out that they were "Cheaper, less liable to expence and Damage by Transport, more hardy and durable" than horses.[77] Nothing seems to have resulted from the suggestion.

Burgoyne in his invasion of New York collected fifty team of oxen from the countryside and used them in the transport service.[78]

The drivers employed in the transport service were hired civilians. While many, if not most, of them were engaged in America, some were hired in England. We have seen that in 1776 the Ordnance department contracted with a Mr. Fitzherbert for a number of wagons for the army in America. He also agreed to supply the drivers. They were to be paid at the rate of 1s. 6d. *per diem* with off-reckonings for clothing and were to enjoy the same

[75] C.O. 5:250, Pownall to Robinson, 7 Jan. 1776. One of the horse contractors was a Scotsman named Fordyce. A London newspaper of 11 Oct. 1776 contains the following notice. "A correspondent asks whether General Howe has any horses to draw his artillery and waggons, without which he will never get to Philadelphia. The horses sent by Mr. Fordyce are all dead. That is a pretty job; but Mr. Fordyce is a Scotchman, and intends to be member for Colchester. He has canvassed the *toone*, and prepared *aw* things in readiness. Contracts are fine things! How many millions of English money will the Scotch profit by in this war!" Quoted in Trevelyan, III, 186-187, note.

[76] W.O. 60:12. When the evacuation of Philadelphia was being contemplated in March, 1778, Amherst recommended that the two regiments of light dragoons (16th and 17th) be sent home unmounted. Their horses were to be kept for the service of the army as baggage horses or for drawing cannon. *Correspondence of Geo. III with Lord North*, II, 153.

[77] C.O. 5:162, Townshend to Germain, 27 Jan. 1776.

[78] *London Gazette*, 28 Oct. 1777.

provisions as the king's troops.[79] Drivers hired in
America were paid between 7d. and 1s. 9d. a day and a
ration of provisions; sleigh-men, 1s. 6d. a day and a ration.[80] In the West Indies, negro slaves were purchased
by the army to assist in transporting foodstuffs.[81]

Between December, 1776, and March, 1780, the average
number of wagons constantly employed by the forces under Howe and Clinton was seven hundred and thirty-
nine; the average number of horses, one thousand nine
hundred and fifty-eight; the average number of drivers,
seven hundred and sixty.[82]

In solving the problem of transport, the rivers, estua-
ries, and lakes of the Atlantic seaboard were a most important factor. In the absence of good roads, abundant
use was made of them for the transport of both men and
matériel. The generals were urged to make good the deficiency in horses and wagons by the use of water transport.[83] The waterways of which the British made most
use were Lakes George and Champlain, the Hudson, the
Delaware, the Richelieu or Sorel, and the St. Lawrence
rivers. While the Hudson and Lakes George and Champlain provided a route across the Northern colonies, the
St. Lawrence formed a vast highway through Canada and
with the Great Lakes made it possible to man and provision the posts in the back country with comparative
ease.[84] Nor were the coastal waters neglected. Men and

[79] W.O. 47:87, Minutes, 6, 20, 27 Feb., 29 June, 1776.

[80] T. 64:102, Day to Robinson, 15 May, 1777; 38 *Commons Journal*, p.
1068.

[81] W.O. 1:51, H. Calder to Jenkinson, 29 Oct. 1779; *ibid.*, General
Vaughan to Jenkinson, 21 Sept. 1780.

[82] 38 *Commons Journal*, p. 1071. See also ''A State of the Number of
Drivers, Horses, and Waggons employed in the Quarter Master Generals
Department'' between 1777 and 1781, in appendix to this chapter.

[83] C.O. 5:93, Germain to Howe, 5 Jan. 1776.

[84] T. 64:102, Day to Robinson, 15 May, 1777, Day to Carleton, 14 Jan.
1777; W.O. 28:7, *passim*.

supplies were constantly shipped up and down the coast in preference to overland transfer.[85] In the South alone complaint was made that the natural facilities for water transport were inadequate. Cornwallis, during his march across the Carolinas in 1781, lamented that while the rivers of Virginia made that province easy of invasion, the total want of interior navigation for more than very small craft rendered the Carolinas difficult to subdue. In invading North Carolina he had hoped to utilize Cape Fear River as a line of communication with the coast, but it was found to be impracticable, owing to the narrowness of the stream and the height of the banks. It was partly for this reason that he retired to Wilmington after the battle of Guilford Court House.[86] Cornwallis and his subordinates, however, seem to have made considerable use of the Santee and Pedee rivers in South Carolina as lines of transport, most of the provisions and stores for the important post at Camden being brought up the former.[87]

For water transport crafts of various kinds were employed—the flatboat, batteau, and sloop being mentioned most frequently.[88] As in the case of wheeled vehicles, some of these were brought over from England; others (doubtless the majority) were obtained in the colonies through purchase, hire, or capture. The garrison at New

[85] See, for example, Howe's operations near New York. ''Minute Book of a Board of General Officers'' (N. Y. Hist. Soc. *Coll.* 1916), p. 71.

[86] C.O. 5:100, Cornwallis to Clinton, 14 July, 1780; *ibid.*, 5:102, 10 Apr. 1781; *ibid.*, 5:101, Cornwallis to Leslie, 12 Nov. 1780; *ibid.*, 5:102, Cornwallis to Clinton, 30 June, 1781.

[87] C.O. 5:100, Cornwallis to Clinton, 6 Aug. 1780; *ibid.*, 5:101, Rawdon to Clinton, 29 Oct. 1780; *Clinton-Cornwallis Controversy*, I, 246.

[88] Mentioned as in use by the garrison at New York, we find the following: armed brig (140 tons, 40 guns); armed schooner (80 tons, 8 guns); 2 sloops (40 and 30 tons each); hulk (180 tons); gunboats (10 oars, one 9-pounder); gun-barges (30 oars, one brass 12-pounder); batteaux (16 oars, one 12-pounder); batteaux (8 oars and 6 oars, unarmed); gun-flats (16 oars, two 12-pounders); crabs; whale-boats (16 oars, one 3-pounder); whale-boats (8 oars, one 1-pounder); scows. W.O. 60:21, *passim.*

York possessed a boat yard where some seem to have been built;[89] and Arnold had a score or more built at Portsmouth during his operations in Virginia in 1781.[90] The hire of a vessel under thirty tons was 3½d. a day per ton; of a vessel of thirty tons and upwards 4d. a day per ton until May, 1777, when it was raised to 5⅓d. a day per ton. Between 1777-1780 the number of vessels employed at different times in the department of the quarter-master general was three hundred and seventeen, and the number of tons 19,558; in the department of the barrack master general, the number of vessels was eighty-five and the number of tons 7,836; in the department of the com-missary general, the number of vessels was two hundred and nine and the number of tons 16,622.[91]

During his campaign in New York in 1776, Howe made frequent use of flatboats, with which he had been supplied from England, in transporting troops on the North and East rivers.[92] Most elaborate preparations with regard to water transport were made for the operations along the Canadian frontier in the same year. The frames of six sloops and eight hundred batteaux were provided by the Admiralty and sent over to General Carleton. The sloops were of about ninety tons each and the batteaux measured from thirty-six to forty feet in length and six to seven feet in width.[93] On being put together many of these craft were dragged up the Richelieu with prodi-gious labor, and were used for conveying the expedition

[89] W.O. 60:12, 21, *passim; ibid.,* 60:20, *passim.*

[90] *Clinton-Cornwallis Controversy,* I, 323, 325; II, 28.

[91] 38 *Commons Journal,* pp. 1068, 1070. These figures do not include ves-sels imported from England but only those procured in America. They do not refer to the forces in Canada, but only to those south of the St. Law-rence.

[92] *London Gazette,* 21 Sept. 1776; C.O. 5:93, Howe to Germain, 30 Nov. 1776; *ibid.,* 5:93, Germain to Howe, 5 Jan. 1776.

[93] C.O. 5:254, Germain to Admiralty, 15 Jan., 13 Feb. 1776.

up Lake Champlain.[94] Similar preparations were made for Burgoyne's campaign in 1777. Like Carleton he relied upon boats for the transportation of his army up the lakes and down the Hudson. Some two hundred batteaux were actually dragged across from Lake George to the Hudson.[95] For moving them over the portage, a "large machine" of some sort (the records fail to describe it) had been especially constructed by the Ordnance department at the instance of Captain Blomefield of the Artillery, who was familiar with conditions in America,[96] but apparently it did not prove practical, for most, if not all, of the boats were conveyed across the watershed in wagons. In this process many of them were shaken and damaged and had to be recaulked, "a matter of no trivial concern or easy execution," which was confided to several "very expert naval officers" accompanying the troops.[97] St. Leger's expedition up the Oswego River and Lake Oneida and down the Mohawk Valley was also accompanied by boats probably carrying provisions and supplies;[98] and Clinton, in advancing northward from New York with a view to joining Burgoyne and St. Leger, transported his forces up the Hudson by boat.[99] Meantime, Howe was using flatboats and galleys for the transport of men and provisions on the Delaware in the neighborhood of Philadelphia.[100]

It must not be thought that the boatmen employed in the transport service were officially enrolled in the army. On a few occasions (as in the case of Carleton's opera-

94 C.O. 5:125, Douglas to Stephens, 21 Oct. 1776.

95 London Gazette, 25 Aug. 1777.

96 C.O. 5:163, Germain to Townshend, 30 Apr. 1777, Townshend to Germain, 3 May, 1777, Blomefield to Townshend, 4 May, 1777.

97 Burgoyne, State of the Expedition, pp. 21, 144.

98 Fortescue, III, 230.

99 London Gazette, 2 Dec. 1777.

100 London Gazette, 2 Dec. 1777, 9 Jan., 9 June, 1778.

tions on the lakes in 1776), the army boats were manned by seamen from the navy and the ocean transports.[101] As a rule, however, civilian inhabitants were hired for the work. Their wages were 2s. 4d. each a day with a soldier's ration and one-sixth of a quart of rum.[102] In Canada, where scores of batteau-men were hired, the following arrangement was made: Each batteau was worked by four men. They were allowed two pounds of bread, ten ounces of pork, and a certain quantity of peas, each, *per diem*. The "head and stem men" were paid at the rate of 2s. *per diem*, the "middlemen" at the rate of 1s. 6d., Halifax currency.[103] The reputation acquired by the Canadian batteau-men was not enviable. Their thieving propensities were a constant subject of complaint on the part of the commissariat department. Commissary General Day declared that they were "totally unacquainted with business except such part as appertains to fleecing the State, to which they have a great propensity."[104]

That both land and water transport services were often inadequate and the army consequently hampered in its movements, there is considerable evidence. The absence of sufficient means of transport prevented Howe from invading Massachusetts with Boston as a base in 1775-1776.[105] When he was finally obliged to evacuate the town, his departure was delayed in part by deficiency of ton-

---

101 C.O. 5:125, Captain Douglas to Philip Stephens, 21 Oct. 1776.

102 38 *Commons Journal*, p. 1068.

103 T. 64:102, Day to Robinson, 15 May, 1777.

104 T. 64:102, Day to Robinson, 12, 20 June, 1777. Many of the batteau-men were of course French Canadians who were not overenthusiastic about the cause of Great Britain: ''I am pretty certain the Canadians will take no part against us, until French Troops are among them; consequently I think I have little to fear this Year; in the mean time they are very useful in our Transport, and are tolerably obedient.'' C.O. 5:98, Haldimand to Clinton, 19 July, 1779.

105 Fortescue, III, 177.

nage.[106] Clinton gave as one of the reasons for abandon-
ing the Cape Fear expedition (May, 1776) the want of
horses and water carriage.[107] Prior to his New York campaign of 1776, Howe presented to Germain an estimate of
the horses and wagons required. His demands were refused, and he was bidden to rely as much as possible upon
water transport. Thus, according to his own calculations,
his army entered upon the campaign only partly
equipped.[108] A small provision train was sent out later
but the wagons proved "to be totally unfit for the Country, being too heavy and made of bad materials. . . ."[109]
In 1777 Howe again requisitioned the government—this
time for three hundred horses. The reply was that only
one hundred could be sent owing to the expense and
hazard of the transatlantic journey.[110] Not unlike this
were the troubles of Burgoyne. During the winter of
1776, no measures were taken in Canada to provide
horses, carts, or forage for the proposed invasion of New
York. Not until June, 1777, were contracts for these articles awarded. As a result the movement of the army was
delayed for three weeks and every subsequent operation
retarded; "for the carriages for the transport service being constructed in haste and of fresh unseasoned timber"
were ill-adapted to the exigencies of the time and place
and were almost all destroyed on the road to Fort
Edward.[111] "This circumstance detained the army so long
at Fort Edward that it ultimately occasioned the unfor-

106 *Narrative of Sir William Howe*, p. 3.

107 C.O. 5:93, Clinton to Germain, 3 May, 1776.

108 C.O. 5:92, Howe to Dartmouth, 2 Dec. 1775; *ibid.*, 5:93, Germain to
Howe, 5 Jan. 1776.

109 "Minute Book of a Board of General Officers" (N. Y. Hist. Soc.
Coll. 1916), p. 75.

110 C.O. 5:94, Germain to Howe, 14 Jan. 1777. Clinton was urged to reduce the number of horses. T. 64:107, Robinson to Clinton, 30 Mar. 1781,
26 Mar. 1782.

111 Stedman, *American War*, I, 353.

tunate, ill-conducted expedition to Bennington.'"[112] As late as 20 August, after he had reached Saratoga, Burgoyne reported that only one-third of his horses had arrived. Oxen were collected from the countryside, but they were found inadequate to the business of provisioning the army and forming the necessary magazines.[113] Burgoyne also experienced difficulty in obtaining a sufficient number of drivers; and of those finally engaged, many proved unreliable, deserting him towards the close of the campaign.[114] Similar difficulties beset Augustine Prevost during his operations in the Southern provinces in 1779. In his march from East Florida to Savannah in January of that year, owing to lack of horses, he was compelled to load his supplies on boats and send them along the creeks and waters of the province while leading his army overland. As a result his men were so hard pressed for food that they were driven to living almost wholly on oysters. Later, after his arrival at Savannah, he complained that he was hampered by lack of wagons.[115] And thus the list of examples might be extended.[116]

This state of affairs may be ascribed partly to the natural difficulty of conducting a war in America and partly to corruption and mismanagement.[117] It was rumored at the time that the officers connected with the transport services, commissary generals, barrack master generals, and quartermaster generals, came home with more gold in their pockets than they had when they went

---

[112] Stedman, *American War*, I, 353; Digby, *Journal*, p. 226.

[113] *London Gazette*, 28 Oct. 1777; Lamb, *Journal*, p. 151.

[114] *State of the Expedition*, p. 10; Digby, *Journal*, p. 304.

[115] C.O. 5:98, Prevost to Clinton, 15 Mar. 1779. *Cf.* Fortescue, III, 272-273.

[116] T. 64:106, Paumier to Robinson, 7 Aug. 1779; *London Gazette*, 20 Feb. 1779 (Lieut. Col. Campbell to Clinton, 16 Jan. 1779); C.O. 5:98, Prevost to Clinton, 30 July, 1779; *London Gazette*, 23 Feb. 1779.

[117] 38 *Commons Journal*, p. 1071.

out or than their slender salaries in America would warrant.[118] They found it to their interest to own a great number of the vessels employed by the army. In placing them at the disposal of the government, they were obliged to contract with themselves. In other words, the same person employed by and acting for the public contracted on the part of the public with himself for the hire of his own property, and paid himself with the public money entrusted to his charge. "His Trust and Interest draw opposite ways," declared a parliamentary commission appointed to investigate the matter. "His Trust obliges him to be frugal for the Public; to hire at the lowest Price; to take Care that what he hires is complete and fit for Service; to employ as few Vessels and Carriages and for as short a Time as possible: But his Interest leads him not to spare the Public Purse; to let to Government at the same fixed Price, all the Vessels, Carriages, and Horses, he can collect, by whatever means procured, or at however low a Price he may have purchased them; and whatever may be their Condition or Difference in Point of Goodness, to keep them continually in Pay, whether wanted, or employed, or not, and for as long a Time as he can contrive; and his last Advantage may be, the suffering them to be taken or destroyed by the Enemy, to entitle him to the Value from the Public. In such a Contest between Duty and Interest, it is not uncharitable to suppose the Public Interest will frequently be sacrificed to private Emolument.'"[119] It was computed that an officer who owned fifty large wagons and two hundred horses, as a few of them did, and who hired them to the government might net a yearly profit of over £9,000. Had the vehicles

---

[118] 38 *Commons Journal*, p. 1069. *Cf.* Jones, *History of New York*, I, ch. 16, ''Base Transactions of Commissaries, Quarter masters, and Barrackmasters, and Engineers, in America.''

[119] 38 *Commons Journal*, p. 1069.

supplied by the quartermasters and commissaries proved serviceable, less objection might have been found. Many of them, however, were hardly fit for use. Cornwallis was finally obliged to issue an order (23 December, 1780) forbidding the quartermaster general from having any property in the wagons employed by his army. By such a measure alone could abuses be prevented.[120] The conclusion seems to be that mismanagement and corruption were at work not only in the provisioning of the army but also in the transport service.

[120] 38 *Commons Journal,* p. 1071.

CONCLUSION

THE failure of British arms in the American Revolution cannot be ascribed to want of courage on the part of officers and men. No braver troops ever shed their blood for the flag of England than those who thrice charged up Bunker Hill or attacked the American lines at Saratoga. The failure was due partly to inept generalship, partly to natural difficulties, and partly to maladministration. In this study emphasis has been laid upon the last two factors. The blunders of British generals have frequently been stressed, but the negligence, corruption, and inefficiency which pervaded the administration of the army and the manifold natural obstacles that stood in the way of an attempt to suppress rebellion in America have rarely been accorded adequate recognition.

As regards the matter of natural difficulties, indeed, the king's troops had more to contend with than their opponents. As has been pointed out, they were separated from their ultimate base by the broad expanse of the Atlantic. Supplies had to be brought a distance of three thousand miles by water. In these days of steam-propelled ships, it is no small achievement, as the recent war demonstrated, to man and provision an army at such a distance. Infinitely more difficult was it in the era of laggard sailing vessels, which were at the mercy of every wind. Again, America was a vast country. To conquer it, as one British statesman declared, was like trying to conquer a map. The distances were great and the roads were poor. A thinly populated region, it could yield but scanty supplies of food to an invading army. There were no large fortified towns the possession of which would give control over a wide area. Colonial society was so loosely organized that the capture of New York or Philadelphia brought no such results as the capture of Berlin or Paris would bring in a European war.

Such natural obstacles might indeed have been triumphantly surmounted by an efficient system of military administration. But efficiency, in the sense of the word to-day, was practically unknown throughout British officialdom at the time of Germain and North. With the business of military administration distributed among a half-dozen jealous departments, it is sometimes remarkable that the troops received any food and clothing at all. The absence of centralized authority, the want of departmental harmony, the clashing of various boards, the jealousies of high officials, all combined to reduce the chances of military success to the lowest terms. Considering England's administration of colonial affairs in the past, however, there was after all nothing very surprising in this mismanagement. Colonial affairs had rarely been subject to a really efficient system of control. Divided authority, interdepartmental friction, clumsy methods of business, ignorance and incompetence had characterized the rule of the mother country from the foundation of the colonies. The ineptitude displayed by the home government in military affairs during the American Revolution may thus be viewed merely as another manifestation of a long-standing evil.

ILLUSTRATIVE APPENDICES

CHAPTER I

A GENERAL SURVEY OF THE BRITISH ARMY AT THE OUTBREAK OF THE REVOLUTION

HOUSEHOLD INFANTRY, 1775[1]

1st Foot Guards	1,649
2d Foot Guards (Coldstream)	1,058
3d Foot Guards	1,058

INFANTRY REGIMENTS OF THE LINE ON THE ENGLISH ESTABLISHMENT, 1775[2]

No. Foot		*No. Foot*	
1st (2d Batt.) (Royal)	477	*19th*	477
3d (Buffs)	477	*21st* (Royal North Brit-	
4th (King's Own) .	477	ish Fusileers) . .	477
5th	477	*23d* (Royal Welsh Fu-	
7th (Royal Fusileers)	477	sileers)	477
8th	477	25th	477
10th	477	*26th*	477
11th	477	*27th* (Inniskilling) .	335[3]
12th	477	*29th*	477
13th	477	*30th*	477
14th	477	*31st*	477
16th	477	32d	477
18th (Royal Irish) .	477	36th	477

[1] For lists of regiments and their numbers, see *Court and City Register,* 1775, and *Army List,* 1775.

[2] Regiments italicized saw service in America during the Revolution. For data, see Chichester, *passim;* W.O. 1:890, Estimate of Clothing Tonnage, 25 June, 1776; *ibid.,* 4:273, Barrington to Gage, 31 Aug. 1775; *London Gazette,* 10 Oct. 1776, and *passim;* Lamb, *Memoir,* 110-111; Belcher, I, 339.

[3] Three companies of the 27th were on the Irish Establishment.

INFANTRY REGIMENTS OF THE LINE ON THE ENGLISH
ESTABLISHMENT, 1775 (Continued)

No. Foot		No. Foot	
38th	477	59th	477
41st	482[4]	60th (2 batt's) (Royal	
43d	477	American) . . .	955
47th	477	64th	477
48th	477	65th	477
50th	477	66th	477
51st	477	67th	477
52d	477	69th	477
56th	477	70th	477
58th	477	O'Hara's Corps . .	214[5]

INFANTRY REGIMENTS OF THE LINE ON THE IRISH
ESTABLISHMENT, 1775

No. Foot		No. Foot	
1st (1st Batt.) (Royal)	477[6]	37th	474
2d (Queen's Royal) .	477	40th	474
6th	474	42d (Royal Highland)	474
9th	474	44th	474
15th	474	45th	474
17th	474	46th	474
20th	474	49th	474
22d	474	53d	474
24th	474	54th	474
27th (3 cos.) (Innis-		55th	474
killing)	142[7]	57th	474
28th	474	61st	477
33d	474	62d	474
34th	474	63d	474
35th	474	68th	474

[4] Col. Wren's regiment of invalids for garrison duty.

[5] In computing the number of regiments on the Establishment, I have for convenience regarded O'Hara's corps as one regiment.

[6] The 2d battalion was on the English Establishment.

[7] The other companies were on the English Establishment.

CAVALRY REGIMENTS ON THE ENGLISH ESTABLISHMENT, 1775

Household

1 Regt. Horse Guards	362
1 Regt. Horse Grenadier Guards	353
1 Royal Regt. Horse Guards	319

Regiments of the Line

1st Dragoon Guards (The King's)	345
2d Dragoon Guards (The Queen's)	231
3d Dragoon Guards (The Prince of Wales's)	231
1st Dragoons (Royal)	231
2d Dragoons (Royal North British)	231
3d Dragoons (King's Own)	231
4th Dragoons	231
6th Dragoons (Inniskilling)	231
7th Dragoons (The Queen's)	231
10th Dragoons	231
11th Dragoons	231
15th Dragoons (The King's)	231
16th Dragoons (The Queen's)	231

CAVALRY REGIMENTS ON THE IRISH ESTABLISHMENT, 1775

1st Horse	214
2d Horse	214
3d Horse (Carabineers)	214
4th Horse	214
5th Dragoons (Royal Irish)	245
8th Dragoons	231
9th Dragoons	231
12th Dragoons	231
13th Dragoons	231
14th Dragoons	231
17th Dragoons	231
18th Dragoons	231

STAFF OF ENGINEERS IN CANADA, 1776-1778[8]

Major General and Commanding Offi-
cer . . . . William Phillips
Lieutenant Col. . . . . . . Forbes Macbean
Chief Engineer . . . . . . Harry Gordon
Lieutenant of Engineers . . . 7
Adj. . . . . Molesworth Cleiland
Q.M. . . . . Sam'l Rimington
Fire Master . . . . Wm. Houghton
Draughtsman . . . . Lieut. Chas. Wintersmith
Comm'y and Paymaster . . . . Alex'r Shaw
Ass't Comm'y . . . . Kenman Chandler
Surgeon . . . . Gervas Wylde
Surgeon's Mates 3
Clerks of Stores . . . . . . 4 (number variable)
Carpenters 5
Conductors 12
Comm'y of Horse 1
Ass't to Comm'y of Horse . . . 1
Nurse to Hospital 2
Smiths, Wheelers, Masons, Collar
   Makers, Miners

STAFF OF ENGINEERS AT NEW YORK, 1774[9]

Commanding Officer of Artillery . . . Samuel Cleaveland
Engineer Extra. and Capt. . . . . . John Montrésor
Engineer in Ord'y 1
Draughtsman 1
Ass't Chaplain 1
Surgeon 1
Barrack Master of Albany 1
Commissary and Paymaster 1
Clerks of Stores 2
Conductors 8
Carpenters 4
Wheeler 1
Collar Maker 1
Smiths 3
Cooper 1
Armourer 1
Nurse 1

[8] W.O. 54:689.   [9] W.O. 54:689.

GENERAL VIEW OF THE FACINGS, &c. OF THE SEVERAL MARCHING REGIMENTS OF FOOT, AS FIXED BY HIS MAJESTY, DECEMBER 19, 1768[10]

Colour of Facings	Rank and Title of the Regiments	Distinctions in the same Colour	If Gold or Silver Hat Lace &c. for the Officers	Colour of the Waistcoats, Breeches, and Lining of the Coats	Colour of the Lace
Blue	1st, or the royal regiment		Gold	White	White, with a blue double worm
Blue	2d, or the Queen's royal regiment		Silver	White	White, with a blue stripe
Blue	4th, or the King's own regiment		Silver	White	White, with a blue stripe
Blue	7th, or royal fuzileers		Gold	White	White, with a blue stripe
Blue	8th, or King's regiment		Gold	White	White, with a blue and yellow stripe
Blue	18th, or royal Irish		Gold	White	White, with a blue stripe
Blue	21st, or royal North-British fuzileers		Gold	White	White, with a blue stripe
Blue	23d, or royal Welch fuzileers		Gold	White	White, with red, blue, & yellow stripes
Blue	41st, or invalids		Gold	Red	Plain button-hole
Blue	42, or royal Highlanders		Gold	White Waistcoats and linings of coats. No breeches.	White, with a red stripe
Blue	60th, or royal Americans		Silver	White	White, with two blue stripes

[10] T. Simes, *Military Guide*, I, 302-304. These regulations were in force in 1775.

Regiment	Facing	Shade	Lace		Flag
6th regiment	Yellow	Deep yellow	Silver	White	White, with yellow and red stripes
9th regiment	Yellow		Silver	White	White, with two black stripes
10th regiment	Yellow	Bright yellow	Silver	White	White, with a blue stripe
12th regiment	Yellow		Gold	White	White, with yellow, crimson, and black stripes
13th regiment	Yellow	Philemot yellow	Silver	White	White, with a yellow stripe
15th regiment	Yellow		Silver	White	White, with a yellow and black worm and red stripe
16th regiment	Yellow		Silver	White	White, with a crimson stripe
20th regiment	Yellow	Pale yellow	Silver	White	White, with a red and black stripe
25th regiment	Yellow	Deep yellow	Gold	White	White, with a blue, yellow, and red stripe
26th regiment	Yellow	Pale yellow	Silver	White	White, with one blue, and two yellow stripes
28th regiment	Yellow	Bright yellow	Silver	White	White, with one yellow and two black stripes
29th regiment	Yellow		Silver	White	White, with two blue, and one yellow stripe
30th regiment	Yellow	Pale yellow	Silver	White	White, with a sky-blue stripe
34th regiment	Yellow	Bright yellow	Silver	White	White, with a blue and yellow worm, and red stripe
37th regiment	Yellow		Silver	White	White, with a red and yellow stripe
38th regiment	Yellow		Silver	White	White, with two red, and one yellow stripe
44th regiment	Yellow		Silver	White	White, with blue, yellow, and black stripes
46th regiment	Yellow		Silver	White	White, with red and purple worms
57th regiment	Yellow		Gold	White	White, with a black stripe
67th regiment	Yellow	Pale yellow	Silver	White	White, with a yellow, purple, and green stripes
5th regiment	Green	Goslin green	Silver	White	White, with two red stripes
11th regiment	Green	Full green	Gold	White	White, with two red and two green stripes
19th regiment	Green	Deep green	Gold	White	White, with two stripes, red and green
24th regiment	Green	Willow green	Silver	White	White, with one red and one green stripe
36th regiment	Green		Gold	White	White, with one red and one green stripe
39th regiment	Green		Gold	White	White, with a light green stripe
45th regiment	Green	Deep green	Silver	White	White, with a green stripe
49th regiment	Green	Full green	Gold	White	White, with two red and one green stripe

GENERAL VIEW OF THE FACINGS, &c. (Continued)

Colour of Facings	Rank and Title of the Regiments	Distinctions in the same Colour	If Gold or Silver Hat Lace &c. for the Officers	Colour of the Waistcoats, Breeches, and Lining of the Coats	Colour of the Lace
Green	51st regiment	Deep green	Gold	White	White, with a green worm stripe
Green	54th regiment	Popinjay green	Silver	White	White, with a green stripe
Green	55th regiment	Dark green	Gold	White	White, with two green stripes
Green	63d regiment	Very deep green	Silver	White	White, with a very small green stripe
Green	66th regiment	Yellowish green	Gold	White	White, with one crimson & green, & one green stripe
Green	68th regiment	Deep green	Silver	White	White, with yellow and black stripes
Green	69th regiment	Willow green	Gold	White	White, with one red and two green stripes
Buff	3d reg. or the Buffs		Silver	Buff	White, with yellow, black, and red stripes
Buff	14th regiment		Silver	Buff	White, with a blue and red worm, and a buff stripe
Buff	22d regiment	Pale buff	Gold	Pale buff	White, with one blue and one red stripe
Buff	27th or Innisk. reg.		Gold	Buff	White, with one blue and one red stripe
Buff	31st regiment		Silver	Buff	White, with a blue & yellow worm, & small red stripe
Buff	40th regiment		Gold	Buff	White, with a red and black stripe
Buff	48th regiment		Gold	Buff	White, with a black and red stripe
Buff	52d regiment		Silver	Buff	White, with a red worm, and one orange stripe
Buff	61st regiment		Silver	Buff	White, with a blue stripe
Buff	62d regiment	Yellowish buff	Silver	Yellowish buff	White, with two blue, and one straw-coloured stripe

Facing	Regiment	Lace colour	Metal	Ground	Lace stripe
White	17th regiment	Greyish white	Silver	Greyish white	White, with two blue, and one yellow stripe
White	32d regiment		Gold	White	White, with a black worm and a black stripe
White	43d regiment		Silver	White	White, with a red and black stripe
White	47th regiment		Silver	White	White, with one red and two black stripes
White	65th regiment		Silver	White	White, with a red and black worm, and a black stripe
Red	33d regiment		Silver	White	White, with a red stripe in the middle
Red	53d regiment		Gold	White	White, with a red stripe
Red	56th regiment	Purple	Silver	White	White, with a pink-colour stripe
Red	59th regiment	Purple	Silver	White	White, with a red and yellow stripe
Black	50th regiment		Silver	White	White, with a red stripe
Black	58th regiment		Gold	White	White, with a red stripe
Black	64th regiment		Gold	White	White, with a red and black stripe
Black	70th regiment		Gold	White	White, with a narrow black worm stripe
Orange	35th regiment		Silver	White	White, with one yellow stripe

DAILY PAY OF EACH RANK IN HIS MAJESTY'S LAND FORCES ON THE BRITISH ESTABLISHMENT[11]

	Royal Reg. of Horse-Guards		Dragoons		Foot-Guards		Foot	
	F. Pay	Subsist.	F. Pay	Subsist.	F. Pay	Subsist.	F. Pay	Subsist.
	£ s d	£ s d	£ s d	£ s d	£ s d	£ s d	£ s d	£ s d
Colonel and Captain	2 1 –	1 11 –	1 15 –	1 6 6	1 19 –	1 10 –	1 4 –	– 18 –
Lieutenant Colonel and Captain	1 9 6	1 2 6	1 4 8	– 18 6	1 8 6	1 1 6	– 17 –	– 13 –
Major and Captain	1 7 –	1 1 6	1 – 6	– 15 6	1 4 6	– 18 6	– 15 –	– 11 6
Captain	1 1 6	– 16 –	– 15 6	– 11 6	– 16 6	– 12 6	– 10 –	– 7 6
Captain Lieutenant or Lieutenant	– 15 –	– 11 6	– 9 –	– 7 –	– 7 10	– 6 –	– 4 8	– 3 6
Cornet h. gds. & dr. Ens. f. g. or 2d Lt. f.	– 14 –	– 11 –	– 8 –	– 6 –	– 5 10	– 4 6	– 3 8	– 3 –
Chaplain	– 6 8	– 5 –	– 6 8	– 5 –	– 6 8	– 5 –	– 6 8	– 5 –
Adjutant (Solicitor in foot-guards the same)	– 5 0	– 4 6	– 5 –	– 4 6	– 4 –	– 3 –	– 4 –	– 3 –
Quarter-Master	– 8 6	– 6 6	– 5 6	– 4 –	– 4 –	– 3 –	– 4 8	– 3 6
Surgeon	– 6 –	– 4 6	– 6 –	– 4 6	– 4 –	– 3 –	– 4 –	– 3 –
Surgeon's Mate					– 3 –	– 3 –	– 3 6	– 3 –
Drum-Major					– 1 –	– 1 –		
Deputy Marshal					– 1 –	– 9		
Serjeant	– 3 –	– 2 6	– 2 9	– 2 3	– 1 10	– 1 4 4/7	– 1 6	– 1 –
Corporal (Kettle-drum in horse-gds. the same)	– 3 –	– 2 6	– 2 3	– 1 9	– 1 2	– 10	– 1 –	– 8
Drummer			– 2 3	– 1 –	– 1 2	– 8 4/7	– 1 –	– 8
Trumpeter	– 2 8	– 2 –						
Private Man	– 2 6	– 2 –	– 1 9	– 1 5	– 10		– 8	– 6
Allowance on the Establishment to — Colonel (per troop or company)	– 4 –		– 2 6	– 1 2	– 1 7 3/4	– 6 4/7	– 1 2	– 6
Ditto for Hautbois (per troop or company)			– 2 –	– 1 6				
Captain	– 4 –	– 4 –	– 2 4	– 2 4	– 1 1 1/2		– 1 –	– 1 –
Agent	– 2 –	– 2 –	– 1 2	– 1 2	– 6 3/4	– 6 4/7	– 6	– 9

11 *Court and City Register*, 1776, p. 170.

OF THE PAY OF THE ARTILLERY, *PER DIEM*[12]

	£	s	d
Colonel	2	4	0
Lieutenant Colonel	1	0	0
Major	0	15	0
Captain	0	10	0
Captain Lieutenant	0	6	0
First Lieutenant	0	5	0
Second Lieutenant	0	4	0
Serjeant	0	2	0
Corporal	0	1	10
Bombardier	0	1	8
Gunner	0	1	4
Matross	0	1	0
Drummer	0	1	0

PRICES OF COMMISSIONS, 1766[13]

First and Second Troops of Horse-Guards

Commissions	Prices	Difference in value between the several commissions in succession
First Lieutenant-colonel . . .	£5,500	£ 400
Second Lieutenant-colonel . . .	5,100	800
Cornet and Major	4,300	200
Guidon and Major	4,100	1,400
Exempt and Captain	2,700	1,200
Brigadier and Lieutenant or Adjutant and Lieutenant	1,500	300
Sub-brigadier and Cornet . . .	1,200	1,200
		£5,500

[12] Duncan, *History of the R. A.*, I, 436.
[13] Simes, *Military Guide* (1776), I, 347-349.

PRICES OF COMMISSIONS, 1776 (Continued)

Dragoon Guards and Dragoons

Commissions	Prices	Difference in value between the several commissions in succession
Lieutenant-colonel	£4,700	£1,100
Major	3,600	1,100
Captain	2,500	1,100
Captain-lieutenant	1,400	250
Lieutenant	1,150	150
Cornet	1,000	1,000
		£4,700

Foot Guards

Lieutenant-colonel	£6,700	£ 400
1st Major ⎫ 2d Major ⎬ with rank of Col. . .	6,300	2,800
3d Major ⎭		
Captain	3,500	900
Captain-lieutenant with rank of Lieutenant-colonel	2,600	1,100
Lieutenant with rank of Captain .	1,500	600
Ensign	900	900
		£6,700

Marching Regiments of Foot

Lieutenant-colonel	£3,500	£ 900
Major	2,600	1,100
Captain	1,500	700
Captain-lieutenant	800	250
Lieutenant	550	150
Ensign	400	400
		£3,500

CHAPTER II

THE ADMINISTRATIVE MACHINERY OF
THE ARMY

COMMISSION OF THE SECRETARY AT WAR[1]

George R

GEORGE the Third by the Grace of God King of Great Britain France and Ireland Defender of the Faith etc. To Our Right Trusty and Welbeloved Councillor Thomas Townshend Esqr. Greeting. We being well satisfied with your Loyalty Integrity and Ability do hereby constitute and appoint you Secretary at War to all Our Forces raised or to be raised in Our Kingdom of Great Britain and Dominion of Wales You are therefore by Virtue of this Our Commission to receive the said Place into your Charge and you are diligently to intend the Execution thereof and faithfully and duly to execute and perform all things incident and belonging thereto and you are to observe and follow such Orders and Directions as you shall from Time to Time receive from Us or the General of Our Forces for the Time being according to the Discipline of War in pursuance of the Trust reposed in You and Your Duty to Us. Given at Our Court at St. James's the twenty seventh day of March 1782 in the Twenty second Year of Our Reign.

By His Majesty's Command

Shelburne

The Right Hon'ble Thos Townshend   Secretary at War

[1] W.O. 25:37, p. 1.

George R.

Whereas it has been represented unto Us that the under-mentioned Arms are wanting for the respective Regiments of Horse and Dragoons against each of their names set down to replace the like number broke and lost at the battle of Fontenoy, and at the skirmish at Clifton. Our Will and Pleasure therefore is that out of the Stores remaining within the Office of Our Ordnance under your charge, you forthwith cause the said Arms to be delivered to the respective Colonels or to their order, and you are to take the usual Indents for the same, and insert the charge thereof in your next Estimate to be laid the Parliament. And for so doing this shall be as well to you as to all other Our Officers herein concerned a sufficient Warrant.

Given at Our Court at Kensington, the 29*th* day of August, 1746, in the 20*th* year of Our reign,

By his Majesty's command,
"Holles Newcastle.

*To our right trusty and right entirely
beloved cousin and councillor, John
Duke of Montagu, Master-General of
Our Ordnance.*

	Carbines	Pairs of Pistols	Bayonets
Earl of Hartford's	84	80	..
General Honeywood's	29	21	..
Major-General Bland's	33	16	43

2 Clode, I, 674.

CHAPTER III

THE RECRUITING OF THE ARMY

PERIOD OF ENLISTED SERVICE[1]

War Office, December 16, 1775.

It is His Majesty's Pleasure, That, from the Date hereof, and during the Continuance of the Rebellion now subsisting in North America, every Person, who shall enlist as a soldier in any of His Majesty's Marching Regiments of Foot, shall be entitled to his Discharge at the End of Three Years, or at the end of the said Rebellion, at the Option of His Majesty.

By His Majesty's Command,

Barrington

ENLISTMENT OF CRIMINALS[2]

Shrewsbury, 18 Aug. 1778, Mr. Ashby, Deputy Sheriff of Shropshire to Barrington.

". . . I presume to mention to your Lordship that seven desperate Rogues included in H. M's conditional pardon . . . dated July 9th last remain in Salop Gaol to be delivered over to such Person or Persons as shall be duly authorised to receive them on condition of their enlisting and continuing to serve H. M. in his Land Service —, their names are John Williams otherwise Williamson for a Highway Robbery, Edward Williams and John Humphreys being found at large being sentenced to be

[1] *London Gazette,* 12-16 Dec. 1775.
[2] W.O. 1:995.

transported, Abraham Jones for a Highway Robbery, Thomas Herbert for Sheepstealing, William Bennett for Shoplifting and Thomas Jarvis the Younger for Burglary. . . .''

Weston House, 10 Sept. 1778, Mr. Godschall [J. P.?] to Barrington.[3]

''John Quin an Irish American 29 years of Age near six feet high very dirty and ragged seemingly of slow understanding was this morning convicted before me of Orchard Robbing. He is willing to serve as a soldier. I have therefore committed him to the House of Correction in Guildford to await your Orders. . . .''

Henley, 6 Aug. 1779, T. Cooper, Under Sheriff of Berks, to Jenkinson.[4]

''This day received a Letter from General Smith the High Sheriff of Berks desiring me to inform you of the Names of the several Convicts who had received Sentence of Death but were pardoned on Condition of entering into the Service.

''At the Summer Assizes 1778 Robert Thacher Received Sentence of Death for a Highway Robbery but has since been reprieved till his Majesty's Pleasure concerning him be known and still remains in the Gaol of the County of Berks. . . .

''At the last Assizes for Berks the three following Persons received Sentence of Death William Hughes for Sheep and Horse stealing William Marriott and William Abby for Horse stealing but were all reprieved before the Judges left the Town and are exceedingly proper Fellows either for the Land or Sea Service . . .''

3 W.O. 1:997.
4 W.O. 1:1004.

FORM OF BEATING ORDER[5]

G. R.

These are to authorise you by beat of drum or other-wise, to raise so many volunteers in any county or part of our kingdom of Great-Britain, as are or shall be want-ing to recruit and fill up the respective companies of our ——— regiment of foot, under your command, to the number allowed upon the establishment; and you are to cause the said volunteers, to be raised and levied as aforesaid, to march under the command of such Commis-sion or Non-commissioned Officer, in such numbers and at such place, to any place or port you shall think proper; and all Magistrates, Justices of the Peace, Constables, and all others Our civil Officers whom it may concern, are hereby required to be assisting unto you in providing quarters, impressing carriages, and otherwise as there shall be occasion; and for so doing, this Our order shall remain in force for twelve months from date hereof, and no longer.

Given at Our Court at St. James's, this ——— day of ——— 17— in the ——— year of Our reign,

By his Majesty's command.

Copy of a Letter from the Secretary at War to the Honourable William Gordon, dated 19th December, 1777.[6]

War Office, 19th December 1777

Sir

I am commanded by the King to acquaint you, that H's Majesty approves of your Proposal for raising a Regi-ment of Foot in the Highlands of *Scotland;* to consist of Eight Battalion Companies, One Company of Grena-diers, and One of Light Infantry. The Battalion Com-panies to consist each of 1 Captain, 2 Lieutenants, 1

---

[5] T. Simes, *Military Guide*, I, 243-244.
[6] 36 *Commons Journal*, pp. 613-614.

Ensign, 5 Serjeants, 5 Corporals, 2 Drummers, and 100 private Men; the Grenadier Company of 1 Captain, 3 Lieutenants, 5 Serjeants, 5 Corporals, 2 Drummers, 2 Pipers, and 100 private Men; the Light Infantry Company of 1 Captain, 3 Lieutenants, 5 Serjeants, 5 Corporals, 2 Drummers, and 100 Private, with the usual Staff Officers. The Regiment to have the Field Officers under mentioned; *viz.* One Lieutenant Colonel and One Major, each having also a Company; and One Major without a Company, receiving an Allowance of 10s *per Diem* in lieu thereof, and 5s *per Diem* as Major; but in case of the Death or Promotion of the additional Major, the Pay of such Major is to cease upon the Establishment.

The Regiment to be under your Command as Colonel Commandant, with the Command of a Company.

I am to inform you, that Levy Money will be allowed you at the Rate of £3 *per* Man, for 1,082 Men; and that His Majesty has been pleased to direct, that the Pay of the Regiment shall take place from the Date of your Beating Order; and shall be allowed you in Aid of Recruiting, on Condition that you do render an exact Account of the said Levy Money, and Pay, that shall be issued to you, charging against it Five Guineas for each Man reviewed and approved, together with the Subsistence of the Non-commissioned Officers and private Men, from the Day of their respective Attestations; and if there should be any Balance remaining it is to be considered as a Saving to the Public, to be hereafter disposed of as shall be thought proper.

No more than three Guineas will be allowed to be given to each Recruit.

None are to be inlisted under Five Feet Four Inches, nor under Eighteen Years, or above Thirty.

It is required, that the Regiment shall be actually raised and approved (after being reviewed by a General Officer) within Four Months from Date hereof.

I have represented to His Majesty, that you humbly hope you shall be indulged in recommending the Officers, being such as are well affected to His Majesty, and most likely, by their Interests and Connections, to assist in raising the Corps without Delay; but that you do not desire any Commissions for them until the Regiment shall have been raised and approved.

You will therefore be pleased to send me, for His Majesty's Consideration, a List of such Persons as you propose for Officers; who, if they meet with His Royal Approbation, may be assured that they shall have Commissions as soon as ever the Regiment is completed. And I am to acquaint you, it is His Majesty's intention that the Companies which shall be first raised shall entitle their Captains and Subalterns to Seniority in the Regiment, according to their respective Ranks, and the different Periods at which the said Companies shall be completed.

I am to inform you that in case the Persons approved by the King for the Rank of Major should be of less than Five Years standing in the Army as Captains, they are to pay £300 each for their Commissions; which sums are to be carried in Aid of the Charges brought on the Public for Levy Money, and credited to the General Account.

I am likewise authorized by His Majesty to acquaint you, the Officers will be entitled to Half Pay in case the Regiment shall be reduced after it has been established.

I have the King's Commands to add, that as Orders are given for several other Highland Corps, it is His Majesty's Intention, that their Seniority in the Army shall be determined by the Periods at which they shall be respectively completed.

I have the Honour to be,

Sir, etc.

Barrington

Honourable Colonel *William Gordon*

Like Letter, of same Date, to *John Mackenzie,* Esquire.
Like Letter, dated the 25th December, 1777, to Colonel
James Murray.
Like Letter, dated the 3d of January, 1778, to Colonel
Francis McLean.

Copy of a Letter from the Secretary at War to the
Mayor of *Liverpool,* dated 8th January, 1778.[7]

War Office, 8th January 1778.

Sir,

I am commanded by the King to acquaint you, that His
Majesty approves of the very handsome Proposal made
by the Gentlemen of *Liverpool,* through their Committee,
for raising a Regiment of Foot at their own Expence; the
Regiment to consist of Eight Battalion Companies, One
Company of Grenadiers, and One of Light Infantry. The
Battalion Companies to consist each of 1 Captain, 2 Lieutenants, 1 Ensign, 5 Serjeants, 5 Corporals, 2 Drummers, and 100 private Men; the Grenadier Company of 1
Captain, 3 Lieutenants, 5 Serjeants, 5 Corporals, 2
Drummers, 2 Fifers, and 100 private Men; the Light Infantry Company of 1 Captain, 3 Lieutenants, 5 Serjeants, 5 Corporals, 2 Drummers, and 100 Private, with
the usual Staff Officers. The Regiment to have 1 Colonel
Commandant, 1 Lieutenant Colonel, and 1 Major, each
having also a Company.

The Non-commissioned Officers and private Men are to
receive Pay from the Days of their respective Attestations.

No more than Three Guineas Bounty Money will be
allowed to each Recruit.

None are to be enlisted under Five Feet Four Inches,
nor under Eighteen Years, or above Thirty.

[7] 36 *Commons Journal,* p. 616.

It is required, that the Regiment shall be actually raised and approved (after being reviewed by a General Officer) within Four Months from the Date hereof. I have represented to His Majesty, that Commissions are not desired for the Officers until the Regiment shall be reviewed and approved.

The List of the Gentlemen recommended through the Committee for Commissions has been laid before the King, and honoured with his Royal Approbation; and they may be assured that they shall have the Commissions as soon as ever the Regiment is raised and approved.

I am likewise authorized by His Majesty to acquaint you, that the Officers will be entitled to Half Pay in case the Regiment shall be reduced after it has once been established.

I am to add, that it is his Majesty's Pleasure, that from the Date hereof, and during the Continuance of the Rebellion now subsisting in *North America,* every Person who shall enlist as a Soldier in any of His Majesty's Marching Regiments of Foot, shall be entitled to his Discharge at the end of Three Years, or at the end of the Rebellion, at the Option of His Majesty.

I have the Honour to be,

Sir, etc.

Barrington.

Worshipful the Mayor of *Liverpool.*

CHAPTER IV

THE PROVISIONING OF THE ARMY

ACCOUNT OF PROVISIONS RECEIVED BY DANIEL
CHAMIER, COMMISSARY GENERAL IN NORTH
AMERICA, BETWEEN 6 FEB. 1775 AND
9 JAN. 1778[1]

Kind of Provision	Amount	Value		
		£	s	d
Bread	2,032,538 lbs.	17,240 :	5 :	6½
Beer	106 tuns 24 gals.	267 :	6 :	7
Spirits	61,282 gals.	6,894 :	8 :	3¼
Wine	14,851 gals.	1,206 :	13 :	6
Beef	159,287 lbs.	9,789 :	10 :	3¼
Pork	231,910 lbs.	9,421 :	7 :	3¼
Flour	271,443 lbs.	1,888 :	8 :	1
Suet	3,238 lbs.	53 :	19 :	6
Raisins	23,010 lbs.	349 :	5 :	2
Pease	9,572 bush.	1,905 :	14 :	4½
Oatmeal	122,059 gals.	4,130 :	5 :	1
Rice	75,077 lbs.	727 :	11 :	10
Oil	12,641 gals.	2,554 :	11 :	2
Butter	17,933 lbs.	485 :	14 :	0
Cheese	7,909 lbs.	111 :	4 :	5
Vinegar	10,739 gals.	288 :	12 :	9
Butt Staves	40			
Puncheon Staves	137			
Hogshead Staves	100			
Half-Hhd. Staves	580	15 :	9 :	4½
Barrel Staves	90			
Headings	40			
Casks	3,221 tuns			
Hoops	27,534	5,504 :	12 :	1¼
Bags	12,491	676 :	11 :	11
Jars	397	198 :	10 :	0
Coals	687 chal.	1,134 :	15 :	9
Sugar	9,004 lbs.	176 :	17 :	3¼
Barley	22,332 lbs.	139 :	11 :	6
Salt	32 Bush.	6 :	2 :	1½
Fish	8,352 lbs.	33 :	8 :	1¾
		65,200 :	16 :	0

[1] W.O. 60:11.

Account of Provisions etc., Decayed

Kind of Provision	Amount	Value		
Beef	1,128 lbs.	17	: 15	: 10½
Pork	140 lbs.	1	: 18	: 5¼
Raisins	769 lbs.	5	: 8	: 2
Oil	104 gals.	15	: 12	: 0
Butter	176 lbs.	1	: 18	: 3¼
Bags	157	–	–	–
Jars	1	10	:	

ACCOUNT OF PROVISIONS RECEIVED BY COMMISSARY GENERAL DANIEL WEIR AT NEW YORK BETWEEN 7 OCT. 1774 AND 5 SEPT. 1781[2]

Kind of Provision	Amount	Value		
		£	s	d
Bread	512,182 lbs.	4,020	: 9	: 6
Spirits	42,655 gals.	5,687	: 7	: 0
Beef	42,832 lbs.	2,699	: 6	: 2
Pork	83,269 lbs.	3,469	: 11	: 1¾
Flour	164,884 lbs.	1,099	: 10	: 8
Raisins	2,574 lbs.	45	: 19	: 3
Pease	1,148 bush.	242	: 9	: 2
Oatmeal	12,007 gals.	422	: 14	: 1
Rice	91,557 lbs.	897	: 5	: 1½
Oil	2,385 gals.	531	: 15	: 4¼
Butter	14,516 lbs.	463	: 14	: 6½
Cheese	251 lbs.	3	: 10	: 7½
Vinegar	4,618 gals.	125	: 0	: 2
Casks	1,052 tuns	1,778	: 2	: 1
Hoops	12,233			
Bags	3,994	216	: 6	: 10
Jars	84	42	: 0	: 0
Candles	120 doz.	40	: 5	: 0
Sauerkraut	123 barr.	215	: 5	: 9
		22,000	: 12	: 5½

2 W.O. 60:11.

ABSTRACT OF PROVISIONS SHIPPED FOR NEW YORK AND PHILADELPHIA IN 1776, 1777, 1778, INCLUDING THE REMAINDER OF THE PROVISIONS CONTRACTED FOR IN 1778 BUT NOT YET SAILED FROM CORK. (LONDON, 15 JANUARY, 1779)[3]

	Beef lbs.	Pork lbs.	Bread & Flour lbs.	Pease bush.	Oatmeal & Rice lbs.	Butter lbs.	
			B 4,821,978				N.B. The Quantity lost or taken on the Voyage to America does not amount to above 12 or 14 days Consumption.
105 Ships dispatched in 1776	1,825,731	7,067,572	9,847,744	76,732	1,722,583	782,249	
11 Ships sailed from Cork 6 May 1777	304,290	1,210,088	1,336,440	7,175½	299,195	128,909	
8 " " " 19 " "	229,950	1,084,096	1,755,376	5,650	535,561	89,340	
10 " " " 20 June "	305,970	898,256	1,506,400	2,816	631,561	131,402	
6 " " " 14 July "	132,300	578,592	1,683,024	1,544	369,824	34,797	None of the Supplies to Canada, Nova Scotia, or the Floridas are included hereof.
8 " " " 30 Oct. "	136,240	727,168	1,249,360	11,154¼	217,864	65,000	
7 " " " 16 Aug. "	86,310	554,960	1,362,984	15,071½		36,882	
8 " " " 12 Sept. "	200,130	678,520	1,395,240	18,115	48,750	104,724	
3 " " " 18 Dec. "	152,565	388,336	289,240	256	196,672	12,473	
2 " " " " "	281,424	721,760					
8 " " " 25 Feb. 1778	194,055	813,986	1,962,612	11,130½	34,020	122,403	A fleet of 10 victuallers is now lying at Cork if they have not already sailed.
7 " " " 10 Apr. "	129,675	193,648	1,634,968	3,579	44,226	40,108	
6 " " " 31 May "	136,448	545,992	1,217,600	7,060		54,405	
6 " " " 28 June "	277,830	937,490	1,076,320	9,916¼		109,172	
13 " " " 31 July "	518,280	916,680	2,900,560	22,691½	188,912	147,240	
5 " " " 12 Oct. "	153,300	607,360	1,517,320	5,708¼	107,296	42,725	
8 " " " 11 Nov. "	284,970	997,148	2,167,760	760¼		118,948	
8 " " " 15 Dec. "	341,670	592,274	1,580,320	7,097¾	176,064	114,856	Orders are given for dispatching 4 Months compleat provisions for 32,000 Men from Cork to New York in Feb. 1779.
Ships at Corke as per Estimate, but the exact Return not recorded	—	985,432	1,958,012	24,962¼	287,826	18,329	
Total	5,691,138	20,499,358	40,372,338	231,419¾	4,860,354	2,154,052	
Which would supply 40,000 Men for		1,039 Days	1,009 Days	1,282 Days		1,005 Days	

[3] T. 64:107, Robinson to Clinton, 19 Jan. 1779 (enclosure).

EXAMPLE OF A PROVISION CONTRACT[4]

Articles of Agreement Indented and made and concluded this 2d April 1776 in the Sixteenth Year of the Reign of Our Sovereign Lord George the third by the Grace of God King of Great Britain France and Ireland Defender of the Faith and so forth, By and Between the Right Honorable the Lords Commissioners of his Majesty's Treasury on the Part and behalf of his Majesty of the one part and Arnold Nesbit, Adam Drummond and Moses Franks Esqrs. on the other part.

Whereas it is thought Necessary that a Contract should be entered into with some fit and responsible persons for furnishing a Quantity of Provisions for the supply of the Troops on Service in America such Provisions to be delivered into Store Houses at Corke at such Times as the said Lord Commissioners shall Appoint.

And Whereas Proposals have been made to the said Lords Commissioners by the said Arnold Nesbit Adam Drummond and Moses Franks for performing the said Service Which proposals the said Lords Commissioners have on the part and behalf of his Majesty thought fit to Accept upon the terms Limitations and restrictions herein After mentioned.

Now this Indenture Witnesseth that the said Arnold Nesbit Adam Drummond and Moses Franks Do for themselves, their Heirs Executors and Administrators promise Covenant Contract and Agree with the said Lords Commissioners of his Majesty's Treasury that they the said Arnold Nesbit Adam Drummond and Moses Franks shall and will deliver or cause to be delivered at their own Costs Charges and Risques into Storehouses to be provided at His Majesty's Expence such Respective

[4] T. 64:106, pp. 64-67.

Quantities as the said Lords Commissioners shall direct
and Require of good wholesome and sound Provisions of
a Quality and condition fit for the purpose of exporting
to America for the use of his Majesty's Troops there
serving under Genl Howe of the kinds herein After mentioned as will be sufficient to Victual 12000 Men from the
1st Day of January 1776 to the 1st day of May 1777 in
the following Proportions that is to say for each Person
to be Victualled for several days and so for every seven
days, Successively, Seven pounds of Bread or in lieu
thereof Four pounds of Pork Six Ounces of Butter three
Pints of Pease One pound of Flour or in lieu thereof Half
a Pound of Rice or half a Pound of Oatmeal and the said
Arnold Nesbit Adam Drummond and Moses Franks further Covenant and Agree that they will during the Continuance of ye Present Contract furnish upon due Notice
given to them such Quantities of the said several Articles
of Provisions as shall from time to time be Required and
Demanded of them by the said Lords Commissioners and
deliver the same into his Majesty's Storehouses at Corke
at their own Expence And in Case any of the said Provisions shall be found bad in their kind or unfit for the purpose before mentioned by the Person or Persons to be
Appointed for inspecting or examining the same such
provisions shall not be suffered to be put into the Storehouses but the like Quantity of ye like Articles of Provisions good wholesome and Sound shall be furnished in
lieu thereof at the Expence of the said Contractors And
the said Arnold Nesbit Adam Drummond and Moses
Franks do likewise agree that all the Provisions to be delivered into his Majesty's Storehouses at Corke shall be
packed in the best Manner and most suitable for the intended Service, And the Lords Commissioners on the behalf of His Majesty Do covenant promise and Agree that
the said Arnold Nesbit Adam Drummond and Moses

Franks their Heirs Executors and Administrators shall be Allowed and Receive for the Provisions so delivered into his Majesty's StoreHouses at Corke at and after the Rate of 5¼d p. Ration upon Producing Certificate signed by the Commanding Officer and Commissary of Stores at Corke or some Person or persons as shall be Appointed for that purpose which Certificates are to specify the Quantities of Provisions which shall have been delivered and that the same were in good Order and Condition And the said Lords Commissioners do likewise Covenant and Agree that they will bear harmless and indemnify the said Arnold Nesbit Adam Drummond, Moses Franks from all Losses and Damages that may happen to the said Provisions after being delivered into the Store Houses at Corke and also in regard to the payment of any Custom House Duties for or upon any of the said Provisions to be delivered pursuant to this Contract and it is hereby declared and Agreed by and between the said Parties to these Presents that the same and the several Articles and things Contained therein shall Continue and be in force for and during the space of Sixteen Calendar Months that is to say for and from the first day of January 1776 to the first day of May 1777 exclusive.

Lastly it is Covenanted and Agreed between the Parties to these Presents that the said Lords Commissioners of His Majesty's Treasury or any of them shall not be liable in any of their Persons or Estates to any Action of Covenant or other Action whatsoever by Reason or Means of their being on his Majesty's behalf made parties to this Contract In Witness whereof the said Lords Commissioners of his Majesty's Treasury and the said Arnold Nesbit Adam Drummond and Moses Franks have hereunto interchangeably put their Hands and seals the Day and Year first. Above Written

North C Townshend Beauchamp Cornwall

Forage

It will be Necessary to begin the Campaign with Six Months Forage in the Magazines which cannot be procured in this Country in its present Situation therefore it must be looked for from Europe.

Hay

Rhode Island from the best information can supply fifteen Thousand Tons of Hay in Season, but still great difficulties will arise in procuring it if the Inhabitants of that Island are inimical, as you must depend upon them to cut and cure the Hay. The same Observation will answer with respect to Long Island, and Statten Island, in the Province of New York. Therefore upon this uncertainty the dependence upon Magazines must be upon Europe.

Forage

The army being in the field may furnish itself with green forage from the Middle of June to the Middle of September.

Oats and Bran

Canada is able to Supply the Articles of Oats and Bran, but the length and uncertainty of the Voyage is such, that it is thought these articles may be brought from England or Ireland, full as Cheap, and with this advantage that Oats in particular are far superior in Quality. . . .

Head Quarters Boston Nov. 27th 1775.

[5] C.O. 5:92, p. 721. Apparently drawn up for the perusal of Lord Dartmouth.

THE DUTIES OF A COMMISSARY GENERAL[6]

Instructions to be observed by our Trusty and Welbeloved Nathl Day Esqr. in the execution of his Commission, under our Sign Manual bearing date 20th day of March 1776 whereby he is appointed Commissary of Our Army in Canada.

You shall forthwith repair to the District described in your Commission as afores'd & take upon you the inspection, supervision, & direction of all Commissaries, & Deputy Commissaries, & Ass't Commissaries, of every description, & all their subordinate Officers, Ministers, & Agents whatsoever now or hereafter belonging to, or attending upon our Army that now is or shall be in Canada, subject nevertheless in all things to such Orders as you shall from time to time receive from us, or from our high Treasurer, or the Commissioners of our Treasury, for the Time being or from the Commander in Chief of our said Army.

You are from time to time to appoint any one, or more of Deputy Commissaries, or Assistants whom you shall think fit to preside over, take care of, superintend, aid, & assist in the securing and management of Magazines and Depots of Provisions and Forage for the use of the said Army, and also the conduct and Establishment of the Bakery, as the exigency of the Service may require.

You are to take charge of all Provisions which shall arrive in Canada for the use of our Army there and superintend the distribution thereof to the Troops. And you are to follow all such Rules and Orders touching the Providing and distribution of Fresh Provisions as you shall receive from the Commander in Chief of our said Army for the time being.

You are to make up monthly Accounts of all Provisions and Supplies which shall be received for the use of Our

6 T. 64:104.

Army, and of the expenditures thereof, and what shall remain in Store, with an Account of the Number of the Rations drawn and of the Officers, Private Men and all others victualled, distinguishing their Rank and situation, and you are from time to time and by every opportunity to make exact and true returns thereof to Our High Treasurer or Commissioners of the Treasury for the time being and you are also from time to time to impart to Our High Treasurer or Commissioners of the Treasury for the time being all material transactions arising within the Charge of the Commissariat, attending our said Army, Given etc.

COMMISSION OF COMMISSARY GENERAL
DANIEL WIER[7]

George R

George the Third by the Grace of God King of Great Britain, France, and Ireland, Defender of the Faith, etc. To our Trusty and Welbeloved Daniel Wier Esqr. Greeting: We do by these Presents constitute and appoint you to be Commissary General of Stores, Provisions and Forage to Our Forces serving within Our Colonies in North America, lying upon the Atlantick Ocean from Nova Scotia on the North to West Florida on the South, both inclusive, now under the Command of Our Trusty and Welbeloved Sir William Howe, Knight of the Bath, Major General of Our Forces, and General of Our Forces in North America only; You are therefore carefully and diligently to discharge the Duty of Commissary Genl. of Stores, Provisions and Forage for Our said Forces, by doing and performing all and all manner of things thereunto belonging; And We do hereby authorize and impower you to inspect the buying & delivering of Stores, Provisions and Forage for the use of Our said Forces,

7 W.O. 25:33, p. 120.

whether the same be done by Contractors or others, and likewise to settle and adjust all accounts relating thereunto; And you are to observe and follow such Orders & directions from time to time as you shall receive from Us, the Commander in Chief of our said Forces, or any other superior Officer, according to the Rules & Discipline of War. Given at Our Court at St. James' the First day of February 1777, in the Seventeenth Year of Our Reign.

By H. M. O.

Geo. Germain

Daniel Wier Esqr Commissary General of Stores, Provisions and Forage to the Forces in No. America now under the Command of General Sir William Howe.

CHAPTER V

THE PROBLEM OF TRANSPORTATION

NUMBER OF SHIPS AND TONNAGE IN SERVICE OF THE ORDNANCE DEPT., 1 JAN. 1776–31 DEC. 1783[1]

Year	Ships	Tons
1776	25	7,164
1777	12	5,363
1778	10	2,377
1779	13	5,628
1780	10	4,676
1781	18	5,092
1782	22	9,634
	110	39,934

ACCOUNT OF TRANSPORTS CONTRACTED FOR BY ORDNANCE DEPT. BETWEEN SEPTEMBER 1775 AND SEPTEMBER 1777[2]

Date	Ships' Names	Ton-nage	Pd. or contracted to be pd.		Remarks
1775			s	d	
Sept. 13	Charming Sally	174	10		Discharged
15	Russia Merchant	243	10		
Oct. 1	Hope	2676$\frac{61}{94}$	10		Taken
Nov. 3	John and William	130	10		
10	Noble Bounty	273	10		
Nov. 24	Carcass Tender	130	10		
1776					
Jan. 24	Woodland	222	11		Discharged
"	Prince George	192	11		
"	Helen	195	11		

[1] 40 *Commons Journal*, p. 138.
[2] W.O. 55:371, pp. 193-194.

ACCOUNT OF TRANSPORTS CONTRACTED FOR (Continued)

Date		Ships' Names	Ton-nage	Pd. or contracted to be pd.		Remarks
Jan.	24	Fleetwood	219	11		Discharged
"	"	Devonshire	179	11		
"	"	Friendship	199	11		
"	"	Hopewell	339	11		
"	"	Prince of Wales	201	11		
Mar.	1	June	300	11		
	15	Rebecca	190	11		
Apr.	2	Cadiz Packet	200	12 : 6		
	3	Union Success	254	12 : 6		
	29	Samuel and Elizabeth	195	11		
Aug.	1	Nottingham	271	12 : 6		
Sept.	2	Priscilla				Strongly fitted and armed.
	–	Unity				
	–	Aston Hall	370	12 : 6		
	–	Richmond	350	12 : 6		Discharged at Dominica.
	6	Lord Townshend	700	14		Very strongly fitted and armed.
	15	Lord Amherst	715	14		Do.
1777						
Feb.	4	Brilliant	800	14		Very strongly fitted and armed
	–	Price Frigate	330	12 : 6		Do.
	6	Lord Howe	720	14 :		"
Mar.	4	Emanuel	160	14 : 6		Discharged
	9	Andrew	300	14 : 6		Very strongly fitted and armed
May	13	Speke	700	12 : 6		Do.
	16	Commerce	400	12 : 6		Discharged
	–	Martha	320	12 : 6		"
	–	Friendship	330	12 : 6		"
July	25	Earl of Bathurst	737	14		Very strongly fitted and armed
Aug.	7	Earl of Cornwallis	400	13		Do.
Sept.	25	Adventurer	374	13		"

EXPENCE OF OCEAN TRANSPORT SERVICE[3]

1779	£	s	d
Cost of Troop Transports . . .	499,193	: 17	: 1
" " Victuallers	131,387	: 8	: 7
1780			
Cost of Troop Transports . . .	548,745	: 4	: 1
" " Victuallers	275,233	: 0	: 10
1781			
Cost of Troop Transports . . .	433,650	: 12	: 10
" " Victuallers	478,913	: 5	: 2
1782			
Cost of Troop Transports . . .	408,629	: 10	: 0¼
" " Victuallers	480,514	: 19	: 5
1783			
Cost of Troop Transports . . .	405,147	: 12	: 10
" " Victuallers	323,963	: 11	: 4

COMMISSION OF THE WAGGON MASTER GENERAL[4]

George R.

George the Third by the Grace of God, King of Great Britain France and Ireland Defender of the Faith etc. To our Trusty and Welbeloved Major Robert Molleson Greeting We do by these Presents constitute and appoint you to be Waggon Master General to Our Army serving in North America. You are therefore carefully and diligently to discharge the Duty of Waggon Master General by doing and performing all and all manner of things thereunto belonging; And you are to observe and follow such Order and Directions from time to time as you shall receive from Us Our Commander in Chief of Our Army serving in North America or any other your Superior Officer, according to the rules and Discipline of War.

[3] Adm., Navy Board, 3526.
[4] W.O. 25:37, p. 94.

Given at Our Court at St. James's the First day of July One Thousand Seven Hundred and Eighty two. In the Twenty Second Year of Our Reign.

By His Majesty's Command

Thos. Townshend

Major Robert Molleson Waggon Master General to the Army Serving in North America.

ACCOUNT OF THE NUMBER OF VESSELS, WITH THE AMOUNT OF THE HIRE, EMPLOYED IN THE DEPARTMENT OF THE QUARTER MASTER GENERAL IN NORTH AMERICA, FOR EVERY QUARTER, FROM THE 25TH OF DECEMBER 1776 TO THE 31ST OF MARCH 1780[5]

	Periods	No. of Vessels	Amount of the Hire		
			£	s	d
	Between 25th December 1776 and 31st March 1777	63	4,042	– 15 –	5¼
Sir William Erskine, Quarter Master General	1st April and 30th June 1777	45	2,987	– 2 –	1½
	1st July and 30th September 1777	46	4,110	– 4 –	3½
	1st October and 31st December 1777	103	14,108	– 12 –	7¾
	1st January and 31st March 1778	41	5,847	– 10 –	2
	1st April and 30th June 1778	122	18,775	– 12 –	9¾
	1st July and 30th September 1778	72	9,924	– 10 –	11
	1st October and 31st December 1778	91	11,897	– 14 –	9¾
	1st January and 31st March 1779	60	9,429	– 7 –	11½
	1st April 1779 and 30th June 1779	68	13,039	– 1 –	4¾
Lord Cathcart, Acting Quarter Master General	1st July and 30th September 1779	70	11,575	– 4 –	7
	1st October and 31st December 1779	59	10,249	– 1 –	11
	1st January and 31st March 1780	62	11,406	– 19 –	9¼
			£127,483	– 18 –	10¼

[5] 38 *Commons Journal,* p. 1104.

ACCOUNT OF THE NUMBER OF WAGGONS, HORSES, AND DRIVERS
WITH THE AMOUNT OF HIRE, EMPLOYED IN THE DEPART-
MENT OF THE QUARTER MASTER GENERAL IN NORTH
AMERICA, FOR EVERY QUARTER, FROM THE 25TH DECEMBER
1776 TO THE 31ST OF MARCH 1780[6]

	Periods	No. of Waggons	No. of Horses	No. of Drivers	Amount of Hire		
					£	s	d
Sir William Erskine, Quarter Master General	Between 25th December 1776 and 31st March 1777	523	1,176	458	13,666	– 3 –	—
	1st April and 30th June 1777	763	2,082	817	28,238	– 14 –	—
	1st July and 30th September 1777	1,376	3,111	1,440	23,631	– 13 –	—
	1st October and 31st December 1777	798	1,880	798	28,785	– 12 –	—
	1st January and 31st March 1778	748	1,810	750	27,281	– 12 –	6
	1st April and 30th June 1778	897	2,128	899	31,498	– 2 –	8
	1st July and 30th September 1778	709	1,893	793	27,821	– 15 –	11¾
	1st October and 31st December 1778	640	1,809	642	24,161	– 12 –	2
	1st January and 31st March 1779	523	1,515	524	21,555	– 19 –	2
	1st April and 30th June 1779	604	1,723	607	24,532	– 8 –	6
Lord Cathcart Acting Quarter Master General	1st July and 30th September 1779	646	2,014	687	27,712	– 7 –	9
	1st October and 31st December 1779	699	2,164	740	29,729	– 15 –	9
	1st January and 31st March 1780	690	2,147	731	29,819	– 12 –	1
					£338,435	– 8 –	6¾

[6] 38 *Commons Journal*, p. 1109.

PROPORTION OF BAT-HORSES PER OFFICER IN
BURGOYNE'S EXPEDITION[7]

To a field officer . . . . 3 per battn 6
A captain   . . . . 2 "   "   12
A subaltern . . . . 1 "   "   16
A surgeon and mate . . . . 2 "   "   2
A chaplain . . . . 1 "   "   1
A quarter master . . . . 1 "   "   1
For carrying the company's tents . . . . .
   2 horses to each company   . . . . .   "   "   16
         Total per Battn   54

N.B.   This calculation was made upon eight companies to a
battalion, in which 2 field officers' companies are included.

The horses for the five British battalions of the line, in
which two field officers' companies are included.

The horses for the five British battalions of the line, upon
calculation, amount to 272
   Gen. Fraser's corps, reckoned to be equal to four battalions   216
   Five German battalions, @ 70 horses per battalion, that
being the difference in proportion to their strength . . . 350
   Breyman's corps 100
                                               ‾‾‾
         Total for the regts. of the regs. 936

      Staff
2 M. Gens 12
4 Brigs   16
Brit. Q.M.G. and asst's. 12
Ger. " " " "   "   "   12
The Hospital 30   82
                                            ‾‾‾

      Irregulars
Canads. — Inds. — and Provs. 200
Artificers 50   250
Recapit. of whole distrib.   ‾‾‾‾‾‾‾
                                           1268

[7] State of the Expedition, pp. 145-146, note.

PROPORTION OF WAGGONS AND OTHER NECESSARIES, FOR
SUCH BRITISH REGIMENTS AS ARE DESTINED TO ACT
ON THE COAST OF THE ATLANTICK THE ENSUING
CAMPAIGN. JANY. 6, 1776[8]

Waggons for every Batt'n of 677 with Harness compleat
for four Horses to each Waggon . . . . } 4
Sunks for the Bat-Horses of each Batt'n Vizt. . . .
   2 per Comp'y for the Men's Tents and Blankets
     and   . . . . } 22
   2 for the Medicine Chests with Collars and Wanties
     compleat   . . . .
Water Decks of painted Oil Cloth   22

For the 42d Reg't Establishment 1,168 men

Waggons   6
Sunks   32
Water Decks   32

For the 71st Reg't of 2 Batt'ns Establishment 2,298

Waggons   12
Sunks   64
Water Decks   64

The Seven Reg'ts now about to sail under the Command of
Earl Cornwallis have received the following proportion of Necessaries Vizt.

Waggons with Harness compleat for three Horses to
   each Vizt.   1
Waggons for the use of their Hospital   2
Sunks for Bat Horses   22
Water Decks   22
Therefore there wants to compleat to their proportion of
Necessaries per Batt'n as follows:
Waggons   3
Sets of Harness for Waggons and the two Hospital
   Waggons   15

8 W.O. 1:890, pp. 1-5.

It is understood that the Treasury mean to order a
number of Draught and Bat-Horses, to be bought up for
the Service in North America: And that the Ordnance
are to send over, such proportion of Horses, as may be
judged requisite for drawing the Artillery: That the
Waggons and Harness, would be most conveniently provided by the Ordnance; That the Treasury are to give Directions for supplying the Blankets and Watch Coats;
and that the War Office, is to order the sunks, Water
Decks, etc. along with the Ordinary Camp Necessaries.

It is supposed, that, exclusive of the two Regiments
now Prisoners there will be in North America next Campaign, 43 British Batt'ns Vizt. 42 Regiments of one Battalion each, and the 71st Regiment of two Batt'ns. Of this
number it is probable that there may be 5 Batt'ns in Detached Garrisons, which may not immediately require
Waggons, so that there will remain 38 Batt'ns to be provided.

Waggons with 4 Sets of Harness

		Wag's.	*Harness*
For 35 Batt'ns at 4 each		140	560
1 " 42 Reg't.		6	24
2 " 71 Reg't.		12	48
38 Total		158	632
Of this Number the 7 Reg'ts under Earl Cornwallis have received		9	27
There remains to be provided for the			
Infantry		149	605
And for the two Reg'ts of Light Dragoons 4 each		8	32
		157	637

RETURN OF DRIVERS, HORSES, AND WAGGONS, DELIVERED BY
THE QUARTER MASTER GENERAL TO THE ARMY UNDER
GENERAL HOWE BETWEEN 1 APRIL AND 30 JUNE 1777[9]

Distribution	Drivers	Waggons	Horses	Commencing	Ending	At per Day s/
Commander in Chief (Howe)	6	6	12	May 10	June 30	72/
Lord Cornwallis	3	3	6	Apr. 1	" "	36/
Major General Vaughan	3	3	6	Apr. 1	" "	36/
Major General Grant	3	3	6	Apr. 1	" "	36/
Major General Grey	2	2	4	Apr. 14	" "	24/
Brigadier General Agnew	2	2	4	Apr. 1	" "	24/
Brigadier General Matthew	2	2	4	Apr. 1	" "	24/
Brigadier General Leslie	2	2	4	Apr. 1	" "	24/
Quarter Master General and Family	3	3	6	Apr. 1	" "	36/
Adjutant General and Family	2	2	4	Apr. 1	" "	24/
Hospital	4	4	8	Apr. 3	" "	48/
Engineer's Department	8	8	32	Apr. 1	" "	144/
Pontoon Waggons	64	32	128	Apr. 2	" "	672/
Flat Boat Waggons	44	22	132	Apr. 3	" "	594/
Maj. Hollands Corps of Pioneers and Guides	2	2	4	Apr. 1	" "	24/
16th Regt. Light Dragoons	7	7	14	Apr. 4	" "	84/
17th " " "	7	7	14	Apr. 2	" "	84/
1st Battalion Light Infantry	10	10	20	Apr. 1	" "	120/
2d Battalion Light Infantry	10	10	20	Apr. 1	" "	120/
British Rifle-men	2	2	4	Apr. 2	" "	24/
Queen's Rangers	5	5	10	Apr. 3	" "	60/
1st Battalion Grenadiers	10	10	20	Apr. 1	" "	120/
2d Battalion Grenadiers	10	10	20	Apr. 1	" "	120/
Guards, 2 Battalions	16	16	32	Apr. 2	" "	192/
4th Regt.	5	5	10	Apr. 5	" "	60/
5th "	5	5	10	Apr. 2	" "	60/
7th "	5	5	10	May 11	" "	60/
10th "	5	5	10	May 11	" "	60/
15th "		5	10	Apr. 1	" "	60/
17th "	5	5	10	Apr. 1	" "	60/
23rd "	5	5	10	Apr. 3	" "	60/
26th "	5	5	10	May 11	" "	60/

[9] 38 *Commons Journal*, pp. 1104-1106. These statistics do not include the
Hessian corps. See also pp. 1106-1109.

RETURN OF DRIVERS, HORSES, AND WAGGONS, (Continued)

Distribution		Drivers	Waggons	Horses	Commencing		Ending		At per Day
									s
27th "		5	5	10	Apr.	3	June 30		60/
28th "		5	5	10	Apr.	1	" "		60/
33rd "		5	5	10	Apr.	1	" "		60/
35th "		5	5	10	Apr.	2	" "		60/
37th "		5	5	10	May 11		" "		60/
38th "		5	5	10	May 11		" "		60/
40th "		5	5	10	Apr.	1	" "		60/
42nd "	Two Battalions	10	10	20	Apr.	3	" "		120/
44th "		5	5	10	Apr.	2	" "		60/
46th "		5	5	10	Apr.	1	" "		60/
49th "		5	5	10	Apr.	3	" "		60/
52nd "		5	5	10	May 11		" "		60/
55th "		5	5	10	Apr.	2	" "		60/
64th "		5	5	10	Apr.	1	" "		60/
71st "	Three Battalions	16	16	32	Apr.	1	" "		60/
Artillery		46	46	92	Apr.	1	" "		552/

A STATE OF THE NUMBER OF DRIVERS, HORSES AND
WAGGONS EMPLOYED IN THE QUARTER MASTER
GENERAL'S DEPARTMENT IN THE FOLLOWING
YEARS[10]

Distribution		Drivers	Horses	Waggons
In	1777	823	2092	763
	1778	874	2086	874
	1779	740	2164	699
	1780	731	2146	690
	1781	623	1979	620

N.B. A no. of Horses and Waggons were taken from the Rebel
Country in the Years of 1777 and 1778 which if brought into
Acc[t] would make one fourth more than what is charged for in
the subsequent Years.

[10] "Minute Book of a Board of General Officers" (N. Y. Hist. Soc. *Coll.*,
1916), p. 226.

In 1779 the Pontoon Train was ordered to be completed which with the arrival of the 76th, 80th, 82nd and 84th Regiments from Europe, the Troops from Rhode Island, and the Flank Companies from Halifax as also the increase of the Provincial Corps, caused an additional number of Horses to be employed that year.

BIBLIOGRAPHY

In the following list no attempt has been made to compile an exhaustive bibliography, only those works being included which were especially serviceable in preparing this work. With a few exceptions, the list includes no material not specifically cited in the footnotes. In general, critical comment has been confined to works that were particularly helpful.

MANUSCRIPT SOURCES

Additional Manuscripts (British Museum).

> Volume 37833, fo. 1 and fo. 43, contains several important letters from George III to John Robinson, secretary of the Treasury board, respecting the provisioning of the forces in America during the war.

Admiralty Papers. Manuscripts in the Public Record Office.

> For the student of the British army in the American Revolution, the chief value of the Admiralty Papers lies in the data which they contain regarding the transportation and convoying of troops and supplies from England to America. The following groups of documents were found especially useful:

> Adm. 1:4288. 1778-1782. Letters from the Treasury to the secretary to the Admiralty.

> Adm. 2:244-259. 1776-1783. Letters from the lords of the Admiralty to the secretary of state and to other departments.

> Adm. 3:81. 1775-1783. Admiralty Board Minutes.

>> The most important transactions of the Admiralty are here recorded. The minutes afford a convenient means of tracing the board's relations with the army.

> Adm. Navy Board, 279-280. 1767-1779. Promiscuous letters as to transports.

A rather important group of documents relating to army transport.

Adm. Navy Board, 3525-3526. 1776-1778. Papers relating to the charge of transports.

Adm. Navy Board, 2592-2614. 1775-1783. Minutes of the Navy board.

The minute books record the most significant measures adopted by the Navy commissioners. After 1779, when the latter took charge of a large part of the ocean transport service for the army, the minute books become exceedingly important to the student of military affairs.

Adm. Victualling Minutes, 72-96. 1775-1783. Minutes of the board and committees.

Since the victualling commissioners were charged with the business of stocking transports with provisions, their books and papers are of considerable value in studying the ocean transport service.

Adm. Victualling Out-Letters, 27-31. 1775-1783. Letter-Books of out-letters.

Adm. Medical Minutes, 49-50. 1773-1783. General minutes of the board of commissioners for sick and wounded seamen and exchange of prisoners of war.

The minutes are essential for an understanding of the functions of the Medical board and its relations to the army.

Audit Office Papers. Manuscripts in the Public Record Office (London).

Declared Accounts, Bundles, 197-208. Declared Accounts of army contractors.

These papers are useful in studying army contracts. The names of the contractors, the goods they supplied, and the dates of the contracts are here recorded.

Colonial Office Papers. Manuscripts in the Public Record Office. C.O. 5:92-103. 1775-1783. Military Correspondence.

These letters are chiefly from Generals Gage, Haldimand, Howe, Clinton, and Carleton, though the collection also includes many letters from the secretary of state for the colonies to the commanders in America. The entire set of letters is of the utmost importance as regards the organization of the army. There are, in particular, many suggestive passages respecting problems of food supply and transport.

C.O. 5:119-132. 1771-1781. Entry Books of letters from the secretary of state for the colonies to the lords of the Admiralty, together with originals of letters received by the secretary from the Admiralty.

Volume 125 contains important data relative to the organization of the transport service in Carleton's expedition on Lake Champlain in 1776. The other volumes contain similar material.

C.O. 5:161-166. 1772-1781. Correspondence of the secretary of state for the colonies with the Ordnance office.

These volumes deal largely with the relation of the Ordnance department to the transport service both on land and on sea. In volumes 163-164 are many letters from Captain Dickinson, who had charge of the shipping hired by the department.

C.O. 5:254-262. 1775-1782. Departmental correspondence of the secretary of state for the colonies.

Volumes 254-255 (1775-1782). Out-letters to Admiralty; volumes 256-257 (1775-1782), in-letters from War Office and Ordnance board; volume 258 (1776-1781), in-letters from the Treasury; volumes 259-260, in-letters from the Admiralty; volumes 261-262, out-letters to the War Office and Ordnance board. These letters are useful in a study of army transport. Volume 250 describes the wagons built for the army by the Ordnance department. Volume 254 treats of the arrangements made to transport Carleton's forces up Lake Champlain in 1776. The problem of draught horses for the troops in America is dealt with in the correspondence with the Treasury.

Treasury Papers. Manuscripts in the Public Record Office.

T. 1:512-519. 1775-1783. Original correspondence or Treasury Board papers.

These bundles of papers contain documents of a varied character—letters, accounts, reports, lists, petitions, and memorials. The documents cover a wide range of miscellaneous topics relative to the army in America. Considerable data may be found regarding victualling and transport.

T. 29 :44-53. 1774-1783. Treasury Board minutes.

It is safe to say that for a study of the British army in the American Revolution no minute books equal in importance those of the Treasury board. The lords commissioners had close interest in the welfare of the army, since they made the contracts for provisions and certain articles of clothing and for the transportation of certain classes of *matériel*. The minute books constitute an unusually complete record of the board's policy and action and, being carefully indexed, are readily used.

T. 64 :101. 1772-1776. Letter and Account Book of commissariat supplies to the troops in North America.

This and the succeeding volumes, T. 64 :102-107, 114, 117-120, form the chief source of information respecting the provisioning of the forces in America.

T. 64 :102-103. 1776-1777. Copies of letters from Nathaniel Day, commissary general to the army in America, to Secretary Robinson and others, and answers thereto.

T. 64 :104. 1776-1781. Copies of letters from Secretary Robinson to Nathaniel Day.

T. 64 :105. 1777-1783. Copies of letters from secretaries Robinson, Rose, Burke, and Sheridan of the Treasury board, to Haldimand.

T. 64 :106-107. 1774-1777, 1778-1783. Letters to and from commanders-in-chief in America.

T. 64 :114. 1778-1779. Correspondence book and accounts of commissariat supplies, touching the army during the American War.

T. 64 :117. 1776. Copies of letters from the Treasury to Anthony Merry, merchant of London, relating to the transportation of cattle, sheep, hogs, dispatched from Wales.

T. 64 :118. 1776-1777. Copies of letters from Daniel Chamier, commissary general of stores and provisions to the army in America, to Secretary Robinson, and copies of the answers.

T. 64:119. 1777-1783. America: Out-letters and observations. Copies of letters from Secretary Robinson to Daniel Wier, Peter Paumier, and Brook Watson, commissaries in America, with many enclosures, tables, letters, and the like. A valuable supplement to the preceding volumes.

T. 64:120. 1779. Correspondence and account book of Peter Paumier, deputy commissary in Georgia.

T. 64:200. 1779-1780. Copies of letters from the commissioners of the Navy to the lords of the Treasury, relative to the victualling of transports. Feb. 3, 1779-Sept. 19, 1780.

This volume and the succeeding one, T. 64:201, constitute the chief source of information relative to the work of the Navy board in connection with ocean transport.

T. 64:201. 1779-1781. Copies of letters from Secretary Robinson to the Navy board on the victualling service. Jan. 30, 1779-Aug. 21, 1781.

War Office Papers. Manuscripts in the Public Record Office.

W.O. 1:10-13. 1776-1783. Letters and enclosures, from officers in America to the secretary at war.

This group of documents contains many letters from the commanders in America—Howe, Clinton, Carleton, and Haldimand. The letters deal chiefly with such items as ammunition, clothing, food, housing, and sickness.

W.O. 1:50-52. 1768-1783. Letters and papers from the West Indies.

Useful for an understanding of military conditions in the British islands.

W.O. 1:616. 1778-1780. Letters from General Amherst, commander-in-chief in England, to Secretary Barrington.

Largely concerned with drafting and recruiting.

W.O. 1:678-682, 684. 1756-1784. Letters from the secretary of state and the Treasury to the secretary at war.

Many of their letters deal with ocean transport.

W.O. 1:683. 1776-1781. Letters from Lord George Germain, secretary of state for the colonies, to Secretary Barrington, concerning American affairs.

This correspondence occasionally contains valuable data respecting the state of the recruiting.

W.O. 1:823-826. 1763-1784. Letters from the Treasury to the secretary at war.

These letters supplement W.O. 1:678-682, 684, regarding problems of ocean transport.

W.O. 1:890. 1776-1783. Statistics relative to the forces in America and the West Indies.

This volume includes lists of camp necessities and equipage, such as wagons, blankets, tents, canteens, haversacks, etc.; names of transports and victualling ships; hospital and medical returns.

W.O. 1:991-1020. 1776-1783. Miscellaneous letters to the secretary at war.

These volumes throw light on many different aspects of military administration. They are especially useful as showing the methods of recruiting and the actual working of the Press Acts of 1778 and 1779.

W.O. 3:1-6. 1767-1778. Letter-books of the commander-in-chief and adjutant general of the army in Great Britain.

Volume 5 contains the letters from Edward Harvey, adjutant general during the early years of the Revolution, to various general officers. It is very useful for a study of the recruiting and augmenting of the army.

W.O. 4:273-275. 1775-1784. American letter-books.

These volumes contain dispatches of the secretary at war to commanders and general officers in America. They deal with a great variety of routine matters such as leaves of absence, promotions, exchanges, warrants for pay, warrants for courts-martial, etc.

W.O. 4:965-967. 1778-1781. Press Act letter-books.

These volumes are the chief source of information relative to the operation of the two press acts, 18 Geo. III, c. 53, and 19 Geo. III, c. 10. They should be supplemented by W.O. 1:991-1008.

W.O. 24:480-523. 1774-1783. Registers of military establishments.

These ledgers contain yearly lists of the established regiments. The lists give not only the number of men on the rolls of each regiment but also the number of companies, battalions, commissioned and non-commissioned officers of each rank, and drummers, which composed each regiment. They constitute a mine of information respecting regimental organization.

W.O. 25:32-37. 1772-1783. Commission books. Series I.

W.O. 25:91-95. 1775-1783. Commission books. Series II.

These books, as the titles indicate, contain the commissions of officers connected with the army. They are especially helpful in determining the functions of numerous special officials appointed in connection with the work of recruiting, provisioning, and transporting the forces.

W.O. 28:2-10. 1777-1783. Headquarters records, America.

This group contains many letters and returns of a miscellaneous character, which deal with such subjects as hospitals, engineers, artillery, ordnance, rations, forage, pay, appointments, courts-martial, and provincial corps.

W.O. 47:85-102. 1775-1783. Ordnance board minutes.

The minute books are essential to an understanding of the functions of the Ordnance department. Valuable data may occasionally be found in them relative to the engineers and artillery, both of which fell within the jurisdiction of the Ordnance board.

W.O. 54:689. 1774-1792. Miscellaneous registers, pay lists, etc.

W.O. 55:369-376. 1774-1783. Entry books of warrants and orders in Council.

Volumes 371 and 374 contain important lists of transports employed by the Ordnance department during the war.

W.O. 60:11-33. 1774-1781. Commissariat accounts.

This collection of documents is of marked importance. It includes a large number of books, ledgers, and statistical charts, kept by the commissariat department in New York. Many of these date from the period of Brook Watson, who was commissary general in New York at the close of the war. They are of much value for the flood of light which they throw on the problems of transport and food supply and on the relation of these problems to the fortunes of the war.

Wier-Robinson Correspondence. *Copies of Letters from Dan'l Wier Esq Commissary to the Army in America to J. Robinson Esqr Secretary to the Lords Commissioners of the Treasury and Copies of Letters from John Robinson Esqr in Answer thereto in the Year 1777.*

> A folio volume of 125 pages recently acquired by the Pennsylvania Historical Society and graciously opened to the inspection of the author by Dr. Montgomery, the librarian. Said to have been prepared for Lord North's examination, it contains many illuminating letters and tables of statistics relative to the provisioning of Howe's army during the campaign of 1777.

GENERAL COLLECTIONS OF PRINTED SOURCES

Acts of the Privy Council, Colonial Series, 1766-1783, edited by J. Munro (Hereford, 1912).

Annual Register, 1774-1783 (London, 1775-1785), 10 vols.

Army Lists, 1775-1783 (London, 1775-1783), 9 vols.

> Yearly lists of all commissioned officers. They are of assistance in tracing the regimental growth of the army from 1775 to 1783. Regiments are often referred to in the documents not by number but by the name of the colonel. This is frequently confusing, especially as new colonels were constantly being appointed. If the colonel's name be known, the *Army Lists* enable one to determine the proper number of his regiment.

Calendar of Home Office Papers, of the Reign of George III, 1760-1775, edited by J. Redington (vols. I, II) and R. A. Roberts (vols. III, IV), London, 1881-1889, 4 vols.

> These volumes occasionally shed light upon various aspects of army administration.

Calendar of Treasury Books and Papers, 1729-1745, edited by W. A. Shaw (London, 1897-1903), 5 vols.

> These volumes illustrate some aspects of the relationship of the Treasury board to the army.

Court and City Register, 1774-1783 (London, 1774-1783), 10 vols.

    Yearly registers of the incumbents of the various public offices. Helpful in studying the administrative personnel and system of the army. The volumes also contain lists of the established regiments, with statements regarding their location and numbers.

Dartmouth Manuscripts, in 11th, 14th, and 15th *Reports* of Historical Manuscripts Commission (London, 1887, 1895, 1896), 3 vols.

    Contain several important references to the plan of taking Russian troops into British pay in 1775-1776.

Journal of the House of Commons, 1547-1803, reprinted by order of the House (London, 1803), 57 vols.

    Aside from its general importance as a means of tracing military legislation, the *Commons Journal* is valuable in studying the army for two reasons. In the first place, it contains the annual army estimates, which enable one to determine in any given year (1) the geographical distribution of the army, (2) the total strength of the army, (3) the strength of every established regiment. In the second place, the *Journal* contains copies of the agreements entered into by the crown on the one hand and by towns or individuals on the other relative to raising regiments for service in the war.

    The *Journal* also contains the ''Reports of the Commissioners of Accounts,'' *q.v.*

Journal of the House of Lords. Vols. 34-39 cover the period, 1774-1783.

London Gazette, The. London, 1775-1783.

    An official organ of the government, issued weekly and containing military proclamations, lists of promotions, excerpts from the dispatches, and other official matter regarding the forces.

Reports of Parliamentary Committees:

    ''Report from the Committee appointed to consider the State

of His Majesty's Land Forces and Marines, 1746,'' in vol.
II of *Reports from Committees of the House of Commons*
(1803).

A very minute and useful account of the army clothing system.

''Report from the Select Committee, to whom it was referred
to consider and examine the accounts of Extraordinary
Services incurred and paid, and not provided for by Parliament, which have been laid before the House of Commons in
the year 1776, 1777, and 1778'' (London, 1778).

This report is exceedingly useful for the study of provision
contracts and the victualling system. It devotes considerable attention to the rum contracts. For the sake of
brevity it is referred to in the footnotes as ''Report on
Army Extras.''

Fifteen Reports from the commissioners of accounts, 1780-
1787, in vols. 38-42 of the *Commons Journal.*

Many of these reports contain valuable data respecting the
administration of the army. They amply repay examination. Worthy of especial note are the 4th, 5th, 6th, and 7th
reports, dealing with the paymaster general and the
transport service. The appendices to the reports include
many letters, commissions, statistics, and memoranda,
which are not to be found in the manuscript official records.

''Report from the Committee appointed to consider the Ordnance Estimate of 1783.''

Yields a few bits of information relative to the artillery at
the close of the war.

Thirty-six Reports from the select committee on finance, 1797-
1798, in vols. XII-XIII of the *Reports from Committees of
the House of Commons* (1803).

The following reports contain much useful information regarding the administration of the British army at the
time of the American Revolution: the 17th Report, on the
Admiralty and Navy board; the 18th, on the Transport
office; the 19th, on the War office; the 20th, on the Barrack office; the 32d, on the Victualling office; the 33d, on

the Medical board; the 34th, on Chatham Chest, Greenwich Hospital, and Chelsea Hospital; the 35th, on army expenditure; the 36th, on the secretary at war, judge advocate general, and commissary general of musters.

Statutes at Large, Ruffhead's edition (London, 1763-1800), 18 vols.

CONTEMPORARY LETTERS, MEMOIRS, NARRATIVES, PAMPHLETS, AND MILITARY WORKS

A Representation of the Cloathing of His Majesty's Houshold [sic] *and of all the Forces upon the Establishment of Great Britain and Ireland,* 1742.

A View of the Evidence (London, 1783).

Contains the evidence of various officers before a committee of the House of Commons appointed in 1779 "to examine into the conduct of Sir William Howe, Lord Howe, and General Burgoyne." Considerable information relative to army organization in America.

Bew, J., *A Letter to the Author of a Pamphlet entitled Considerations upon the different modes of finding recruits for the army* (London, 1776).

Burgoyne, John, *A State of the Expedition from Canada* (London, 1780).

An invaluable source of data respecting the organization of Burgoyne's forces on his ill-starred expedition from Canada in 1777. The account deals very minutely with the problems of transport and food supply.

Burgoyne, John, *Orderly Book,* edited by E. B. O'Callaghan (Albany, 1860).

This volume contains a considerable amount of minute information relative to regimental organization.

Cadell, T., *Considerations upon the Different Modes of Finding Recruits for the Army* (London, 1775).

Cornwallis, Charles, *Correspondence of Charles, first marquis Cornwallis,* edited by Charles Ross (London, 1859), 3 vols. These volumes add little to the official dispatches.

Correspondence of George III with Lord North, edited by W. B. Donne (London, 1867), 2 vols.
These letters are invaluable for the light which they throw on the military policy of the king and his relations to the army during the period, 1775-1783. His attitude on the question of "raising men for rank" is fully revealed.

Digby, (Lieut.) William, *Journal,* edited by James Phinney Baxter (Albany, 1887).

Hadden, James M., *Journal,* edited by H. Rogers (Albany, 1884).
Hadden was an officer of the artillery in Burgoyne's army in 1777. His *Journal* is one of the chief sources of information respecting that branch of the service.

Howe, (Sir) William, *Narrative* (London, 1781).
Like Burgoyne's *State of the Expedition from Canada,* Howe's account of his career in America incidentally throws considerable light on the organization of the British forces.

Howe, (Sir) William, *Orderly Book,* edited by B. F. Stevens (London, 1890).
Contains a quantity of minute information regarding regimental organization, courts-martial, camp life, etc.

Jones, Thomas, *History of New York during the Revolutionary War,* edited by E. F. DeLancey (New York, 1879), 2 vols.
Although the author of this work was a judge, he did not write judicially. If allowances are made for prejudice, however, the work becomes a useful contemporary account of the British occupation of New York. Especially worthy of note is the chapter on the "Base Transactions of Commissaries, Quartermasters, Barrackmasters, and Engineers, in America." It places His Majesty's forces in a bad light, but much of the data is confirmed by other contemporary sources.

Kemble Papers, in New York Historical Society *Collections* for 1883 and 1884 (New York, 1884-1885), 2 vols.
Kemble was deputy adjutant general from 1773 to 1779 un-

der Gage, Howe, and Clinton. Besides his journals, these volumes contain the army orders of the generals whom he served. They are thus a most valuable source of data regarding many aspects of British army organization.

Lamb, R., *Journal* (Dublin, 1809).

Lamb, R., *Memoir* (Dublin, 1811).
Lamb was a sergeant in the 9th Foot. He participated in Burgoyne's campaign, 1777. His *Journal* and *Memoir* are among the few works that furnish a picture of the life of the British soldier as drawn by himself.

Minute Book of a Board of General Officers of the British Army in New York, 1781. New York Historical Society *Collections,* 1916. New York, 1916.
Invaluable in the study of provisioning and transport.

Montrésor, John, *Journals,* edited by G. D. Scull, in New York Historical Society *Collections* for 1881 (New York, 1882).
As an officer of the engineers in America at the time of the Revolution, Captain John Montrésor was in a position to furnish much information respecting that branch of the service. The above-named volume also contains the journal of his father, Colonel James Montrésor, who served as an engineer in America at the time of the French and Indian War.

Observations on the Prevailing Abuses in the British Army, Arising from the Corruption of Civil Government. By the Honourable ***—an Officer (London, 1775).
A warm denunciation of the evils of army life. Interesting as embodying a contemporary point of view.

Pattison, (Major General) James, *Letters.* New York Historical Society *Collections* for 1875 (New York, 1876).
Pattison was colonel in the artillery as well as major general in the king's forces in America. His letters shed light upon many aspects of army organization but are especially valuable in studying the artillery.

Riedesel, Mrs. General, *Letters and Journals,* translated from the original German by W. L. Stone (Albany, 1867).

An entertaining picture of social life in the army during a campaign in America. Madame Riedesel accompanied her husband, General Riedesel, on Burgoyne's famous expedition in 1777. She looks at the army from an interesting angle, that of an army officer's wife. Her comments on the moral tone of Burgoyne and his staff may seem to be the froth of idle gossip, but they are confirmed by other writers.

Schenck, David, *North Carolina, 1780-1781* (Raleigh, 1889).

Simcoe, John G., *Military Journal* (New York, 1844).
Although chiefly concerned with the history of a provincial corps, this work contains occasional references to the organization of the regular forces.

Simes, Thomas, *Military Guide* (London, 1776), 2 vols.
Simes' *Military Guide* was intended to be a *vade mecum* for British officers. Volume I contains model forms for all kinds of military papers and reports; regulations regarding reviews, camps, hospitals, tactics, etc.; and charts and orders relative to uniforms in the British service. Volume II is a military dictionary in which the meaning of many contemporary military terms may be ascertained.

Stedman, Charles, *History of the American War* (London, 1794), 2 vols.
Disappointingly meagre in its yield of facts respecting British army organization during the war.

Stevens, Benjamin F., *The Clinton-Cornwallis Controversy* (London, 1888), 2 vols.
A reprint of six controversial pamphlets written by Clinton and Cornwallis relative to the Yorktown campaign, with lengthy transcripts from their dispatches. The volumes occasionally yield material relative to the feeding and transport of the troops during the southern campaigns.

Tarleton, Banastre, *History of the Campaigns of 1780-1781 in the Southern Provinces of North America* (Dublin, 1787).
The many valuable documents in this volume occasionally offer data respecting the organization of the forces under

Cornwallis, though emphasis is laid chiefly upon military operations.

Walpole, Horace, *Last Journals* (London, 1910), 2 vols.

SECONDARY WORKS

Andrews, Charles M., *Guide to the Manuscript Materials for the History of the United States to 1783, in the British Museum, in Minor London Archives, and in the Libraries of Oxford and Cambridge* (Washington, D. C., 1908).

Andrews, Charles M., *Guide to the Materials for American History to 1783, in the Public Record Office of Great Britain* (Washington, D. C., 1912-1914), 2 vols.
These volumes chart a sea of documents. The notes and introductions, especially to the War Office and Admiralty papers, are replete with data not elsewhere accessible in print, relative to the organization and administration of the royal forces during the eighteenth century. The functions and relations of the various boards and officers concerned with military affairs are instructively set forth.

Barrington, Shute, *Political Life of William Wildman, viscount Barrington* (London, 1814).
This is an excellent biography of an official who was vitally connected with the administration of the British army during the early stages of the Revolution. The author demonstrates most conclusively Barrington's disapproval of the king's policy regarding the colonists, and shows that like Lord North he begged repeatedly to be allowed to resign. These facts become of considerable importance in interpreting Barrington's career as secretary at war.

Belcher, Henry, *First American Civil War* (London, 1911), 2 vols.
This work is of little value as regards the history of battles and campaigns, because the author has based his account largely on histories the accuracy of which is now discredited. It contains, however, two admirable chapters

on the "Forces of the Crown" in the eighteenth century, which lay particular emphasis upon the social aspects of the army, the classes from which it was recruited, the hardships and amenities of military life, and the character of officers and men. The author shows considerable acquaintance with contemporary material of an unofficial character, such as letters, newspapers, and memoirs. The appendix to volume I contains a valuable table showing the history of every British regiment in the war.

Butler, L., *Annals of the King's Royal Rifle Corps* (London, 1913), 2 vols.

This account of the 60th Royal American Regiment, which played an important part in the Revolution, is one of the best regimental histories.

Calver, William L., "The British Army Button in the American Revolution," Pt. I. New York Historical Society Quarterly *Bulletin,* vol. VII, No. 1, April, 1923, pp. 10-23.

Calver, William L., "Belt Plates and Badges of the British Army in the American Revolution." New York Historical Society Quarterly *Bulletin,* vol. VIII, No. 4, January, 1925, pp. 91-108.

Cannon, Richard, *Historical Records of the British Army; comprising the history of every regiment in His Majesty's service* (London, 1834-1850), 71 vols.

Few of these histories deal with the Revolutionary careers of British regiments. Such volumes as do so, however, enable one to follow the story of the regiment in America and sometimes yield useful data relative to its orgin. Much of Cannon's material has been epitomized by Chichester with important additions in his *Records and Badges of the British Army, q.v.* The records of the 71st, 72d, and 73d regiments were found especially helpful.

Carrington, Henry B., *Battles of the American Revolution* (New York, 1876).

Channing, Edward, *History of the United States* (New York, 1905-1912), vol. III.

Volume III contains a brief but excellent summary of the character of the British army at the time of the Revolution.

Chichester, Henry M., *Records and Badges of the British Army* (London, 1902).

An invaluable compendium of British regimental history. It comprises in concise terms most of the material to be found in the Cannon series (*q.v.*) and additional facts gleaned from unofficial regimental histories and contemporary sources. A noteworthy feature of the work is the bibliographical notes which follow the record of each regiment.

Clode, Charles M., *Military Forces of the Crown* (London, 1869), 2 vols.

An invaluable treatise on the legal and administrative aspects of the army. The appendices contain much illustrative material gleaned from documentary sources.

Connolly, T. W. J., *History of the Sappers and Miners.* 2d ed. (London, 1857), 2 vols.

Curtis, Edward E., "The Provisioning of the British Army in Boston," *Magazine of American History,* June-July, 1915.

De Fonblanque, Edward B., *Episodes from the Life and Correspondence of John Burgoyne* (London, 1876).

Dictionary of National Biography, edited by Leslie Stephen and Sidney Lee (London, 1885-1890), 63 vols.

These volumes contain excellent vignettes of many of the British commanders.

Duncan, Francis, *History of the Royal Regiment of Artillery* (London, 1879), 2 vols.

Volume I contains many curious and interesting facts gleaned from official and unofficial sources relative to the career of the royal artillery in America, 1775-1783. The author has treated his subject in a lively, vivacious manner.

Eelking, Max von, *Die Deutschen Hülfstruppen im Nordameri-kan Befreiungskriege* (Hanover, 1863).

> Contains a quantity of interesting and valuable data respecting military affairs, most of which the author secured from the letters and diaries of Hessian soldiers who served in America. Much light is incidentally shed upon the organization of the British forces. Although the author is strongly biased in favor of the German auxiliaries, his conclusions regarding the value of their service to England during the struggle are based upon such a wealth of contemporary evidence that they cannot be lightly dismissed as mere prejudice.

Farmer, Henry George, *Memoirs of the Royal Artillery Band, its Origin, History, and Progress. An Account of the Rise of Military Music in England* (London, 1904).

> Very helpful in tracing the history of military music in the British army at the time of the American Revolution.

Farrow, Edward S., *Military Encyclopedia* (New York, 1885).

Fisher, Sydney G., *The Struggle for American Independence* (Philadelphia, 1908), 2 vols.

> Chapter XLII contains a good summary of the strategic problems which confronted the British army in attempting to subdue America. Fisher's character sketches of the British generals are suggestive.

Fortescue, J. W., "A Chapter on Red Coats," *Macmillan's Magazine*, September, 1893.

Fortescue, J. W., *History of the British Army* (London, 1899-1920), 10 vols.

> Volume III treats of the Revolution. Although written from the British standpoint, it is by all odds the best purely military account of the war. No other printed work contains an equal amount of information based on documentary sources relative to the administration and organization of the forces during the period from 1775 to 1783. I

have had occasion to use many of the same documents as Mr. Fortescue and can testify to his thoroughness and accuracy.

Fortescue, J. W., *The British Army, 1783-1802* (Edinburgh, 1905).
This volume contains a most valuable survey of army organization at the close of the Revolution.

Frothingham, Richard, *History of the Siege of Boston* (Boston, 1873).
Occasionally yields data relative to the provisioning of the British garrison.

Goodenough, W. H., and Dalton, J. C., *Army Book of the British Empire* (London, 1893).

Greener, William, *The Gun* (London, 1835).
Chiefly valuable for its minute description of Ferguson's breech-loader, which was used by some of the troops in British service.

Grose, Francis, *Military Antiquities* (London, 1801), 2 vols.
The main emphasis of this well-known work is laid upon the history of the British army during the middle ages and the sixteenth and seventeenth centuries. It contains some useful data, however, respecting the pay, clothing, and equipment of the forces during the latter half of the eighteenth century.

Hatch, Louis C., *The Administration of the American Revolutionary Army*, Harvard Historical *Studies*, X (New York, 1904).
Valuable for the purpose of comparing the organization of the American army with that of the British.

Johnston, Henry P., *Yorktown Campaign* (New York, 1881).

Johnston, Henry P., *Battle of Harlem Heights* (New York, 1897).

Kappey, J. A., *Military Music* (London, 1894).

King, C. Cooper, *Story of the British Army* (London, 1897).
The author of this work gives a popular and rather super-
ficial account of the army during the Revolution.

Lecky, W. E. H., *The American Revolution:* Edited by J. A.
Woodburn (New York, 1907).
Occasional passages may be found relative to the military
measures of the government during the war. Political conditions as they affected the army are touched upon.

Lloyd, Ernest M., *A Review of the History of Infantry* (New
York, 1908).
Explains the tactics of British infantry at the period of the
war and traces the war's effect on them.

Lowell, Edward J., *The Hessians* (New York, 1884).
This work compares unfavorably with Max von Eelking's
Die Deutschen Hülfstruppen.

Maitland, Frederick W. *Constitutional History of England*
(Cambridge, 1908).

Memorial History of Boston, edited by Justin Windsor (Boston,
1880-1881), 4 vols.

Nevill, R., *British Military Prints* (London, 1909).

Oman, C. W. C., *Wellington's Army* (New York, 1912).
By the time of Wellington, army conditions had not changed
radically since the American Revolution. Many methods
and customs prevalent in 1775 were still in vogue in 1805.
With certain allowances this work is a rich mine of information regarding the army in the last quarter of the
eighteenth century.

Porter, (Maj. Gen.) Whitworth, and Watson, (Sir) Charles M.,
History of the Corps of Royal Engineers (London, 1889-
1913), 3 vols.
Contains considerable information relative to the part
played by the engineers in the American Revolution.

Richards, Walter, *Her Majesty's Army* (London, 1888-1891), 3 vols.
> A popular account of the regiments composing the British army at the time of Queen Victoria. The volumes are occasionally helpful in tracing regimental history.

Rogerson, W., *Historical Records of the Fifty-Third* (London, 1890).

Sawyer, Charles Winthrop, *Firearms in American History, 1600-1800* (Boston, 1910).

Scott, Sibbald D., *The British Army, its Origin, Progress, and Equipment* (London, 1868-1880), 3 vols.
> These volumes deal mainly with the state of the army in the seventeenth century.

Skrine, Francis H., *Fontenoy* (London, 1906).
> Devotes several pages to an excellent description of the British soldier's uniform and equipment at the middle of the eighteenth century.

Smythies, R. H. R., *Historical Records of the 40th Regiment* (Devonport, 1894).

Stocqueler, Joachim H., *History of the British Army* (London, 1871).
> This work is a somewhat bald *résumé* of the history of the British army from 1660 to 1868. The author limits his narration to military operations, and eschews practically all reference to the administrative history of the army.

Stryker, William S., *Battles of Trenton and Princeton* (New York, 1898).
> The method of provisioning the British forces in New Jersey at the time of the battles of Trenton and Princeton receives some treatment. The appendix contains several documents illustrative of the process.

Trevelyan, George Otto, *The American Revolution* (New York, 1905-1912), 4 vols.
> Contains several pages, based on contemporary sources, describing the character of the army officers. Also valuable

for occasional quotations relative to the army from contemporary newspapers. In my footnotes this work is referred to simply as "Trevelyan." The work noted below is referred to by its full title.

Trevelyan, George Otto, *George the Third and Charles Fox* (New York, 1912-1914), 2 vols.

Wheeler, Owen, *The War Office, Past and Present* (London, 1914).
Of but little value for our period.

Williamson, J., *Treatise of Military Finance* (London, 1782).
Invaluable in the study of military finance.

INDEX